C000089244

Xavier's Legacies

Asian Religions and Society Series

Edited by Kevin M. Doak

Xavier's Legacies: Catholicism in Modern Japanese Culture

UBCPress · Vancouver · Toronto

© UBC Press 2011

All rights reserved. No part of this publication may be reproduced, stored in a retrieval system, or transmitted, in any form or by any means, without prior written permission of the publisher, or, in Canada, in the case of photocopying or other reprographic copying, a licence from Access Copyright, www. accesscopyright.ca.

21 20 19 18 17 16 15 14 13 12 11   5 4 3 2 1

Printed in Canada on FSC-certified ancient-forest-free paper (100% post-consumer recycled) that is processed chlorine- and acid-free.

Library and Archives Canada Cataloguing in Publication

Xavier's legacies : Catholicism in modern Japanese culture / edited by Kevin M. Doak.

(Asian religions in society series, 1705-4761/1925-0126)
Includes bibliographical references and index.
ISBN 978-0-7748-2021-9 (bound); ISBN 978-0-7748-2022-6 (pbk.)

1. Catholic Church – Japan – History. 2. Catholic Church – Japan – Influence. 3. Catholic Church – Social aspects – Japan. 4. Japan – Religious life and customs. I. Doak, Kevin Michael II. Series: Asian religions in society

BX1668.X39 2011   282'.52   C2010-907361-4

e-book ISBNs: 978-0-7748-2023-3 (PDF); 978-0-7748-2024-0 (epub)

Canadä

UBC Press gratefully acknowledges the financial support for our publishing program of the Government of Canada (through the Canada Book Fund), and the British Columbia Arts Council.

We acknowledge support in the form of a publication subvention from the Nippon Foundation Endowment, Georgetown University.

UBC Press
The University of British Columbia
2029 West Mall
Vancouver, BC V6T 1Z2
www.ubcpress.ca

This volume is dedicated to John W. Witek, SJ (1933-2010),

Professor of Asian History at Georgetown University for over thirty-five years. Without his inspiration and guidance, this book would never have seen the light of day.

Requiescat in pace, Father Witek.

Contents

Figure and Tables

Figure

Tables

Acknowledgments

So many people have contributed in so many ways to bringing this volume to fruition that it would be impossible to thank them all. But I would be particularly remiss not to mention the following: Archbishop Giuseppe "Joseph" Pittau, SJ; William J. Farge, SJ; Paul Anderer; Kristine Dennehy; Kevin J. Hanlon, MM; Hose Mitamura; John W. O'Malley, SJ; Alvaro Ribeiro, SJ; Jean-Philippe Mathy; Kazuko Okazaki; Junji Hiroshima; Yukihiko Hirata; Fumiaki Shinozaki; Andrew Barshay; Emily Andrew and Megan Brand (my editors at UBC Press); the anonymous readers for the press; and especially John W. Witek, SJ, without whom this project would never have happened but who, sadly, did not live to see publication of this book. I certainly do not mean to imply that any of those listed above agree with all or any of the points made in this volume, but all had some influence on its development, and the volume is better for their input. I wish to acknowledge their contributions and thank them for their ideas and suggestions. *Ad Majorem Dei Gloriam!*

Xavier's Legacies

This image is a work by an anonymous Japanese artist working from plates imported from Europe and was completed in Japan probably in 1622. However, it was lost and not discovered until 1920 in the Higashi family home in Takatsuki and is now a Japanese National Cultural Treasure, housed in the Kobe City Art Museum. As such, it captures in one picture the many words of this volume that try to explain what "Xavier's legacies" in modern Japanese culture can mean.

Source: Portrait of St. Francis Xavier, SJ (1506-52), Important Cultural Treasure, Kobe City Museum, Kobe, Japan.

Introduction: Catholicism, Modernity, and Japanese Culture

Kevin M. Doak

Catholicism reached Japan in 1549 when Francis Xavier, SJ, landed at Kago--shima City.[1] It was 15 August, the Feast of the Assumption of the Blessed Virgin Mary. Xavier remained in Japan for two years and three months, and with the help of a native Japanese convert, Anjirō (Yajirō), he translated into Japanese the Gospel of St. Matthew, the Apostles' Creed, cardinal Church teachings, and various prayers. He travelled throughout the country, even to the capital city, Kyoto, converting Japanese to the faith everywhere he went. It is estimated that, in those few years, Xavier converted 800 Japanese and established good relations with influential men such as the Buddhist monk Ninjitsu and Shimazu Takahisa, Lord of Satsuma, and Ōtomo Yoshi-shige, Lord of Bungo, who would later convert to the faith.[2] Not only did Xavier plant the seeds of Christianity in Japan, but he also laid the founda-tions for the field of Japanese studies by taking up the study of the Japanese language and with his insightful writings on the character of the Japanese people, their cultural, social, and political institutions. In his wake, other Jesuits built on those foundations, including João Rodriquez, SJ, whose 1608 *Arte da lingoa de Iapam* was "the starting point of the scientific study of Japanese as a language."[3] During what has come to be called "the Christian century," Catholic influence on Japanese culture was surprisingly deep. Not only did samurai (including the Taikō Hideyoshi) adopt Western dress (including Christian symbols), food, and drink, but some even adopted Christian names. There has long been speculation that the tea ceremony, as reconstituted by Sen no Rikyū (1522-91), was influenced by the rituals of the Catholic Mass.[4] It is a matter of historical record that five of Rikyū's seven top disciples were Christians or allies of the Christians, including Hosokawa Tadaoki, whose wife was the famous Gracia Hosokawa.[5] It has been estimated that by the 1630s there were 760,000 Catholics after only eighty years of missionary work, nearly 6.3 percent of the total population. As Miyazaki Kentarō notes, that is approximately ten times the percentage of Catholics in present-day Japan.[6]

One of the greatest challenges for historians of Christianity's influence on Japanese culture is to assess the impact of Catholicism during the "closed country" period of 1640 to 1873. Once systematic persecution began in 1614, at least 2,138 Catholics were martyred (of that number, 71 were Europeans).[7] However, these figures might be gross underestimations as they reflect only the numbers found in available public records of persecutions of Catholics. Presumably, many Catholics were caught and tried during the Tokugawa period, but we will never know since hidden Christians were almost never publicly identified as Christians but were tried on other, vague charges. These numbers do not include periodic persecutions prior to 1614, including the notorious crucifixion of the Twenty-Six Martyrs of Nagasaki in 1597, nor do they include the estimated 27,000 people who were slaughtered in the Christian-led Shimabara Uprising of 1637-38. The best estimation is that between 1600 and 1873 the number of Catholics in Japan declined from as many as 760,000 to about 50,000.[8] How many of them were executed, how many apostatized, or how many simply drifted away over the years is impossible to know. But since about half of the surviving Catholics refused to unite with the Church after 1873, the actual number of Japanese Catholics who survived the long period of persecution to form the basis of the modern Catholic Church in Japan was probably only about 20,000. We do know that in 1876, when early-Meiji-period persecutions had ended, there were 18,435 Catholics in Japan.[9] We may never know what happened to hundreds of thousands of Catholics over the course of the two centuries when Japan was closed to Christianity.

Because of the difficulty in assessing the position of Catholicism during the Tokugawa period, and because of the salience of Catholicism in the decades prior to the closing of the country, historians have tended to limit their interest in Catholicism in Japan to the "Christian century" from 1549 to 1650. Thereafter, Christianity is not seen as playing a major role in Japanese culture until the advent of the West after 1854 (mainly in the form of British and American forces). Consequently, Christianity in modern Japan is largely told as a story of the advent of Protestantism, which is often presented as a more "modern" alternative to the Catholic Church.[10] From this perspective, the intellectual and cultural options facing Japanese in the modern period were (1) secular materialism in the vein of Fukuzawa Yukichi (which ultimately came to include social Darwinism, Marxism, and a range of modern "scientific" forms of materialism); (2) Protestant Christianity;

and (3) a possible third option by those who sought to make Buddhism a modern Japanese religion.[11] From this modernist perspective, Catholicism is relegated to a thing of the past or, when it is unavoidably visible, regarded as a strange, marginal, and largely "French" thing (because of the monopoly that French missionaries had over the Catholic Church in modern Japan until the twentieth century) of little consequence to modern Japanese society and culture.

This volume presents a different, and long overdue, perspective: far from being marginal or irrelevant, Catholicism has provided Japanese from the mid-nineteenth century to the present with an important, alternative way of negotiating with modernity. Because Catholicism had established roots in Japanese tradition for over 300 years when Protestant missionaries arrived, it offered a unique relationship with what, after the nineteenth-century advent of "civilization and enlightenment," would be deemed "Japanese tradition." From this Catholic vantage point, Japanese tradition was neither something to leave behind nor something to cling to in the face of the challenges of modernity: it had encompassed the Catholic faith centuries earlier, even as both the Church and Japanese culture had grown in subsequent years. This depth of investiture in Japanese tradition gives Catholicism in modern Japan a very different cultural significance than that of Protestantism. But because Catholicism was reintroduced to Japan in the late nineteenth century by French missionaries – thus drawing on the prestige of all things Western at that time – Catholicism also presented nineteenth-century Japanese with a way of being fully modern that, at the same time, was grounded in over 300 years of Japanese tradition and history. Moreover, as a minority cultural form in Japan, it presents comparative social scientists and historians with an excellent opportunity for rethinking a theory of modernization that all too often posits a binary opposition between tradition as indigenous and modernity as Western (i.e., what might be called the "missionary thesis"). In late-nineteenth-century Japan, Catholicism had a stronger claim on indigenous identity than the newly arrived Protestantism, and a modernity that was heavily informed by the latter was more easily criticized as a particularist and contingent ideology deeply connected to a specific Western modernity. From the perspective offered by this book, we gain a better understanding of the appeal of Catholicism not merely among the farmers and fishermen who might have felt left out of the main benefits of the modern transformation of Japanese society but also among the social elite – especially diplomats, intellectuals, and even the imperial household – who not only benefited from the modern transformation but also could draw from the moral resources of the Catholic

Church in helping to steer Japan away from the extremes of a nineteenth-century modernism that had few roots in Japanese cultural tradition.

As a result of the tendency to relegate Catholicism in Japan to the "Christian century," studies on Christianity in modern Japan often work from an implicit narrative of the initial missionary conquest in the sixteenth century, the subsequent failure of Japan to embrace Christianity (*sakoku*), and the dominance of secularization in the modern period (with a small but vocal Protestant intellectual group as the exception that proves the rule). In this narrative – whose influence extends beyond religious history to inform much of Japanese studies – modern Japan signifies the dominance of secularism or, in a different inflection, the dominance of Protestantism among the few Japanese Christians who struggle against both secularism and indigenous cults, notably the tennō-sei. This is a surprising narrative since the actual number of Catholics in Meiji Japan compared favourably to Protestants: the Catholic missionaries started with an advantage of thousands, perhaps tens of thousands of *kakure kirishitan* (hidden Catholics), so it is not surprising that Catholics significantly outnumbered Protestants in the early Meiji years. Yet, even after thirty years of intense activity by Protestant missionaries, the number of Catholics was certainly not marginal: by the early twentieth century, Catholics still were nearly double the number of Protestants (58,261 to 31,631).[12] Yet, from most histories, one gets the impression that Catholicism simply disappeared in Japan sometime during the early seventeenth century. At most, literary scholars are aware of Endō Shūsaku as a quixotic Catholic writer whose historical novels frequently focus on the "Christian century" (thereby reinforcing the putative ties of Catholicism to Japan's premodern past). In contrast, historians of modern Japan know of many Protestant Japanese intellectuals, especially of the Meiji period (e.g., Ebina Danjō, Nitobe Inazō, Niijima Jō, Uchimura Kanzō). But little is known of Catholic Japanese from the late nineteenth century to the present. This is a shame since, as this volume reveals, Catholic Japanese have had a tremendous impact on their society and culture in the modern and contemporary periods, especially in the fields of literature, philosophy, education, science, diplomacy, and politics.[13] For example, it is striking that Japan has had more Catholic prime ministers (Hara Kei, Yoshida Shigeru, Asō Tarō) than the United States has had Catholic presidents – yet how many people know this? How widely is it known that the current empress was raised and educated as a Catholic (and undoubtedly baptized) and thus likely has baptized her son, the crown prince?[14] How much information do we have on key diplomats, intellectuals, and novelists (other than Endō) whose Catholic values have had tremendous influence on contemporary Japanese culture and society? Truth be told, not much.

Catholicism, Modernity, and Japan

To appreciate what the Catholic difference meant to Japanese in the middle to late nineteenth century, we need to take a broad perspective on the events, ideas, and people whose influence forged the particular constellation of Catholicism in modern Japan. This broad view needs to include the teachings of the Catholic Church on modernism as well as the cultural, social, and political orientations of the French Catholics who had exclusive rights over missionary activity in Japan at this time. In addition, we need to consider the difference between the approaches of Protestant missionaries who saw Japan as virgin territory and Catholic missionaries' concern to locate the long-rumoured *kakure* Catholics and, once found, serve their needs at a time when it was illegal for Christians to minister to Japanese. We need to recognize the complex role of French diplomats who enjoyed particularly close relations with the *bakufu*, the very authorities responsible for the laws that oppressed Japanese Catholics, and how this affiliation with *bakufu* retainers encouraged a positive view of Catholicism after the Restoration, when those retainers suddenly found themselves on the losing side of the modern transformation.

For the origins of Catholicism in modern Japan, we must begin in Paris. In 1653, only a few years after the close of the "Christian century" in Japan, the Paris Society for Foreign Missions (Société des missions étrangères du Paris; MEP) was established with the goal of sending missionaries to Asia. Indeed, until Spanish Dominicans arrived in Japan in 1904, MEP had exclusive rights to Catholic missionary work in Japan, much as the Jesuits had during the sixteenth century. Exercising that right was not easy, as the imprisonment and death of the missionary Giovanni Battista Sidotti in 1715 demonstrated. But MEP never lost sight of the goal of returning to the orphaned Catholics in Japan, and in 1825 the Asiatic Society of Paris published *Eléments de la grammaire japonaise*, M.C. Landresse's edited French translation of Rodriguez's *Arte da lingoa de Iapam*. In 1832, a real opportunity to return to Japan seemed at hand when the Vatican placed Korea and the Ryūkyū islands under MEP's authority as an apostolic vicariate. Finally, the 1842 Treaty of Nanking provided a means of exercising this opportunity, particularly when it was followed by the Treaty of Whampoa on 24 October 1844, securing Chinese toleration of Catholicism. Earlier, on 28 April of that year, Theodore-Auguste Forcade, MEP, and a Chinese convert, Augustin

Ko, had arrived at Naha City in the Ryūkyū islands, where Forcade devoted himself to the study of the Japanese language for the next two years (one can assume that he already had the benefit of Rodriguez's grammar of the language). This moment marks, in a sense, the return of Catholic missionaries to Japan, as the Ryūkyū islands were at that time a kingdom that, while neither Chinese nor Japanese, enjoyed close ties to the Satsuma domain. In 1846, Pope Gregory XVI elevated Japan to the status of apostolic vicariate and appointed Forcade in charge as "bishop of Samos." Bishop Forcade immediately tried to enter Nagasaki but was not permitted to land. The following year he visited the pope in Rome but due to illness was not able to return to Asia.

The first Catholic missionaries to set foot on Japanese soil (excepting Okinawa) since Sidotti were Eugene Emmanuel Mermet de Cachon, MEP, and Prudence-Séraphin-Barthélemy Girard, MEP, who accompanied Baron Gros on his mission to conclude a Treaty of Commerce and Friendship with Japan in 1855. Mermet went to Hakodate, where he served the French Catholics in the foreign concession there while teaching French to Japanese. Girard remained in Yokohama, where in January 1862 he built the first Catholic church there. Hundreds, perhaps a thousand, Japanese flocked to the building to admire its unusual architecture, statues, and paintings. In case the Christian message was not sufficiently conveyed through the visual aids, Girard also preached in Japanese to a broad spectrum of society: peasants, merchants, and even samurai. One month later thirty-six of his Japanese followers were arrested for violating the prohibition against the "evil cult" and sentenced to death. After intervention by the head of the French diplomatic mission, De Bellecourt, the Japanese officials agreed to release the thirty-six on the condition that Girard no longer preach in Japanese. He might have felt compelled to accept this compromise, but he also appealed directly to officials back in Paris to urge Emperor Napoleon to intercede on behalf of religious freedom in Japan.

The issue of religious freedom was a major point of debate among Catholic theologians in the first half of the nineteenth century. Although the current status of the scholarship on these French missionaries does not permit us to draw direct lines of influence, an understanding of issues debated among French Catholic priests and theologians during the years when the missionaries received their training helps us to understand the preconceptions that they brought with them to Japan. The critical years were from 1835 to 1865. The earliest MEP missionaries to come to Japan had their theological training in the late 1830s (e.g., Forcade, Furet, Mermet de Cachon), but they were not the ones who stayed the longest or had the greatest influence on

Japanese converts. Girard and Pierre Mounicou were both ordained in the momentous year 1848, but neither remained in Japan after the prohibition on Christianity was lifted in 1873, limiting their influence on Japanese converts. The three most influential of the early generation of missionaries were Bishops Bernard Petitjean (1829-84), Joseph Laucaigne (1838-85), and Jules Cousin (1842-1911). All three were in Japan during the "closed country" period when Christianity was illegal, and all three served as bishops in Japan well into the 1880s (in the case of Bishop Cousin, until 1911). Bishops Laucaigne and Petitjean are known for their early catechisms (1865 and 1868, respectively) and Bishop Cousin for his influence in training Japanese priests. They received their theological training in Paris between 1850 and 1865, precisely when the issue of religious freedom, the authority of the pope, the limitations on national authority, and related issues were hotly debated among leading Catholic intellectuals.

It is safe to assume that the most important intellectual influence on these early missionaries to Japan was that of the Dominican priest Jean-Baptiste Henri Dominique Lacordaire. Lacordaire has been called "the greatest pulpit orator of the nineteenth century" and, along with Félicité Robert de Lamennais, dominated French Catholic theology of the early nineteenth century.[15] Lamennais had outlined a rational, common-sense foundation for the one true religion, and he joined with Lacordaire after the Revolution of 1830 in founding a journal, *L'avenir* ("The Future") to promote this rational philosophical defence of religious liberty of people against the extremes of French nationalism (Gallicanism). In this sense, Lacordaire and Lamennais were allies in supporting ultramontanism (defence of the pope and the magisterium of the Church as universally valid). But when Pope Gregory XVI condemned the excessively populist and modernist ideas in *L'avenir*, Lamennais hardened his position, ultimately leaving the Church, while Lacordaire repented and was soon invited by the archbishop to deliver a series of lectures from the pulpit of the Cathedral of Notre Dame. These lectures, which took place regularly between 1835 and 1852 (with an interval of a few years), were attended by the most influential men in France, and we can be sure that they were widely discussed among seminarians, priests, and others in Paris. Most important to the Church was that Lacordaire found a way to respond from within the Church to the challenges represented by the rise of populism in the 1848 Revolution, in contrast to Lamennais, who was unable to resist those pressures. Most relevant for MEP was Lacordaire's homiletic innovation: rather than preach to the converted, as was the custom, he emphasized apologetics, a defence of the Church with the unbeliever as the intended audience. Lacordaire exemplified how to "take the Church to the peoples," and he did so with what was regarded as heroic style and passion. In his last lecture, delivered in 1853, he attacked the Second Empire of Napoleon III and because of this critique was forced to leave Paris. In his latter years, he taught patriotism and religion in a military school, and in his last year he was rewarded with a seat in the academy, thus raising him to the height of respectability in French society.

What are we to make of this Catholic intellectual milieu out of which MEP missionaries came to Japan? In the first place, Lamennais probably had much less influence on them than Lacordaire, since he had renounced his priesthood and the Church decades earlier. To young French seminarians with an eye to spreading the faith in Asia, surely Lacordaire was a real cultural hero, a defender of the Church in the face of the challenges of modernism, populism, and extreme nationalism. But Lacordaire was also a complex man: a republican Catholic, an ultramontanist who rejected monarchy. There is reason to believe that his nuanced response to modernity – accepting some parts, rejecting others – would appeal to young priests. But there is equal reason to believe that Lacordaire was also influential among missionaries who listened deeply to his lectures on the need to engage those who did not believe and to defend the faith from false beliefs and paganism.

But of course we should not conclude that intellectual reasons were the only motivations for young French priests to leave their country for the distant Far East. A more religious motivation likely came from the widely publicized and numerous accounts of MEP missionaries martyred in the Far East between 1815 and 1862. These martyrdoms "were described in Europe by books, pamphlets, annals, and journals, arousing the pity of some and the anger of others, and inspiring numerous young men either with the desire for martyrdom or that of evangelization."[16] Or, of course, both. Nor can we discount the possibility that many young priests responded to these martyrdoms at least as much from a sense of outrage over the violations of the right to religious freedom as from a longing for the purity of faith or a nostalgia for an earlier, premodern Church. Modern and antimodern attitudes overlapped in the lectures of Lacordaire and in the implicit lessons of these martyrdoms. But both were specifically Catholic experiences and Catholic values that stood in sharp contrast to a much less critical view of modernity that stemmed from the growing influence of liberal theology among nineteenth-century Protestant thinkers.

The most important influence in shaping attitudes toward modernity among nineteenth-century Catholic missionaries to Japan was the official

Church engagement with the modernist ideas spawned by the 1848 Revolution. In this sense, the French theological debates of Lamennais and Lacordaire were part of this broader picture. The year following the 1848 Revolution the Provincial Council of Spoleto pushed for an official Church response to new arguments being raised against the Church, and Pope Pius IX was petitioned to provide guidance on how a Catholic should respond to these new ideas circulating throughout Europe. Preparation for what would later be known as the Syllabus of Errors began as early as 1852, and in 1860 the bishop of Perpignan issued "Pastoral Instructions on Various Errors of the Present" to his clergy. These instructions were the basis for reflection by 300 bishops who gathered in Rome in 1862 for the canonization of the twenty-six Japanese martyrs who had been crucified in 1597. Surely, French missionaries interested in propagating the faith in Japan paid attention to this episcopal meeting in Rome and, at the same time, were not able to ignore the Church's response to these new, modern heresies. On 8 December 1864, the Feast of the Immaculate Conception, Pius IX had the syllabus sent to all the bishops of the Church, who in turn were responsible for ensuring that all their clergy – especially missionaries – were familiar with it.

It is not known how long it took for the Syllabus of Errors to reach missionaries in Japan at the time, but certainly warnings against modern heresies (including the heresy of modernism itself) would have been familiar to priests and seminarians in France from 1849 to 1864. The canonization of the twenty-six Japanese martyrs in Rome on the eve of issuing the syllabus brought to the fore the connection between the past and the present: the willingness of the sixteenth-century martyrs to shed their blood in defence of the Church and the need in the nineteenth century to protect the Church from modernist heresies. The risks of martyrdom were never far from the Catholic experience in Japan during the 1860s. Of course, murder and assassination were threats facing all Westerners in Japan during the early 1860s, but martyrdom was implicitly a characteristic of the Catholic experience due to the continued presence of hidden Japanese Catholics who, if discovered, faced immediate execution. At a time when most Protestant ministers focused on servicing their Western brethren,[17] Catholic missionaries also felt a serious obligation to seek out the existing Catholic Japanese and provide for their sacramental needs. Many questioned whether any Catholic had survived the 200 years of persecution, but the French missionaries were fired up with a zeal for discovering the long-lost legacy of St. Francis Xavier, SJ. The legend of these hidden Catholics certainly gave rise to a strong desire to discover them, if they indeed existed, but it also encouraged an effort to return to the past, to encounter the Catholic faith centuries before the corruptions of modernity had begun to influence the Church. But did these crypto-Catholic Japanese even exist, or was this merely another myth like that of Prestor John?

A moment that would forever change the history of Catholicism in Japan, and shape Japanese Catholic attitudes toward modernity, took place on a spring day in Nagasaki in 1865. Here is what happened at the Ōura Catholic Church, as recalled by the principal witness, Father Bernard Petitjean:

> On March 17, 1865, about half past twelve, some fifteen persons were standing at the church door. Urged no doubt by my guardian angel, I went up and opened the door. I had scarce time to say a Pater when three women between fifty and sixty years of age knelt down beside me and said in a low voice, placing their hands on their hearts:
>
> "The hearts of all of us here do not differ from yours."
>
> "Indeed!" I exclaimed. "Whence do you come?"
>
> They named the village, adding, "All there have the same hearts as we."
>
> Blessed be Thou, O my God, for all the happiness which filled my soul! What a compensation for five years of barren ministry! Scarcely had our dear Japanese opened their hearts to us than they displayed an amount of trustfulness which contrasts strangely with the behaviour of their pagan brethren. I was obliged to answer all their questions and to talk to them of O Deusu Sama, O Yasu Sama, and Santa Maria Sama, by which names they designated God, Jesus Christ, and the Blessed Virgin. The view of the statue of the Madonna and Child recalled Christmas to them, which they said they had celebrated in the eleventh month. They asked me if we were not in the seventeenth day of the Time of Sadness (Lent); nor was Saint Joseph unknown to them; they call him O Yasu Sama no Yofu, "the adoptive father of our Lord." In the midst of this volley of questions, footsteps were heard. Immediately all dispersed; but as soon as the newcomers were recognized, all returned laughing at their fright.
>
> "They are people of our village," they said, "They have the same hearts as we have."
>
> However, we had to separate for fear of awakening the suspicions of the officials, whose visit I feared.[18]

Father Petitjean had discovered the hidden Christians, Catholics who had kept alive their faith for over 200 years without the help of priests or any sacrament save baptism! He soon found that they had quite accurately maintained key teachings of the Church, including the Apostles' Creed, prayers (in both Latin and Japanese) such as the Our Father, the Hail Mary, the fifteen decades of the rosary, and how to confess one's sins, and other details of Catholic life that had been transmitted to their ancestors no later than the early seventeenth century.[19] The entire Catholic Church was elated by the news of the discovery of the Japanese Catholics, and, in recognition of the importance of this work, Father Petitjean was elevated to bishop of Japan on 22 June 1866. Until Japan was divided into two vicariates in 1876 (at his request), Bishop Petitjean had apostolic authority over all Catholics in Japan.

This sensational moment is known as "the discovery of the hidden Christians." But as Jennes has pointed out, it is more accurate to say that it was the Japanese Catholics who "discovered the missionaries and recognized them as the legitimate successors of the Padres, preaching the same Faith that had been announced to their forefathers, and for which they had suffered martyrdom and persecution for over two hundred years."[20]

Jennes's perspective helps us to understand the complex attitude that both missionaries and Japanese Catholics had toward the modern era, which was about to dawn on Japan. Whereas for Protestants (both missionaries and Japanese) the Meiji Restoration of 1868 marked a fresh baseline, a new beginning as it were, Catholics already owed much to the past. For all the persecution under Tokugawa rule, the *ancien regime* was analogous to medieval Europe in the sense that there was no schism among Japanese Christians at this time: if one was Christian, one was Catholic. This relationship with the past was also expressed in the Japanese language used to refer to Catholicism and Protestantism in the Meiji period: the former was called *kyūkyō* ("old doctrine") and the latter *shinkyō* ("new doctrine"). Most importantly, among the estimated 50,000 hidden Catholics who now gradually came out in the open, and even among the roughly 25,000 of them who immediately reunited with the Church,[21] traditional Japanese culture had been deeply enmeshed with the practice of their faith. For them, learning a foreign language such as English, cutting one's hair, or wearing Western clothes were not historically linked to the practice of their Catholic faith. Moreover, their faith was connected to a heroic moment in the past, when the great St. Francis Xavier and other Jesuits had sacrificed so much to transmit the enduring truth of their faith, not to mention the sacrifices (often in blood) paid by their ancestors for their Catholic beliefs. For most Japanese Catholics in the late nineteenth century, and especially for those in western Japan, the past was a fecund period of religious belief, the present was significant to the extent that it remained faithful to the past and brought them priests, and the future was a very uncertain proposition (until 1873, their faith was still illegal). Whatever they may have come to know about Pope Pius IX's Syllabus of Errors, they were not positioned particularly well to embrace modernity without reservation.

But there was no overlooking the modernity in these French missionaries with their strange clothes and long, dark beards. (Those crypto-Catholics who rejected the French missionaries and modernity clung to their past practices and became *hanare* or "schismatics.") The world had not yet changed in 1865, but certainly the present promised certain advantages over the immediate past for those crypto-Catholics who united with the Church. For one thing, Catholics could now receive the sacraments from priests, and they flooded into the Ōura Church from surrounding villages for Mass and prayer. The *bakufu*'s prohibition against the Christian religion was still in effect, however, and in 1867 leaders of the Urakami Christians (so-called from the area where they lived) were imprisoned, and eventually 3,304 of these Catholics were forcibly removed from their homes and dispersed over twenty-one separate provinces in western Japan. This "fourth Urakami" persecution took place right through the years of the Meiji Restoration, beginning under the *bakufu* but mainly taking place in the early years of the Meiji "modern" government that began with Shinto nationalist aspirations of a restoration of the emperor as a Shinto priest-ruler. Finally, in 1873, after intense diplomatic pressure from Western powers, including France, the ancient signboards prohibiting Christianity came down, and the Catholics were allowed to return home. By then, at least 664 of the group had died. Modern Japan did not begin on an altogether high note for Japanese Catholics. In contrast, the relationship to the new modern society and government for Protestants was considerably different: English (not French) became the language of success and power for Meiji Japanese, and most Protestant missionaries spoke English and promoted English-language Bibles. For some ambitious young Japanese, the Protestants were at least as attractive for their English lessons as for their doctrinal lectures. But most importantly, the sacrifices of the Urakami Catholics had earned the right of all Christian missionaries to proselytize among Japanese and the right for any Japanese to practise Christianity in whatever form he or she wished. Modernity, for Protestants in Japan, was a much less mixed bag than it was for Catholics.

It is remarkable, then, that even though it was not completely in keeping with the trends of the times the Catholic Church enjoyed significant growth during the early and mid-Meiji period, even before religious freedom was guaranteed by Article 28 of the 1889 Constitution of Greater Imperial Japan. The two dioceses instituted in 1876 were further divided into three dioceses in 1888 and into four dioceses in 1891. Twenty-three Japanese men were ordained priests between 1881 and 1894, many of whom came from families that had held leadership positions in the hidden Catholic communities over the previous centuries. In 1904, Catholics in Nagasaki, with their deep ties to the past, were three times more numerous than Catholics in the rest of Japan, and even as late as 1927 they were still the majority, representing 63,698 of the total 97,581 Catholics in Japan.[22] Two other salient points from the demography of Christians during the late nineteenth century are worth noting in this regard. First, the Catholic Church enjoyed a growth rate of 37 percent during the final decade of the nineteenth century, whereas the Protestant numbers declined 7 percent. Second, the real story is told in the raw numbers: by the early twentieth century, there was nearly double the number of Catholics (58,261) than Protestants (31,631).[23] The point is not "who won" in converting souls to Christ (in fact, there are now slightly more Protestants than Catholics in Japan). Rather, it is to suggest how Catholic attitudes critical of modernism and progressivism were no obstacle to continued growth of the Catholic Church during this period of general intoxication with all things modern.[24] The Catholic Church may well have encompassed one of the broadest yet least studied sources of critical attitudes toward modernity in Meiji Japan.

As noted above, Catholics in Nagasaki represented the majority of Japanese Catholics during this period, and their understanding of the faith was much more tied to tradition than was the case for Catholics in the east and certainly more so than Protestants. Catholic missionaries in Yokohama vied with Protestant missionaries for the educated, modernizing elites, while the Nagasaki Catholics tended to be more rural and uneducated – precisely the social stratum that gained the least during the early stages of modernization in Japan. These differences played out in concrete ways. For example, Catholic missionaries in Yokohama preferred the vocabulary for Catholic terminology that had been worked out in China in preparation for evangelizing in Japan. In the west, Bishop Petitjean insisted on preserving the Portuguese and Latin terminology that was already familiar to the Nagasaki Catholics from their centuries underground.[25] By 1883, however, the newer terminology favoured in the east had won out and was in general use among all Japanese Catholics.

Characteristic of Catholic missionary work, in contrast to Protestant missionary work, was the emphasis on serving the disadvantaged, the poor, orphans, and especially those suffering from Hansen's disease (i.e., leprosy). Most representative was Father Germain Léger Testevuide, MEP, who worked with victims of Hansen's disease at Gotemba. As Ballhatchet notes,

The rural, philanthropic focus ... was probably linked to the conservatism of Catholicism in general and French Catholicism in particular. As a result in the long term converts were likely to be attracted more by Catholic compassion for the poor ... than by its links with the new world view intro- duced as a result of the opening of the treaty ports.[26]

Ballhatchet then points to the Sisters of the Charitable Instruction of the Infant Jesus as an example of reaching out, educating girls from 1872 on (see Ann Harrington's chapter in this volume). Given Ballhatchet's assess- ment of conservative impulses underlying this work in the eastern part of the country, we cannot impose a binary opposition of "traditional Catholi- cism" in the west and "progressive Catholicism" in the east. Testevuide's work was in the greater Tokyo area, and his charity work was not incon- sistent with a critical view of modernism, progressivism, and the state- centred ideologies that were embraced by much of the Meiji elite. Indeed, Catholic charitable work often served to highlight the gaps in modernist politics that often simply ignored the plight of those suffering from disease, poverty, social discrimination, and physical handicaps.

During the late nineteenth century, when liberal theologies were domin- ant in most American Protestant seminaries, the contrast with Catholicism could not have been more stark. Throughout the pontificates of Pius IX (1846-78), Leo XIII (1878-1903), and St. Pius X (1903-14), the Church struggled against a modernism that provided intellectual cover for an atheism often expressed in a narrow scientific rationalism. The First Vatican Council (1869-70) strongly supported the ultramontanists and rejected Gallicanism, but it also emphasized the need for "a proper collaboration between faith ... and reason," noting the continued relevance of both reason and revela- tion.[27] The council neither rejected reason in favour of fideism nor celebrated the modern intoxication with reason as a step beyond what some thought of as the superstitions of the past (i.e., faith). The fight against modernism and atheism in the "age of science" continued to characterize Catholic theol- ogy throughout the late nineteenth and early twentieth centuries. A key moment in this battle was the syllabus of Pius X, "Lamentabili sane exitu," issued on 3 July 1907. It condemned the chief tenets of modernism, a position that was strengthened in November of that year when Pius X "prohibited the defence of the condemned propositions under the penalty of excom- munication."[28] "Lamentabili sane exitu" was followed by the encyclical "Pascendi" of 8 September 1907 and by the oath against modernism, pre- scribed on 1 September 1910 and required of all Catholic priests.

These efforts to resist the extreme claims made in the name of modernism, unpopular as they may have been in Europe, faced additional challenges in Meiji Japan, where all things modern were often celebrated without qualification. Even establishing a Catholic voice in the media was not easy. One reason was that a large percentage of the Catholics in Japan were rural people of limited education, whereas the Protestant missionaries, with their English Bibles and rather uncritical stance toward modernity, found it easier to attract many of Japan's more ambitious young minds. One can debate endlessly whether these social realities limited the number of Catholic intellectuals or whether the Catholic Church's position on modernism and rationalism limited its appeal for Japanese intellectuals. In either case, it is fair to accept Hanzawa's conclusion that no major Catholic intellectual emerged in Japan until the Taisho period (1912-26).[29]

But Hanzawa does not assert that there was no Catholic presence in Japanese culture: rather, his point is that there was no major Japanese intellectual who expressed Catholic views in public discourse during the Meiji period. In fact, Hanzawa details the extensive Catholic media that emerged in the late nineteenth century, especially the influential Catholic newspaper *Kōkyō Bampō* ("The Catholic Monitor") (1881-93) and the magazine *Koe* ("Voice") (1891-present). The force behind the *Kōkyō Bampō* and the leading Catholic influence on Japanese media during the Meiji period was François Alfred Ligneul, MEP (1847-1922). Ligneul came to Japan in 1880 and stayed until 1912, dividing his energies between the Tsukiji seminary, which he headed, serving as spiritual director of the Saint Maur sisters, and developing Catholic publications in Japanese. With Maeda Chōta, one of the first Japanese ordained a priest in the modern period, he co-wrote *Shūkyō to kokka* ("Religion and the State") in 1893 to offer a Catholic refutation of Inoue Tetsujirō's allegation that Christians could not be loyal citizens.[30] Ligneul changed the name of the *Kōkyō Bampō* to the *Tenshu Bampei* ("The Soldier of God") and emphasized apologetics so that Catholics could defend their faith against the challenges of the modern age. *Koe* began in the Osaka Diocese and was designed by Bishop Midon to be "a Voice crying out in the desert ... [to] fight against the invasion and influence of the heretics."[31] Presumably, by "influence of the heretics" he included the Protestants who had become much more active in publications and intellectual work. But these publications were not exclusively directed against fellow Christians. Rather, their harshest adversaries were Japanese: "rationalistic thinkers like Yasui Sokken (1788-1877), materialists such as Katō Hiroyuki and sceptics [sic] like Inoue Tetsujirō [who] began attacking the very bases of religion ... The favorite bone of contention of the sectarians was that the Church was the enemy of science."[32] In this context, the chapter in this volume by James Bartholomew helps to fill an important gap by highlighting the work of Japanese scientists of the time, such as Noguchi Hideyo, Takamine Jōkichi, and Nagai Nagayoshi, who were Catholic.

The first influential Japanese Catholic intellectual was Iwashita Francis Xavier Sōichi (1889-1940). Iwashita attended the Catholic Morning Star (Gyōsei) school in Tokyo and was baptized into the Catholic Church in 1901, his second year at middle school, taking the name of St. Francis Xavier. He then proceeded through the course for modern Japan's intellectual elite, beginning at the First Higher School. While at this school, he organized the Catholic Study Group with five other Morning Star graduates there and worked under the direction of Father Emile Eck, who had taught him at Morning Star. This Study Group, and the Vincent de Paul Society that he established around the same time, became the foundation for the Catholic Youth Association (Kōkyō Seinen Kai), which is credited with the large increase in Catholics in Japan during the mid-1920s.[33]

Iwashita then matriculated at Tokyo Imperial University, where he studied philosophy under the fabled Professor Raphael Koeber, a convert to Catholicism. His classmates included his lifelong friend Kuki Shūzō and other cultural and intellectual luminaries, such as Watsuji Tetsurō, Amano Teiyū, Kojima Kikuo, and Mitani Takamasa, and two years behind him was Tanaka Kōtarō, with whom he often socialized (see my chapter on Tanaka).[34] After graduation, he taught English in Kagoshima and then in 1919 left Japan for postgraduate study with Catholic professors in France, Germany, Belgium, England, and Italy (he turned down a government scholarship and went on his own money as he did not want to be obligated to work as a professor of philosophy at Tokyo Imperial University). While in Europe, Iwashita formed the Bon Samaritain Society with other Japanese, including his Morning Star classmates Totsuka Vincent Bunkyō, a medical student, Ogura Shintarō (who accompanied Iwashita on the trip to Europe), and Hasegawa Luke Ryūzō, who was in Paris to study art. Still in Europe, Iwashita decided to become a priest, so he studied theology at Rome's Angelico University and was ordained in Venice at the San Marco Cathedral in 1925. On his return to Japan that year, he opened his home in Tokyo to Catholic students, promoted the study of Catholicism, published Catholic works at his own expense, and expanded the network of Catholic Study Groups in the region. He served as editor of *Koe, Katorikku Shimbun,* and *Katorikku Kenkyū;* he taught at the Tokyo Seminary; and, even after he became the director of the Kōyama (aka Kamiyama) Resurrection Hospital, caring for victims of Hansen's disease, he made monthly trips back to Tokyo to continue directing the spiritual work of young Catholic students such as Yoshimitsu Yoshihiko (see his chapter in this volume). After a brief trip to China, he fell ill and passed away on 3 December 1940 (the feast day of his baptismal namesake, St. Francis Xavier, SJ). Iwashita was fifty-one years old.

Although his life was short, his influence through the many organizations that he founded or participated in and through his prolific writings was immense. So many Catholics who had a great impact on Japanese culture were influenced by Iwashita that it would be little exaggeration to say that he was the intellectual fount of modern Japanese Catholicism. He certainly articulated in powerful terms the general tendency among many modern Japanese Catholics to adopt a measured critique of modernity. His negative assessment of modernity focused on the ethical pitfalls of modern subjectivism, which Iwashita found particularly troubling in Protestantism. But as Hanzawa also notes, he was not inclined to idealize a Catholic medieval period.[35]

Iwashita's appraisal of modernity can be summarized around two key arguments, one about the limits of science, the other about the limits of individuals. Iwashita was modern enough to accept the legitimate contributions of scientific advances in the modern era, but at the same time he recognized that much of modernism stemmed from an arrogation in the name of science of that which properly belonged to God alone. "All scientific truths," he maintained, "ultimately come back to first principles that are themselves self-evident proofs. Whether we understand the details, we must accept their results ... This acceptance is necessary. However, the Truth which is the object of faith is a mystery concerning God."[36] Iwashita's criticism of scientism (*kagaku shijōshugi*) was based not on an absolute mysticism or even a rejection of science itself but on the argument that scientism was not reasonable. This view enabled, even encouraged, many Catholic Japanese to become scientists without any crisis of religious faith or conscience (see Bartholomew's chapter, this volume). One hallmark of Iwashita's thought was its rigorous application of the principle of reason to the created world as a legitimate means of discovering both nature and the supernatural.

Just as science must not be severed from the broader supernatural world from which it derives its origin and meaning, so too the individual cannot be conceived in radical separation from the community or society. Of course, Iwashita held that this true community was found in the *ecclesia*, the Catholic

Church as founded by Jesus Christ himself. Although the Church was historical in foundation and growth, it was also the sign of God's continuous presence among humans through time. There was nothing here of the modernist assumption of a radical break or discontinuity. Hence, Iwashita rejected the modernist and secularist arguments that (national) society had replaced religious community, and in fact he argued that "what Catholics call the Church is the perfect society. It is an association of people that exists for the achievement of common goals. But it is not an accidental organization ... Christ himself personally established this Church as a society."[37] Precisely for this reason, Iwashita was, as Hanzawa notes, a consistently harsh foe of nationalism, by which he meant *minzokushugi*.[38] This form of ethnic nationalism had emerged in early-twentieth-century Japan as a surrogate for civil society, an often secularized (or Shintoized) form of national society.[39] In essence, Iwashita was implying a sense of the Church as an alternative to modernist society but not one premised on a rejection of history, reason, or awareness of global responsibility. In one way or another, many of these views have been shared by most Japanese Catholics down to the present day.

Legacies of Francis Xavier(s): An Overview of the Chapters
The rest of this volume may be said, in a sense, to explore the legacy not only of St. Francis Xavier, SJ but also of his namesake, Francis Xavier Iwashita. After Harrington's opening chapter, which looks again at the French influence but through the lens of a gendered analysis that focuses on the role of women religious, we take up the role of Catholic scientists (Bartholomew's chapter). Here the reader is invited to keep in mind the issues that Iwashita raised about the positive and negative intersections of science with the Catholic faith as well as his own association with Catholic scientists such as Totsuka Vincent Bunkyō. The next two chapters deal with two intellectuals who were most directly influenced by Iwashita: the legal scholar Tanaka Kōtarō, whose jurisprudence was deeply informed by Iwashita's idea of the *ecclesia* as the perfect society, and Yoshimitsu Yoshihiko, who developed a neo-Thomist critique of modernism. Ikehara's chapter on Kanayama Masahide notes the personal influence of Iwashita and Yoshimitsu on Kanayama and reveals how influential Catholics such as Kanayama and Rear Admiral Stephen Shinjirō Yamamoto (1877-1942) were at the highest levels of Japanese government. Yamamoto's chapter on Father Inoue Yōji introduces a very important contemporary Japanese theologian whose books are popular among Catholic and non-Catholic Japanese.

The chapters by Williams and Sunami look at the extraordinary influence of Catholicism on postwar Japanese fiction. Williams presents a new perspective on Endō Shūsaku, certainly the best-known Catholic writer and possibly the best-known Catholic Japanese. Endō can be considered Iwashita's spiritual grandson, as his spiritual director and house master during university days was Yoshimitsu, who had received his spiritual direction from Iwashita. It is safe to assume that what most Japanese know about Catholicism they have learned from Endō's works. Sunami's chapter, translated into English for this volume, gives us an overview of a contemporary Catholic female writer, Sono Ayako. Sono is not only a popular writer whose works frequently take up Catholic themes in an explicit manner but also the wife of Miura Shumon, himself a Catholic writer and former high-level government official. Sono was baptized Mary Elizabeth Chizuko on 26 September 1948 when she was a seventeen-year-old student.[40] She and her husband are perhaps Japan's most famous and influential Catholic couple.

Finally, Mullins' closing chapter surveys the status of the Catholic Church in Japan today, particularly in light of the sociological and demographic challenges arising from the increased globalizing forces in Japanese society. In the process, Mullins raises an intriguing question that cuts right to the heart of this volume: is there a *Japanese* Catholicism today? And if so, is such a national framework for the Catholic (katholikos = universal) Church necessary in our increasingly globalized world?

As in any anthology, there will inevitably be gaps in our coverage.[41] Some important Catholic Japanese are not included in this volume, as much from the space limits of a single volume as from the particular interests of the contributors. Therefore, before closing this introduction, I will provide a brief overview of some of those Catholic Japanese who did not receive particular attention here but whose Catholicism and influence on modern Japanese culture are matters of public record. I hope that such an overview will provide a broader sense of the extensive impact of Catholic Japanese in various realms of modern Japanese culture and society. Notes for further reading on these Catholics, where available, will also be provided.

Unsung Legacies: Those Left Out

One of the most intriguing cases of a Catholic in modern Japan is that of Yosano Akiko (1878-1942). Yosano is well known as a leading Japanese writer, most famous for her poem "Please Do Not Die" addressed to her brother during the Russo-Japanese War. But it has not been noted in the

major studies of her life that she converted to Catholicism in 1940 and has
passed the faith down through her family to the present.[42] Yosano's contemporary, Yamaguchi Shikazō (1870-1953), was trained in Catholic theology, worked as a journalist for *Koe,* and was an active participant in the
intellectual circles of his time.[43] Another literary figure from Yosano's time,
the translator and literary critic Tsujino Hisanori (1909-37), was converted
by Iwashita, taking the name of St. John shortly before his death at the age
of twenty-seven.[44] At the time of his death, Tsujino was heralded as one of
the brightest literary minds of his time. One of the most active Catholics of
the period was the aforementioned Yamamoto Stephen Shinjirō, who rose
to be a rear admiral in the Imperial Navy and was a close adviser to Emperor
Hirohito. Yamamoto was related to Iwashita: his younger brother Saburō
had married Iwashita's younger sister Masako. He was only one of many
Catholic influences close to the imperial family that Ben-Ami Shillony has
chronicled in his recent book on the Japanese monarchy.[45] In addition to the
current empress, who was raised and educated as a Catholic by her parents,
Prince Asaka Peter Takahiko and his wife, Princess Tōdō Lucy Chikako,
converted to Catholicism in the early postwar years.[46]

Those years were a boon for conversions to Catholicism. Clearly, works
such as Nagai Takashi's *Bells of Nagasaki* helped the cause, for it became not
only a best-selling book but the basis for a popular movie and song, too.
Nagai himself was a powerful metaphor for the spiritual relevance of Catholicism in postwar Japan. He has even been called "the saint of the atomic
wasteland" *(genshino no seija)*.[47] But an equally strong case for canonization
can be made for Kitahara Satoko (1929-58). Her life spans a narrative that
moves from the centre of modern Japan to its margins. Satoko was born
into privilege and affluence, the daughter of a university professor who had
moved into the Suginami suburb of Tokyo. One day, while accompanying
her younger sister to her Catholic school (the Kitahara family was not Catholic, however), she asked one of the nuns there about the faith and soon
found herself taking lessons in Catholicism. She was baptized Elisabeth in
October 1949, and her story might well have ended there, one among a
growing number of middle-class Japanese converts to Catholicism in the
early postwar years. But her conversion was only the beginning. While
staying with her older sister in Asakusa, she was attracted to the figure of
the dishevelled Brother Zeno Zebrowski, who walked the streets minister-
ing to the least fortunate in the city. Soon enough Satoko was working
alongside him and then living among the poorest of the poor in an area of
Tokyo known as "Ant's Town." She helped in every way she could, not

only with their efforts at eking out a living at "rag picking," but also teaching the children of Ant's Town. She was soon known as "Maria of Ant's Town" and beloved by the entire community. In style and substance, Satoko embodied an ambivalence to the modernizing impulses of early postwar Japan. When the city sought to simply brush away the "filth" of Ant's Town, she spoke up for the importance of community and human values that she, Brother Zeno, "Boss" Ozawa, Matsui Tōru, and others had built in the shadows of the new Tokyo. Her dedication to the poor cost her her health, for Satoko developed tuberculosis and died from it in 1958 at the young age of twenty-nine. Her impact on postwar culture was substantial, with books and a major movie about her life, but she remains little known outside Japan due primarily to a lack of English-language works about her.[48]

Across town, yet in an entirely different world, the rising writer Shimao Toshio was struggling with marital difficulties. Shimao began writing personal accounts of these problems in 1955 with "Out of the Depths I Cry" *(Ware fukaki fuchi yori)*, a none-too-thinly veiled reference to Psalm 130. Other than the titles of his works, his writings were hardly Christian in any explicit sense. But his life and his "fiction" merged until the lines were often difficult to perceive. In either case, it was clear to the literary world that Shimao had an affair with another woman, that the anguish it caused seemed connected to his wife Miho's mental instability, and that Miho (and then he) had entered a mental hospital for an extended time. For the next several years, Shimao wrote about this incident in what became known as his "sick wife stories" *(byōsai mono)*, though critics have suggested that they would be more accurately called "sick couple stories" *(byōfu mono)* since Shimao makes it clear that his wife's suffering was inextricably connected to his own sins. These essays were collected in his masterpiece, *The Sting of Death (Shi no toge)*, the title referring to the effects of sin recorded in 1 Corinthians 15:55-56. In fact, Shimao had worked things out with his wife, agreeing to leave Tokyo (and, it seemed, his career) for her hometown on Amami Ōshima, which they did in October 1955. The following year, in Amami, Shimao converted to Catholicism, the faith of his wife's family. Miho followed him back into her childhood faith soon after. Shimao was not only able to rebuild his family life but also went on to have a remarkable career as one of postwar Japan's most important writers, even though he spurned life in Tokyo (de rigueur for any ambitious writer, then or now), choosing to live in the remote islands of western Japan. In marked contrast to Endō, Shimao might be thought of as Japan's best writer who happened to be (a converted) Catholic. Although many literary critics seem unaware of the importance of Catholicism in his works, there is no question that Catholic values shaped his writing, particularly on the sanctity of marriage, the seriousness of sins against chastity, the importance of atonement, and a willingness to eschew the material benefits of modernity to protect these fundamental moral values.

Although Kitahara found an alternative modernity in the ghettoes of Tokyo and Shimao rejected the modern mecca of Tokyo and its materialism, Yamamoto Kōichi (1940-83) represents an even more subtle way in which Catholicism challenged dominant ideas of modernity from the margins of a newly affluent Japan during the 1960s, 1970s, and into the 1980s.[49] He was one of the first Japanese to join the lay Catholic organization Opus Dei ("The Work of God"), and his life story is deeply intertwined with the founding of Opus Dei in Japan. Although this organization and its work are not the usual things found in a cultural history of Japan, they are appropriate since Opus Dei, as a lay organization, by design works to change culture by working from within everyday secular occupations. Assessing its influence on postwar Japanese culture may not be as simple as tracing the work of prominent Catholic Japanese writers and intellectuals, but a full picture of the influence of Catholicism in modern Japanese culture must include consideration of its work.

Opus Dei was founded by the Spanish priest Josémaria Escrivá on 2 October 1928, but it was not until 1958 (the year of Kitahara's death and only two years after Shimao's conversion) that the work began in Japan. Again it was two Spanish priests, José Ramón Madurga and Fernando Acaso, who came to the Osaka area at the request of the local ordinary, Bishop Paolo Yoshigorō Taguchi. Yamamoto began associating with the group in mid-1959. He was baptized on 14 April 1963 and asked to join Opus Dei on 20 October after graduating from Kwansei Gakuin University. (The first Japanese to join Opus Dei, on 28 December 1962, was Sōichirō Nitta, ordained a priest in 1972.) Yamamoto's godfather was Antonio Villacieros, the Spanish ambassador to Japan, and Yamamoto received a grant from the Spanish Embassy to study at the Institute of Spanish Language and Culture at the University of Navarra in 1966 before moving to the Roman College of the Holy Cross, where he studied theology until 1970. After his return to Japan, Yamamoto played a key role at the Opus Dei Seido Language Institute, established in Ashiya in 1962. Although the institute also offered English classes, the most popular language among Japanese students, the linguistic and cultural orientation of Opus Dei was Spanish, making it unusual among such institutions in postwar Japan.

In a sense, we might say that Yamamoto found an alternative modernity in the Spanish orientation of Opus Dei that paralleled the alternative modernity that Catholic Japanese had earlier found in the French orientation of the MEP. In 1971, the Seido Language Institute was absorbed into the newly formed Seido Foundation for the Advancement of Education, which now had a publication department along with the Okuashiya Study Centre, and it soon included Seido Gakuen and a catering school in Nagasaki. During the growth decade of the 1970s, these institutes played a key role in the conversions of many people to Catholicism and influenced many more Japanese who did not convert. Yet what stands out about these activities in a broader historical context is the alternative that they presented to a dominant Anglo-American culture of modernity, one that was especially centred on the Tokyo area. In ways remarkably similar to Kitahara and Shimao, Yamamoto offered Japanese who lived outside this privileged circle of Tokyo a spiritual life that was in certain respects at odds with the dominant American-oriented culture of modern Japan.

As with any thesis, there are limits to my argument about Catholicism as an alternative way of coming to terms with modernity in Japan. Particularly in the wake of the Vatican II reforms, one finds especially in eastern Japan (i.e., the Tokyo region) a greater propensity to embrace various aspects of modernity, if not always modernism, among Catholics.[50] Yet even in Japanese Catholic circles where modernity seems most welcome (often in the form of ecumenical projects, interfaith dialogue, and theological innovations), there remains a different kind of resistance to modernity expressed in various efforts to articulate a quasi-indigenous critique of the West. One of the most intellectually intriguing is the effort by the Dominican priest and Tokyo University professor of philosophy Miyamoto Hisao to reconstruct philosophy on the basis of a Hebraic concept of being *(hayah)* rather than the Greek notion of *ontos*. Miyamoto offers his theory of *hayahtology* as a deconstruction of the Western foundations of modern philosophy in ontology.[51]

This effort to separate Japanese Catholics from the West (if not modernity *tout court*) has in recent years reached the highest levels of Church governance in Japan. When, in preparation for a meeting with the Asian synod, Pope John Paul II sent an outline in advance of the meeting (the *Lineamenta*), the Japanese bishops met to discuss the *Lineamenta* in an extraordinary plenary session on 18-21 February 1997. At that meeting, they rejected the pope's agenda for the synod, declaring that they would present their own issues for discussion. The following quotation from the Japanese bishops' response to the *Lineamenta* speaks for itself:

Since the questions of the *Lineamenta* were composed in the context of Western Christianity, they are not suitable. Among the questions are some concerning whether evangelization is going well or not, but what is the standard of evaluation? ... The judgement [sic] should not be made from a European framework, but must be seen on the spiritual level of the people who live in Asia.[52]

Building on this "Asian spirituality," the Japanese bishops outlined a position that became a major source of tension between the Vatican and the Asian bishops. Criticizing the *Lineamenta* (i.e., Pope John Paul II) for "a certain 'defensiveness' and apologetic attitude," the bishops conceded that

Jesus Christ is the Way, the Truth, and the Life, but in Asia, before stressing that Jesus Christ is the TRUTH, we must search much more deeply into how he is the WAY and the LIFE. If we stress too much that "Jesus Christ is the One and Only Savior," we can have no dialogue, common living, or solidarity with other religions.[53]

The Japanese bishops presented these declarations, along with a list of eight major topics for the Church in Asia, to the Vatican on 23 July 1997.

This context of tensions between the bishops of Asia and the Vatican best explains the publication in 2000 by the Congregation for the Doctrine of the Faith of *Dominus Iesus: On the Unicity and Salvific Universality of Jesus Christ and the Church*. Although certain liberal Catholic theologians, particularly in the West, have often presumed that *Dominus Iesus* was aimed at them (it was, after all, penned by Cardinal Joseph Ratzinger, whom they derisively referred to as "God's Rottweiler"), consideration of the *Lineamenta* controversy in Asia, and of the timing and substance of the document, suggest a broader concern by the Vatican over the unwillingness of Asian bishops to proclaim Jesus Christ as the universal truth for all humans – a non-negotiable for orthodox Catholics, indeed for all orthodox Christians. The matter is brought into greater clarity when one considers that (then) Cardinal Ratzinger also wrote *Truth and Tolerance: Christian Belief and World Religion* in 2002, presenting a book-length critical analysis of the claims of relativism, focusing on arguments for "Asian spirituality" as a limitation on the scope of Catholic dogma.[54]

All this brings us back not to a conclusion but to an informing paradox of Catholicism in modern Japan. Even as many of Japan's Catholic bishops intone a culturalist line of Asian resistance to the presumed dominance of the West, they inevitably fall back on cultural resources for their arguments, which were first articulated by Western, and often Marxist, scholars. Whether cultural Orientalists or revolutionary nationalists, those who have tried to articulate a native non-Western sensibility are often caught in this epistemological dilemma: to free oneself from "the West," one must imbibe more of the Western intellectual and cultural forms of liberation (for a deep critique of this intellectual problem, see Yamamoto's chapter). Critical theorists in Japan who have considerable expertise in Asian history and thought have called into question whether there is in fact something that can be called "Asian values."[55] Yet prelates in Japan, educated mainly in European languages, Catholic dogma, and canon law, seem more susceptible to the seductions first created by the Western imagination of an Asian other. Yet this irony is capped by another: one finds considerable consistency in the cultural theories of Pope Benedict XVI and Yoshimitsu Yoshihiko, who, writing half a century ago, pointed out that culture could never be opposed to the Church; rather, the Church itself constituted a culture of its own that was formed and sustained by historical time rather than by a transcendental cultural essence. Yoshimitsu would have appreciated Pope Benedict XVI's call to retire the outmoded theory of "in-culturation" in favour of a more anthropologically and historically accurate model of "inter-culturation," in which all social and cultural identities are merely historical contingencies dependent on the grace of God.[56]

Notes

1 Francis Xavier, SJ (1506-52), was beatified by Pope Paul V on 25 October 1619 and canonized by Pope Gregory XV on 12 March 1622, a mere seventy years after his death, and thus now is formally known as St. Francis Xavier, SJ. However, I refrain from referring to him as St. Francis Xavier in my narrative when referring to events that happened prior to his canonization. No disrespect for him or the Catholic Church is intended.

2 Jennes, *A History of the Catholic Church in Japan*, 13-16.

3 Boxer, *The Christian Century in Japan*, 195-96.

4 See *God's Fingerprints in Japan* (DVD).

5 There is reason to believe that Hosokawa Tadaoki himself was never baptized. See Boxer, *The Christian Century in Japan*, 185.

6 Miyazaki, "Roman Catholic Mission in Pre-Modern Japan," 7. These figures are contested, however. Some sources have put the total number of Catholics in the early seventeenth century at 1 million (Charles Pierre, SJ), others upward of 700,000 (Alexander Brou, SJ), and others still as low as 200,000 (Bishop Cerqueira). See Jennes, *A History of the Catholic Church in Japan*, 240-42.

7 Boxer, *The Christian Century in Japan*, 448. Jennes, *A History of the Catholic Church in Japan*, 246, counts only 2,126 martyrs in the period 1549-1639 but adds the important caveat that "this number is merely a strict minimum, listing only those martyrs whose name or identification is generally well known; it does not include the 'many others' mentioned in the lists without indicating the number."

8   Fifty thousand Catholics is a Church estimate from 1892 that includes "about half" who were *hanare,* separatists who did not reunite with the Church after 1873. Cited in Cary, *A History of Christianity in Japan,* 288. These *hanare* still numbered about 30,000 as late as 1945, but today only about 1,000 survive, almost all of whom reside in remote areas in and around Kyushu. See Miyazaki, "The Kakure Kirishitan Tradition," 22-23.

9   Van Hecken, *The Catholic Church in Japan since 1859,* 23.

10 See Howes, *Japan's Modern Prophet;* Scheiner, *Christian Converts and Social Protest in Meiji Japan;* Suzuki, ed., *Kindai nihon kirisutokyō meicho senshū* (the thirty-two-volume set of Christian archives from modern Japan, of which only a couple treat Catholicism); and Yamaji, *Essays on the Modern Japanese Church.*

11 See Ketelaar, *Of Heretics and Martyrs in Meiji Japan;* and Thelle, *Buddhism and Christianity in Japan.*

12 Van Hecken, *The Catholic Church in Japan since 1859,* 59. Van Hecken's source for these numbers is Yanagita, *Christianity in Japan,* 48. This is a relative, as well as absolute, numerical superiority of Catholic over Protestant converts to that time, if we consider the generally accepted number of Catholics that came from the *kakure* group to be 18,435 and the number of Japanese Protestants around 1873 to be close to zero. That would yield a Protestant increase of 31,631 and a Catholic increase of 39,826. Of course, there were more than a few Protestant Japanese converts even during the early Meiji years, so the disparate growth rate is probably even greater.

13 This lack of information on Catholicism in modern Japan stems from the fact that there have been few English-language works on Catholicism in the modern period, and those that have been published are mostly out of print and difficult to obtain. Volume 1 of Cary's *A History of Christianity in Japan* is one such treasure trove of information. But it was published in 1909 and is thus quite limited in its coverage of the twentieth century. And even in what it does cover, it focuses on the works of European (mainly French) Catholics working in Japan, and very little space is devoted to Japanese who were Catholic. Another valuable (and out-of-print) source is Jennes, *A History of the Catholic Church in Japan* (1959), but only the last thirty pages cover the post-Edo period, and even then only up to 1873. The most comprehensive study of Catholicism in modern Japan is Van Hecken, *The Catholic Church in Japan since 1859* (1963). It is a chronicle of official Church activities (establishment of dioceses, schools, etc.), with only cursory attention to the role of Japanese Catholics. Drummond, *A History of Christianity in Japan* (1971), provides a historical introduction to the early "Christian century" before turning to his main focus on Protestants in the modern period, offering as an afterthought only thirty pages on Catholicism in the modern period, told mainly from a missionary perspective that (again) largely overlooks Japanese Catholics. This missionary bias even infects Japanese works on Catholicism in the modern period, such as Ikeda's *Jimbutsu chūshin no nihon katorikku-shi* (1998), a wonderfully informative encyclopedia on key individuals in the history of Catholicism in Japan, but it lists only twenty-four Japanese among the sixty-six entries on individual Catholics of the modern period. In contrast, Hanzawa's *Kindai nihon no katorishizumu* (1993), the standard work on the topic of Catholicism in modern Japan, takes up in depth three important Japanese Catholics (Iwashita, Tanaka, and Yoshimitsu) and does so with compelling analyses of their contributions to modern Japanese thought. It is nicely complemented by Kamiya, *Suga Atsuko to kyūnin no rerigio* (2007), which consciously seeks to complete Hanzawa's work by extending the scope of analysis into the postwar period and including discussion on several Japanese women (including the empress of Japan). Also dealing with the postwar period is the controversial two-volume study by Onizuka, *Tennō no rozario* (2006),

which alleges a postwar global conspiracy to convert the Japanese nation to Catholicism. There has been an explosion of interest in Catholicism in Japan in the Japanese media, but unfortunately none of these works is available in English. In that context, I must mention Kevin Hanlon's study based on his personal experience as a Catholic priest in contemporary Japan, supplemented with scholarly analysis of major Catholic works, *Gaikokujin shisai ga mita nihon no katorikku shintō* (2001). Hanlon's book has now appeared in English as *Popular Catholicism in Japan* (2004).

14 Empress Michiko (née Shōda Michiko) was born into and raised by one of Japan's most famous Catholic families. Her marriage to the current emperor was arranged by the Chamberlain Koizumi Shinzō, a Christian. Shillony, *Enigma of the Emperors*, 234. Although Shillony is correct that Koizumi exercised great influence over then Prince Akihito and was a Christian, he does not appear to have been Catholic, as Shillony claims on page 234. Sonoda, *Kakusareta kōshitsu jimmyaku*, 14, claims that Koizumi was "an Anglican, which is quite close to being a Catholic." Director of the Imperial Household Agency Usami Takeshi assured Prime Minister Kishi Nobusuke (who was worried that Michiko was Catholic like the rest of her family) that Michiko (against all probability) had not been baptized, so the marriage could proceed as planned. Shillony, *Enigma of the Emperors*, 236, 239, notes that, even after the wedding, Princess Michiko "kept her Catholic practices and friends." Japanese scholars have been giving renewed attention to Empress Michiko's Catholicism: see Sonoda, *Kakusareta kōshitsu jimmyaku*, 14-40; and Onizuka's two-volume screed, *Tennō no rozario*, 2: 261-343.

15 Scannell, "Jean-Baptiste-Henri Dominique Lacordaire."

16 Launay, "Society of Foreign Missions of Paris."

17 The earliest time of Protestant missionary activity among the Japanese was 1869, though the first Japanese Protestant converts were in 1872, on the eve of the lifting of the prohibition against Christianity. See Scheiner, *Christian Converts and Social Protest in Meiji Japan*, 16.

18 Petitjean, cited in Cary, *A History of Christianity in Japan*, 282-83. The original source is Marnas, *La Religion de Jésus Ressuscitée au Japon dans la seconde moité du XIXe siécle*. The English translation presumably is Cary's. The village was Urakami, and these Catholics were thus known as the Urakami Christians. There is some uncertainty over the identity of the lady who approached Petitjean: most accounts give her name as Elisabeth Dzuru of Hamaguchi, as Van Hecken, *The Catholic Church in Japan since 1859*, does; Fujita, *Japan's Encounter with Christianity*, calls her Yuri Isabelina Sugimoto of Urakami.

19 Japanese copies of these prayers and articles of faith can be found in the appendix of Urakawa, *Nihon ni okeru kōkyōkai no fukkatsu*, 1-62.

20 Jennes, *A History of the Catholic Church in Japan*, 215.

21 These figures for *kakure kirishitan* (crypto-Catholics) and *hanare* (those who refused reunification with the Church after 1865) are from Cary, *A History of Christianity in Japan*, 288. The figure of 25,000 Catholics in the late 1860s seems a reasonable estimate given that we have a rather reliable number of 18,435 Catholics in Japan as of 1876, following the persecutions of 1867-73. And Cary's estimate of the number of *hanare* Christians is reasonable in light of the later estimate of 30,000 *hanare* in Japan during the period 1925-45. The *hanare* community has dwindled to between 1,000 and 1,500 at present. Miyazaki, "The Kakure Kirishitan Tradition," 23. Miyazaki uses the anachronistic term *kakure* ("hidden" or "crypto-") for the group of Christians that after 1865 refused to join the Catholic Church. In fact, they were no longer hidden *(kakure)*, especially after 1873, so the correct term for them is *hanare* ("separate").

22 Van Hecken, *The Catholic Church in Japan since 1859*, 69.

23 Ibid., 59. Van Hecken's source for these numbers is Yanagita, *Christianity in Japan*, 48.
24 The more positive orientation of Protestants toward modernity during the late nineteenth century in contrast to Catholics was by no means limited to Japan. The debate over modernism shaped Catholic-Protestant relations in the United States at the time, as in Europe. Most relevant for Japan was Johann Caspar Bluntschli's condemnation of Catholicism for its anti-modern attitudes. See McGreevy, *Catholicism and American Freedom*, 101-4. Bluntschli's ideas were very popular among key modernizers in nineteenth-century Japan, especially Katō Hiroyuki.
25 Marnas, *La Religion de Jésus Ressuscitée au Japon dans la seconde moité du XIXe siécle*, 550-53.
26 Ballhatchet, "The Modern Missionary Movement in Japan," 41.
27 O'Collins and Farrugia, *Catholicism*, 91.
28 A. Haag, "Syllabus," in *The Catholic Encyclopedia*, 1912.
29 Hanzawa, *Kindai nihon no katorishizumu*, 119-21, cited by Ballhatchet, "The Modern Missionary Movement in Japan," 41.
30 For a discussion and short translation from Ligneul and Maeda's work, see Doak, *A History of Nationalism in Modern Japan*, 98-100.
31 Van Hecken, *The Catholic Church in Japan since 1859*, 132-33.
32 Ibid., 140.
33 Ikeda, *Jimbutsu chūshin no nihon katorikku shi*, 429.
34 Hanzawa, *Kindai nihon no katorishizumu*, 230.
35 Ibid., 228.
36 Iwashita, cited in ibid., 244.
37 Iwashita, cited in ibid., 268-69.
38 Hanzawa, *Kindai nihon no katorishizumu*, 242.
39 On the conceptual proximity of *minzoku* and society *(shakai)* in Japanese discourse, see Doak, *A History of Nationalism in Modern Japan*, 127-63.
40 Tsuruha, *Kami no deku*, 55-56.
41 Some influential and well-known Catholic Japanese who are not treated in any depth in this volume, in addition to those listed below in note 47, include Prime Minister Hara "David" Takashi (1856-1921; baptized 1872), Prime Minister Yoshida Shigeru (1878-1967), and his family. Yoshida had his family baptized but held off his own baptism until his deathbed, declaring that he was going to "steal heaven." He supported the Catholic Church in many ways, serving as co-chair of the fundraising committee to build St. Mary's Cathedral (established 1964). A Mass of Christian Burial was held for Yoshida at St. Mary's with Cardinal Doi presiding. Yoshida's granddaughter Asō Nobuko married Prince Tomohito, and his grandson Asō Tarō became foreign minister of Japan and Japan's third Catholic prime minister. Other influential Catholics in social and political affairs include Sadako Ogata (b. 1927), director of Japan International Cooperation Agency and former UN high commissioner for refugees, and her friend Yamamoto Tadashi (b. 1936), who has served as adviser to Prime Minister Obuchi, worked on the Trilateral Commission, and served as director of the Japan Center for International Exchange. Yamamoto comes from a large and influential Catholic family: his older brother Jōji became a priest, his older sister Yoshiko was a nun and president of Seishin Women's College, and another brother and sister were executives with the Bank of Tokyo. Another influential Catholic businessman in postwar Japan is Koyabashi "Antonio" Yōtarō (b. 1933), who has sat on the board of directors of major corporations such as Xerox, NTT, Sony, GM, and Swiss ABB. Another influential Catholic is Mushakōji Kimihide (b. 1929), who has served as vice-president of the United Nations University. Also,

Motoshima Hitoshi, the mayor of Nagasaki who was shot in 1990 for remarks about the emperor, was a lifelong Catholic (see Field, *In the Realm of a Dying Emperor*). Other influential Catholic literary people include Tanaka Chikao (1905-95, though Tanaka might never have been baptized) and his wife Sumie (1908-2000); Yashiro Shizuichi (1922-98) and his daughter, the actress Mariya Tomoko (b. 1960); Kaga Otohiko (b. 1929); and Takahashi Takako (b. 1932).

42   See http://blogs.yahoo.co.jp/t_kagawa100/1199247.html. Akiko's grandson, Yosano Kaoru, is a Catholic and was a Liberal Democratic Party representative in the National Diet until the upset election of 2009.

43   Ikeda, *Jimbutsu chūshin no nihon katorikku shi,* 340-44.

44   Kamiya, *Suga Atsuko to kyūnin no rerigio,* 201-2.

45   Shillony, *Enigma of the Emperors.*

46   See Van Hecken, *The Catholic Church in Japan since 1859,* 110.

47   Ikeda, *Jimbutsu chūshin no nihon katorikku shi,* 461.

48   In 1973, Takagi Shirō wrote and directed an operetta at the Takarazuka Theatre called "The Town Where Stars Fell," based on Kitahara's life. Kitahara wrote a book on her experience in Ant's Town, *Ari mo machi no kodomotachi* (with a foreword by Tanaka Kōtarō), and Shochiku produced a film on her life, *Ari no machi no maria,* with the film star Chino Kakuko in the lead role. English works on Kitahara are few and far between. The only in-depth study is Glynn, *The Smile of a Ragpicker,* which is out of print and difficult to find. More easily obtained is Taira, "Ragpickers and Community Development."

49   The information below on Yamamoto and Opus Dei in Japan comes from Mélich Maixé, "Koichi Yamamoto (1940-1983) and the Beginnings of Opus Dei in Japan." Since Mélich Maixé does not employ macrons, it is impossible to know whether Koichi and other Japanese names in the article are the correct romanization. Most likely, it should be Kōichi, and that is how I record the name here.

50   Kamiya's *Suga Atsuko to kyūnin no rerigio* is a welcome volume that, in many ways, serves as a necessary complement to Hanzawa's study on prewar Japanese Catholicism, which emphasizes a critical view of modernity. Whereas Hanzawa's objects of study (Iwashita, Yoshimitsu, Tanaka) are mainly on pre-Vatican II Catholic culture, Kamiya's book consciously focuses on post-Vatican II Catholic culture in Japan. In separate chapters, Kamiya introduces journalist and professor Suga Atsuko (1929-98), theologian and educator Inukai Michiko (b. 1921), professor of the history of science Murakami Yōichirō (b. 1936), writer Okawa Kunio (b. 1927), professor of philosophy Onodera Isao (b. 1929), translator and writer Takada Hiroatsu (b. 1900), and writer Serizawa Kōjirō (1897-1993), in addition to the current empress (née Shōda Michiko) and Inoue Yōji and Iwashita Sōichi, who are also discussed in this volume. One weakness of this effort to assert a more positive image of modernism and Catholicism is that the most modernist examples were often not so Catholic. Takada and Serizawa were never baptized, and Suga herself seems to have fallen away from the Church at the end of her life. But Kamiya makes a compelling case that their deep interest in Catholicism and their writings about Catholic values and faith nonetheless play a major role in enhancing awareness of, and respect for, Catholicism among the Japanese public today.

51   See Miyamoto, *Sonzai no kisetsu.*

52   Special Assembly for Asia of the Synod of Bishops, "Official Response of the Japanese Church to the Lineamenta."

53   Ibid. Emphasis is mine, but capitalization is in the original.

54   Ratzinger, *Truth and Tolerance,* especially 85-89, 223-31. Although Pope Benedict XVI (Cardinal Ratzinger) does not directly address Japan in this book, he uses India to

signify the Asian challenge to Western Christianity, a move that seems appropriate given that the challenge to the Vatican was broader than the Japanese bishops but issued in the context of the Asian bishops' synod.

55 See Aoki and Saeki, eds., *"Ajia-teki kachi" to wa nanika.*
56 See Yoshimitsu, *Bunka to shūkyō no rinen;* and Ratzinger, *Truth and Tolerance,* especially 55-79.

1
Catholic Women Religious and Catholicism in Japan: 1872-1940

Ann M. Harrington

One is hard pressed to think of Catholicism in Japan without thinking about St. Francis Xavier, SJ. And thus one is led to think of the Society of Jesus, the Jesuits, and their pioneering work in Japan from 1549 until 1639. This time period, often called Japan's first Christian century, has been studied extensively, and its stories are well known to Japanese and many outside Japan. When Catholicism returned to Japan in the nineteenth century, the Paris Foreign Mission Society priests received permission from the Vatican to be the only order of Catholic priests to proselytize in Japan.[1] The story of the women religious who helped the Paris Foreign Mission Society priests in the last half of the nineteenth century is not so well known.[2] That lack of recognition remains true for those sisters who went to Japan in the twentieth century. All of these women followers of St. Francis Xavier, SJ, who carried the Christian message are for the most part ignored in the study of Catholicism in Japan.

My remarks here focus on the works of sisters during two time periods: the Meiji period (1868-1912), and the prewar Showa period (1926-40). The first women religious to go to Japan, the Sisters of the Infant Jesus from Paris (Soeurs de l'Enfant-Jésus de Paris), also known as the Saint Maur sisters, arrived in Japan in 1872. Mother Saint Mathilde Raclot headed their mission and lived the remainder of her life in Japan. In this early period, I look only briefly at the Saint Maur sisters because I have written of them elsewhere.[3] For the latter period, I explore the mission experiences of the Sisters of the Holy Names of Jesus and Mary from Canada, hereafter referred to as the Holy Names sisters. In 1931, these women religious went to a Japan eager to take its place as an equal to the Western powers and to throw off any vestiges of Western imperialism.

The majority of my information came from the archives of the religious orders under discussion.[4] For the latter period, I also used a study by Hirayama Kumiko, a professor at Kagoshima Immaculate Heart College.[5] In the process of looking at these two orders of religious women, the Saint Maur sisters and the Holy Names sisters, it became clear that these women made significant contributions to Japan. I argue that the history of Catholicism in Japan is incomplete without a study of the works of women religious. Even though the sisters served at the invitation of the priests, they were responsible for many works that were indispensable to the Catholic mission. But the Japan in which the Holy Names sisters arrived in 1931 was quite different from the Japan of 1872. I will explore how Japan's growing militarism impacted the work of the sisters who arrived in the 1930s and show how the influence of the first sisters to go to Japan remained strong some sixty years after their entrance into Japan and proved invaluable to the newly arrived women from Canada and the United States.

The Saint Maur Sisters
The Saint Maur sisters arrived in a Japan that had been forced open by Commodore Matthew Perry of the United States in 1854 and where, for over two centuries, the government had forbidden the practice of Catholicism. The Paris Foreign Mission Society priests gained the approval of the pope to be the only Catholic missionaries in Japan at this time; the exclusive privilege was intended to avoid a repetition of the conflicts that erupted when the Augustinians, Franciscans, and Dominicans joined the Jesuits in proselytizing in Japan toward the end of the sixteenth century. The French priests, though there was tolerance for them in Japan, initially were not allowed to proselytize, but they were allowed to serve the needs only of French Catholics (e.g., diplomats, traders, advisers) who came as part of the nineteenth-century endeavour to open Japan to trade with the Western world. When a series of attacks against Christianity had died down by 1872, the priests carried out their plan of inviting Catholic sisters to join them in Japan for the tasks of opening orphanages, schools, and hospitals, the very types of institutions that reach the everyday lives of Japanese, especially Japanese women and children. Because the sisters were doing similar work in France at the time, they came with great experience and expertise. However, like so many other Westerners of the time, they came with little time to prepare for their biggest challenge – learning the language and the customs of Japan.

The work of these sisters did serve the needs of Japan at this time of rapid industrialization and modernization. Historian Mikiso Hane writes that, "in the city of Tokyo alone, hundreds of babies were abandoned in public places."[6] The sisters looked to this unmet need – one that matched their initial limited Japanese language skills. But they went well beyond this through the years, opening schools and clinics. In 1872, the Tokyo prefectural government abolished the town office that handled relief operations, which directly affected the poor of Tokyo and limited the services available to them.[7] Again, some of these needs were picked up by the sisters. The same is true for the education of girls. Although the government mandated in 1872 education for all Japanese, no provisions were made to pay for it. This resulted in a larger number of boys attending school than girls until the early 1900s. In these early years, there was a disproportionate number of male teachers as well. The sisters' schools helped in this regard, especially in providing schooling for girls who had no money.[8] It is important to add that, in my study of the work of these women, specifically the Saint Maur sisters, I found no indication that conversion to Catholicism was required for access to the services provided. One must concede that, in a semi-colonized Japan struggling to bring itself to equality with the West, the government would not block the type of efforts exercised by the women.

The Sisters of the Holy Names of Jesus and Mary

The Holy Names sisters arrived in Japan in 1931. For an answer to what prompted religious orders of women to go to Japan at that time, we must look at two Church writings. First, Pope Benedict XV wrote an apostolic letter in 1919 "On the Propagation of the Catholic Faith throughout the World."[9] The letter warned of the dangers of nationalism and colonialism so prevalent in the West from the mid-nineteenth century on. Benedict XV warned missionaries against serving the needs of their own country by stating, "we must never forget that a missionary is an envoy not of his own country but of God."[10] But even more important was his "call to missionary orders and institutes and to the whole church to cooperate in the formation of a native priesthood and native episcopacy in as many countries as possible."[11] He worked toward providing practical training for missionaries and improved language instruction. Benedict XV stated that, "once the indigenous clergy has been formed, then the Church has been well-founded and the task of the missionaries has been accomplished."[12] I think that St. Francis Xavier, SJ, would have approved.

Pope Pius XI's encyclical, *Rerum Ecclesiae,* issued in 1926, reminded bishops of the "vast regions which are still deprived of the civilizing influence of the Christian religion."[13] Pius XI stressed the importance "of building up a native clergy," as had his predecessor.[14] In addition, he corrected an assumption from the past: "Anyone who looks upon these natives as members of an inferior race or as men of low mentality makes a grievous mistake."[15] The very presence of the caution speaks volumes about Western attitudes toward Asia. Also, his inclusion of Christianity as a "civilizing" agent of the mission has its own implications and harbours echoes of the very imperialism that he sought to squelch.[16]

Just as the Paris Foreign Mission Society priests had invited the Saint Maur sisters to work in Japan, so too the Canadian Franciscan priests, influenced by the writings of Pius XI and Benedict XV, invited the Canadian Holy Names sisters to Japan. The sisters were reluctant at first because they had just agreed to send sisters to South Africa, and they thought that going to Japan was impossible at that time. But the prefect apostolic, Egide-Marie Roy (1894-1947), a Franciscan in Japan, pleaded for the sisters' help, and a group of four left on 1 November 1931. These sisters were Marie-Edith Brossoit (Mother Edith), Mary Esterwin Redmond, Marie-Veronique du Crucifix Saint-Germain, and Mary Ann Patricia Cuniffe.[17] The priests specifically wanted sisters to teach at a high school for girls in Naze on Amami Ōshima, one of the largest islands in the Ryūkyū island chain off the southern coast of Kyushu, in the province of Kagoshima. This location is especially pertinent to this volume honouring St. Francis Xavier, SJ, because it was at Kagoshima where he first landed in 1549 when he introduced Catholicism into Japan. The circumstances of accepting this school will be treated later.

After their arrival in Japan, the Holy Names sisters spent two years learning the language and culture of the country, a period of time that they admitted was not long enough. Their letters mention that the German Franciscan sisters in Sapporo had spent five years learning the language and culture, and the Religious of the Sacred Heart in Tokyo had spent eight years.[18] The Saint Maur sisters, on the other hand, spent no time learning the language; they moved right into their work on arrival, as was common at that time.

The diaries that the sisters kept describe their travels throughout Japan – visiting schools run by other congregations of women religious, especially those conducted by the Saint Maur sisters.[19] Mentioned often in their writings is the name of Mother Saint Therese Hennecart (1870-1940), the regional superior for the Saint Maur sisters. She arrived in Japan in 1903 and by 1921, as Mother Saint Mathilde Raclot before her, became the sister in charge of her congregation's works in Japan. On an educational trip in July 1933, Sisters Esterwin and Helen Elizabeth Bradley[20] travelled to Yokohama, where they consulted with Mother Saint Therese about taking over the school in Naze on Amami Ōshima. She suggested that they talk with a Mr. Yamazaki, the chief teacher in their Yokohama school as well as their community adviser in all educational affairs. He strongly suggested that they *not* accept an already established school. The sisters travelled on to Sapporo in Hokkaido, where they met the Franciscan Sisters of Saint George, who ran a girls' high school in the area for 750 students. They had thirty-two faculty members, twenty-five of whom were Japanese. The Franciscan bishop of Sapporo, Wenceslas Kinold (1871-1952), described by the sisters as "a venerable old man with many years experience in educational matters of Japan," corroborated the advice given by Yamazaki.[21] As it turned out, the warnings of the two men proved prophetic, as we will see. The sisters returned by way of Tokyo and visited the Seishin Gakuin, run by the Religious of the Sacred Heart, and two other schools conducted by the Saint Maur sisters, one of them, Futaba, with 1,500 students. They stopped in Kobe, Obayashi, and Okayama, where they visited schools run by the Religious of the Sacred Heart, the Dames de Nevers, the Sisters of the Infant Jesus of Chauffailles, and the Sisters of Notre Dame de Namur.

Growing Militarism in Japan

In August 1933, word came from the Holy Names mother house in Canada that the congregation had agreed to take over the school built ten years earlier on the island of Amami Ōshima in the town of Naze by the Franciscan priests from Canada. Why the sisters did not heed the advice of Yamazaki and Kinold, who warned them against taking over an already established school, I do not know. The priests had run into trouble through the years among local folks, who accused them of being spies, so in 1932 they withdrew from running the school and turned it over to the Missionary Sisters of the Immaculate Conception from Canada, who had been working at the school at the invitation of the Franciscan priests since 1926.[22] These sisters had lasted only a short time without the Franciscans. The illness of their superior, and undoubtedly the tensions in the area, caused them to withdraw from the school in mid-year, much to the surprise and chagrin of the priests.[23] Perhaps it was the awkward position in which the priests were left that convinced the Holy Names sisters to help out despite the antagonistic condition and the warnings of their advisers.

It was into this hostile and unstable atmosphere that the Holy Names sisters began their first official work in Japan. In mid-July, Mother Edith and Sister Esterwin travelled to Naze, about 205 miles south of Kagoshima, a trip of eighteen to twenty-two hours by sea. While they were there, the police came to inspect the house and proclaimed that all was in order. On 8 August, the first Holy Names sisters, Sisters Esterwin and Ann Patricia, actually moved to Naze. They were followed by Sister Veronica of the Crucifix, along with two alumnae of the school, Nakamura Kikue and Ikeda Takiko.[24]

An interesting story comes from the letter of Sister Edith Christine Richardson to the mother house in Canada. She remained in Kagoshima City when some of the others had been moved to Amami Ōshima. Right across the street from them, she recounts, lived a relative of the famous Saigō Takamori, a native of Kagoshima, known to all Japanese as one of the leaders of the Meiji Restoration (1868), which brought Japan into the modern, industrialized world. Yet he was also the leader of the Satsuma Rebellion (1877), which provided the last significant but unsuccessful challenge to the new Meiji government. Many Japanese see him as one who exemplified the samurai spirit. Initially, Saigō's relative had been cold and unfriendly to the sisters. A death in the family, however, brought more relatives to Kagoshima, among them a woman from Osaka who was Catholic. She called the sisters and asked to pray in their small chapel and to attend Mass the following morning. The woman was fluent in French because she and her husband (Hiraga) had spent five years in France, so she could converse easily with the sisters. After her departure, her sister, their neighbour, brought the sisters a gift in gratitude for assisting a visiting relative.[25]

In the 8 September 1933 entry in their diary, the sisters recorded the problems in Amami Ōshima. They reported that the story alleging the fathers were spies had taken hold, that Calixte Gélinas (1881-1953), a Franciscan priest and a naturalized Japanese citizen under the name Yonekawa, was really a general and Father Pius a naval officer. Further, their living quarters at the Tamiyama Seminary provided them with an advantageous lookout onto the bay, seen by the Japanese as their first line of defence against a potential American invasion.[26] The sisters noted that there had been numerous articles in the Ōshima newspaper and in an "extra" describing an imaginary state of affairs and the great harm that would be caused if the Catholic girls' school were allowed to continue. The rhetoric against the school was picked up by other newspapers, the *Kagoshima Shimbun* and the *Osaka Mainichi*. On the first night, the sisters' school was surrounded by police.

Also, in a letter dated 8 September 1933, Sister Esterwin reported to the Canadian mother house that the mayor and the entire city council called "and visited in detail, first the school, then the boarding school ... twenty-four of them plus some hangers on."

Before I knew there was a man taking pictures there [in the chapel] ... Finally, the visitors went away, but not until most of them had gone from end to end of the attic! – and all had visited besides, the washroom and pupils' dining room and kitchen. In the last named place I was introduced to the mayor! He was very pleasant, – in fact, most [of] them were – and more than one tried to explain things to the little policeman (Yamamoto-san) who was literally "hopping mad."[27]

On the first day of classes, 8 September, Mr. Ando, the director of the school, asked that pupils assemble "to greet His Majesty, the Emperor ... all, teachers – sisters too – and pupils, turning toward Tokyo and bowing profoundly. They say it is merely saying 'Good Morning' to their common father, the Emperor. I suppose that is all it does mean to most of them. Surely, it meant no more to us."

Even with this display of reverence for the emperor, attacks continued. In another letter from Sister Esterwin, dated 10 September, she mentioned that Miss Ikeda

has had no easy or pleasant time of it here, as the alumnae are not united, but those on her side have finally succeeded in preparing their protest and presenting it to the authorities ... She is very tired with "sodans" (conferences) and listening to Town Council meetings ... Before leaving Friday evening, she had decided to delay her return a little. When she was just about to go, shouting began in the street and approached our gate, "Close the school!" "Tear down the school!" "Director, come out and we'll kill you!" "Teachers, come out!"

It was all started by one man, but he had assembled quite a crowd. By the time the police arrived, all had disappeared. The next day, Saturday, protesters threw stones that crashed on the roof, and on Sunday the newspaper attacks against the school continued. Surprisingly, when the sisters went out for Mass at the neighbouring parish, they were not molested. But so strong were the anti-Catholic feelings that school administrators told students not to wear their uniforms outside the school.[28]

Their troubles were far from over. A letter on 6 October from Sister Esterwin to the mother general in Canada explained that she was writing in French instead of English because fewer Japanese knew French, and she was certain that her letters were being read by the Japanese. She mentioned that the newspaper of 13 September was so violent in its attacks against the school that the police forbade its distribution. By 16 September, the city council had passed a resolution against the school and its director, Ando. "This was a great mishap for us, as we knew that the provincial authorities would soon come from Kagoshima, and thus we were left alone, without experience in these schools in Japan, where everything is minutely regulated."[29]

As events unfolded, however, it became clear that the city council did not have the power to close a school. So Ando returned, and an official inspector from Kagoshima City gave the school a favourable report. The sisters themselves taught English, music, French, typing, and drawing. The government obviously forbade the teaching of religion in the schools, but one of the sisters or the Franciscan priests taught religion either in the convent or in the chapel.[30] As Sister Edith Christine wrote, "It is not easy to constantly keep in mind that we must never speak of God – we who have come so far only to do this!"[31]

Franciscan priest Egide Roy, the bishop of Kagoshima, in his annual report to Rome of 1933-34, described what the sisters had endured from the end of July to the time of his account. He reported that a strong protest had broken out against the school for girls and had quickly become an attack against Catholicism: "I do not hesitate to describe the actions as those of true gangsters of which the sisters and missionaries were the victims until the end of September." And he reported that the causes were four. First, shortly after the Washington Conference (1921-22), where Japanese fortifications of the area were the subject of lively discussion among the powers, the arrival of the priests on the island of Ōshima made some Japanese military men suspicious that the priests were coming to observe their military activities. Second, they also suspected that the missionaries were trying in secret to undermine the Constitution of Japan by their passivity and opposition to things such as the Japanese imperial ancestry and expressions of patriotism and loyalty. Third, the Buddhist priests, shocked by the progress of Catholicism, exploited the naïveté of certain military officers and the extraordinary venality of journalists. And fourth, personal hostilities toward the Franciscan priest Calixte Gélinas, who went to Canada during this time, added an acrimonious series of attacks and calumnies.[32]

From the sisters' diary, it is clear that plans for a school in Kagoshima City were in the works at least by 24 October 1933, and in his account to Rome Roy mentioned that the presence of a Catholic school on a fortified island was among the thorniest of issues between the Franciscan mission and the local authorities. He noted that the Japanese provincial government and the Franciscans had reached a secret agreement to close the controversial school in Naze, but there was approval for a similar school in Kagoshima

City, where the military would not be able to offer serious objections. He also mentioned that the Ministry of Public Instruction gave permission on 14 December to close the Naze school and gave approval on 22 December for the opening of a new school in Kagoshima City.[33]

Mother Saint Therese, their Saint Maur sister mentor, worked with the architect and the sisters to plan the building of the new school. In commenting on her presence, one of the sisters wrote on 21 November that "her sojourn amongst us leaves an impression of profound peace. Contact with her has been a source of edification. What an invaluable assistance she has been on account of her thirty-three years' experience in Japan!"[34] The sisters learned that the Mombusho (Department of Education in Tokyo) had approved the new school, Seimei Kōtō Jogakkō (Holy Names Women's Higher School). As early as 1931, Roy wrote to the general superior of the Holy Names sisters in Canada indicating that he intended to have the school in Naze move to Kagoshima City because of the unrest in Naze, and it was this new school that he saw the sisters running once they had spent more time in Japan.[35] So the sisters on site had begun teaching with less preparation than anticipated, and their experiences demonstrate how they suffered because of it.

One example that the sisters provide of mistakes made due to their lack of understanding Japanese culture is a telling one in terms of the Japan of the time and supports the reasons for the attacks against the school outlined by Roy above. Each school was mandated to have a repository for a copy of the emperor's "Rescript on Education," issued in 1889. As described by the sisters,

> This document is considered sacred, and treated with the utmost reverence and solemnity. The Director of the school, with white gloves, removes the Rescript from an especially prepared repository, and reads it to the faculty and students at every important assembly. All remain standing, motionless with bowed heads during the reading, and the ceremony is closed with the singing of the Japanese national anthem.

The sisters had not yet had time to prepare the repository for the document, so Sister Esterwin had placed it in an upstairs cabinet "on the same shelf with some of the sisters' personal linens." When the inspectors came to see the rescript, they were horrified and took pictures of the items found on the shelf, and the photos became the content of "extras" published in Naze against the sisters. To make matters worse, the sisters had slippers on a bottom shelf in the same cabinet. The writer added, "although all of this may seem trivial to us several decades later, it was considered of major importance in the Japan of 1933, and added weight to the cloud of suspicion and misunderstanding which was eventually to put an end to the work of our Sisters in Ōshima."[36]

But before leaving, there was more work to be done. The sisters of Saint Maur sent a Mr. Maruyama to help settle affairs in Naze. After interviewing the prefectural officials, he realized that there was no hope for keeping the school. In lieu of the old school, the officials gave permission for the new school in Kagoshima City. They had to keep quiet about the new school, but it needed to be ready by April, the beginning of the Japanese school year. The old school would close in March. Not only did the Sisters of Saint Maur lend one of their administrators, but they also lent their name as the sponsor of the new school because the Holy Names sisters had no prestige in Japan, and they were connected to the Ōshima Kōtō Jogakkō, "which the newspapers had succeeded in making a term of opprobrium throughout the country."[37] Further, the Holy Names sisters had no legal standing in Japan because they were not incorporated; the time was not appropriate to do that, and it would be too costly.

Once again the Sisters of Saint Maur came to the rescue. The result was that the school was officially established under the non-profit foundation of the Sisters of Saint Maur. It helped that Mother Saint Therese was well respected in Japan, receiving an audience with the emperor and an imperial decoration. The diary entry goes on to say that the schools of the Saint Maur sisters were large, counting thousands of pupils, many of whom were people of rank and in good repute in the land. The diary records that Mother Saint Therese even called on some of the prominent Kagoshima families, then residing in Tokyo, to gain their support for the "sister school" of their alma mater, as Seimei Kōtō Jogakkō was now called. Maruyama tried to create good relations with the press, the people, and the military.[38] Clearly, the sisters had a lot of help in establishing the new school.

It opened in Kagoshima City in April 1934 in a rented building, the new structure not completed until August. The move to the new building was duly touted on 12 August, with many dignitaries present for the ceremonies. Difficulties continued, however. A military man named Hariguchi prompted the distribution of handbills throughout the city against the sisters and the Franciscan priests. Having gathered a group of 400 men on the evening of 8 December 1935, he made plans to act against Seimei Kōtō Jogakkō. The next day they attacked the principal of the school, Mr. Moriya. The event was described by Sister Helen Elizabeth, a witness: "Mr. Hariguchi had Mr. Moriya in the corner [of his office] and was trying to choke him. Blood was

streaming from the poor man's mouth, and had even spurted on the wall."
She went on to say that "our arch enemy sat down on the stairs and began
reading ... at the top of his voice. In a screaming voice he denounced our
school and its teachers ... unpatriotic was the cry. The school must be
closed!"[39]

Roy realized that the Franciscans were the real target. The antagonism
against the priests continued to such an extent that a Japanese bishop was
named to replace Roy as prefect apostolic, namely, Paul Aijiro Yamaguchi
(prefect from 1936 to September 1937). Franciscan priests withdrew completely from Kagoshima in 1936, as did the Sisters of the Immaculate Conception and the Sisters of Saint Anne. Even a small congregation of Japanese
sisters withdrew. That left the Holy Names sisters as the only religious
congregation remaining in Kagoshima.

As events unfolded, so did attacks against Seimei Kōtō Jogakkō. Protesters
threw stones at sisters on the road and broke windows in the school building, and one sister suffered a knife stab in the arm. There was talk of scandals.
Even the military and the police became anti-school, discussing the presence
of Westerners on top of the hill. One of the sisters described the setting as
follows: "The prospect from the level plateau crowning the hill is natural
beauty that renders one speechless. The city with its environs forms a pen-
insula with the blue waters of the bay on three sides of it." Obviously, for
those concerned about security, the implication here once again is that
Catholics possessed a clear view of Kagoshima Bay and thus posed a threat
to Japanese military manoeuvres.[40] However, in May 1936, new hope arose
when the dispute between Hariguchi and Seimei Kōtō Jogakkō was settled
in favour of the school.[41]

For a time, the school seemed to flourish. The sisters abided by the government's expectations in giving due honour to the emperor and to Japan's
military heroes. For example, when Admiral Tōgō Heihachirō, a famous
naval officer, died in 1934, the sisters participated in the requisite ceremony
to bury a lock of his hair in his native Kagoshima. The pupils from their
school, like all others in Kagoshima, participated in the ceremony.[42] The
school was fully involved in preparations for the visit of the emperor to
Kagoshima. When all schools were asked to house students from neighbouring provinces, the school offered lodging to 250 students and their professors. The military manoeuvres began "when the emperor disembarked from
his war vessel and set his noble feet on Kagoshima soil amid the roar of
welcoming cannons and guns. Thousands of citizens were at the wharf to
receive him."[43] The sisters described the official installation of the imperial
rescript in the school Hoanden, which they now understood more clearly.

And they wrote of the ceremony in honour of the great Meiji emperor. The sisters were advised, they did not say by whom, to show interest in Japan's war effort against China and to host military manoeuvres on the Seimei campus. "What a sight the school grounds presented! Filled with beautiful horses, machine guns, tanks, etc."[44]

The classrooms of Seimei Kōtō Jogakkō were nearly full, but conditions in the country were becoming more sombre. As Japan heightened hostilities with China, the sisters decided not to mention anything political in their writings, and they warned those in Canada and the United States not to mention anything related to international affairs in their letters back. (The sisters believed that the Japanese were reading both their outgoing and their incoming mail.)[45] Often the sisters mentioned that they were under surveillance.[46] By 1940, Yamaguchi, at this point bishop in Nagasaki but still in charge of Kagoshima, informed the sisters that they could not stay in Kagoshima because almost all of Kyushu was considered a strategic zone by the military – especially Kagoshima and its neighbouring towns.[47] Shortly thereafter, the superior general of the Holy Names order in Montreal called the sisters home (14 August 1940). The reasons given were "the alarming newspaper reports concerning Japan, together with the anxiety caused ... by the hostile attitude of Japanese military men toward foreigners."[48]

The school continued, as it does today, under the auspices of the Nagasaki Junshin Seibo Kai (Nagasaki Sisters of the Immaculate Heart of Mary), a congregation of women religious founded by Japanese. The school was renamed Junshin Kōtō Jogakkō (Immaculate Heart Women's Higher School) because Seimei was not appropriate for the times. *Junshin* ("immaculate heart") could be extended to reflect the purpose of this new congregation – to educate women to become pure wives.[49] The congregation had come into existence through the efforts of Japan's first native Japanese bishop, Hayasaka Kyūnosuke, who saw it as his mission to establish a congregation of Japanese women who would be educators. He chose two women to begin this foundation, Oizumi Katsumi and Esumi Yasu. When the women agreed, they were sent to France to study under an established congregation for one year, as required by church law. When they returned in 1934, Bishop Hayasaka declared them an established congregation.

Later the school was moved to another location, and the Kagoshima Medical School moved into the former school buildings. The belief was that it was more important to educate doctors than women. Another reason given was that the gulf was an important training place for Japan's planned attack on Pearl Harbor, and the Kagoshima prefectural government thought that it would be inappropriate for high school students to observe such manoeuvres.[50]

Conclusion

It was the women religious in the nineteenth and twentieth centuries who founded and/or conducted the majority of the Catholic orphanages, schools, clinics, and hospitals in Japan. Although I cannot verify that this number is exact, I can say that there were at least twenty-seven congregations of women religious from the West working in Japan during the years 1872-1941, plus at least eight native Japanese congregations of Catholic women religious in existence. Obviously, the latter were greatly influenced by Western congregations of women. The Saint Maur sisters, who went to Japan in the 1870s, remain active there today, and almost all of their sisters working there are Japanese. They continue to run respected schools in Japan, such as the Futaba school in the Kōjimachi area of Tokyo, where the current empress studied for three years, and the Futaba Denenchōfu school, where Masako, the wife of the crown prince, was educated. And it is the sisters who have moved quickly to staff their educational institutions with native Japanese.

The long presence of the Saint Maur sisters in Japan gave them an appreciation for Japanese culture and religions. When Mother Saint Therese was teaching at Futaba school in Tokyo, she often said to her students, "I did not come to Japan to spread French culture, nor to recruit lightly a number of new Christians. I came to help you become what you want to be: serious-minded, refined, real Japanese women."[51] The fact that she gained great respect in Japan demonstrates her commitment to doing well what she purported to do – provide quality education for Japanese women. The Holy Names sisters were not in Japan long enough to become part of Japan, and thus they relied heavily on the experience and knowledge of Mother Saint Therese and the advisers whom she recommended. Her wise counsel helped them to sustain a quality school in extraordinarily difficult times.

Besides the issue of strong anti-Catholic sentiment in Kagoshima, Japan's growing nationalism and militarism fostered the belief that Japan did not need to rely on foreigners to educate Japanese citizens. The Holy Names sisters were caught in what was one of the most anti-Catholic, anti-foreign parts of Japan at the worst time possible. Catholicism especially came under fire. The Japanese of the Kagoshima area saw Catholicism as a world-wide organization controlled from a single centre. Because the priests were men, the Japanese military believed that they could be spies observing all their military manoeuvres and reporting them to potential enemies. Even when the sisters replaced the priests in the school, the feelings of many Japanese in the area continued to grow more antagonistic toward Catholicism and foreigners. Having endured the entry of Westerners into their country in the second half of the nineteenth century, the Japanese were not about to let them make inroads into national beliefs. One might see this as an attack against Western imperialism. Certainly, preaching religious beliefs that worship a God higher than the emperor seemed dangerous indeed.

Despite the linking of Catholicism and Western imperialism, the former did have a certain prestige among some Japanese. And it is hard to imagine Catholicism in Japan without the schools, hospitals, and social services provided by the sisters. Equally hard to envision is how the priests would have been able to reach women and children as successfully as the sisters were able to do. In the Catholic Church, married or single women did not serve as missionaries to other countries, as did Protestant women, who first came as wives of missionaries and later on their own. Catholic mission work was generally limited to women belonging to religious congregations until the later 1960s, after the Second Vatican Council (1962-65).

Clearly, the work of women religious was vital to Catholicism in Japan. They existed in greater numbers than priests. They lived in community, so they had a built-in support system in moving to a new land. They provided a lived experience for Japanese women interested in joining a religious congregation. They could reach women and children in a way that would have been impossible for the priests alone. In 1940, when the Holy Names sisters turned over their school to the Immaculate Heart sisters, there were 250 pupils, 60 of them studying Catholicism.[52] There is much research yet to be done to bring to light the many works, adventures, and achievements of women religious in Japan, both Western congregations and Japanese congregations.

Notes

1 See Harrington, *Japan's Hidden Christians.*
2 See Harrington, "The First Women Religious in Japan."
3 See Harrington, "French Mission Work in Japan." Two other congregations of women religious from France arrived in 1877 (Soeurs de l'Enfant-Jesus de Chauffailles) and in 1878 (Soeurs de Saint-Paul de Chartres).
4 The archives of the Saint Maur sisters are at their mother house in Paris, France; the archives of the Holy Names sisters are in Longueuil, Canada; and the archives of the Franciscan fathers discussed here are in Montreal, Canada.
5 "Shōwa zenki Kagoshima no katoriku kōtō jogakkō appaku mondai no kenkyū" ("A Study of the Oppression on a Catholic Girls' High School in Kagoshima during the Prewar Showa Era"). This study was sent to me by the author.

6 Hane, *Peasants, Rebels, and Outcastes*, 209.
7 Garon, *Molding Japanese Minds*, 35.
8 Marshall, *Learning to Be Modern*, 75-77. Protestant missionaries from the United States are included in the education of girls at this time. Also, once the government removed the tuition charges for compulsory schooling, the enrolment of girls rose from 70 percent to 90 percent.
9 This letter is identified as *Maximum Illud*.
10 Cited in Pollard, *The Unknown Pope*, 203.
11 Ibid.
12 Ibid., 204. Pollard sees *Maximum Illud* as "the most important church document on the missions until the Second Vatican Council."
13 Pope Pius XI, *Rerum Ecclesiae*, sec. 3.
14 Ibid., sec. 19.
15 Ibid., sec. 26.
16 Patricia Grimshaw puts it well when writing of British imperialism: "An important component of mission development was the discourse of 'the civilizing mission' wherein the benefits of Christianity, education, and Western ways of living in virtuous families came to be accepted as a key objective of imperial outreach." Grimshaw, "Faith, Missionary Life, and the Family," 264.
17 Archives of the Sisters of the Holy Names of Jesus and Mary, Longueuil, Canada. The family names and dates of the sisters provided by the archivist are Catherine Brossoit or Brossois (both spellings are in the archival documents) (1870-1947); Ruth Redmond (1927-61); Gertrude St-Germain (1895-1976); and Terese Cunniffe (1897-1987). Nine more sisters were to follow before World War II: Mary Helen Elizabeth (Frances Bradley 1894-1975); Edith Christine (Edith Richardson 1904-44); Hélène-de-Marie (Léonide Clément 1907-66); M. Louise-de-la Passion (Jeanne Bégin 1903-79); Ida-Marie (Léontine Perron 1906-93); Marie-Pierre-du-Crucifix (Anna Turcotte 1885-1940); Marie-Augustine-de-la-Croix (Bernadette Bédard 1904-77); Mary Elaine (Agnes Duffy 1895-1976); and Marie-Louise-de-Gonzague (Euphrasie Jeannotte 1872-1964).
18 Sister Mary Evangeline, *Four Centuries after Xavier*, 28. This work is built on the diaries and letters of the sisters in Japan during the time.
19 Ibid., 24.
20 Sister Helen Elizabeth Bradley arrived in Japan in 1932 along with Sister Edith-Christine Richardson. See note 17 for a list of all the sisters who served in Japan up to 1940.
21 Archives of the Sisters of the Holy Names of Jesus and Mary, Longueuil, Canada, handwritten account of the sisters' preparation and departure and time in Japan, 23 June-14 July 1933.
22 The goal of this congregation of sisters is the evangelization of non-Christians.
23 Juchereau-Duchesnay, "Rélation Annuelle de la Préfecture de Kagoshima 1932-1933 à la Sacré Congrégation de la Propagande, Rome," 7-8.
24 Japanese names are given in Japanese style, surname first.
25 Sister Mary Evangeline, *Four Centuries after Xavier*, 29.
26 For a discussion of Japanese naval strategy at this time, see Evans and Peattie, *Kaigun*, 286-98.
27 Archives of the Sisters of the Holy Names of Jesus and Mary, Longueuil, Canada, handwritten account of the sisters' preparation and departure and time in Japan, Sister Esterwin quoted, 8 September 1933.
28 Ibid., 10 September 1933.

29   In Sister Mary Evangeline, *Four Centuries after Xavier,* 27. The letter is translated into English in this source.
30   Ibid.
31   Ibid., 29.
32   Archives of the Franciscans, Montreal, Canada, "Rélation-Annuelle 1933-34," sent to the Prefect of the Sacred Congregation of Propaganda in Rome, 29 August 1934, 2-3.
33   Ibid., 3.
34   Archives of the Sisters of the Holy Names of Jesus and Mary, Longueuił, Canada, handwritten account of the sisters' preparation and departure and time in Japan by one of the sisters, not named, 21 November 1933.
35   Archives of the Franciscans, Montreal, Canada, letter to Reverend Mother Marie-Odilon, Superior General of the Holy Names, from Egide Roy, Bishop of Kagoshima, 27 May 1931.
36   Sister Mary Evangeline, *Four Centuries after Xavier,* 28.
37   Archives of the Sisters of the Holy Names of Jesus and Mary, Longueuil, Canada, handwritten account of the sisters' preparation and departure and time in Japan, 17 January 1934.
38   Ibid.
39   Sister Mary Evangeline, *Four Centuries after Xavier,* 51-52.
40   Hirayama, "Shōwa zenki Kagoshima no katoriku kōtō jogakkō appaku mondai no kenkyū," 76; Sister Mary Evangeline, *Four Centuries after Xavier,* 74.
41   Sister Mary Evangeline, *Four Centuries after Xavier,* 59.
42   Archives of the Sisters of the Holy Names of Jesus and Mary, Longueuil, Canada, handwritten account of the sisters' preparation and departure and time in Japan, 18 July 1934.
43   Sister Mary Evangeline, *Four Centuries after Xavier,* 48.
44   Ibid., 101.
45   Ibid., 97.
46   Ibid., 65, 74, 80.
47   Ibid., 125.
48   Archives of the Sisters of the Holy Names of Jesus and Mary, Longueuil, Canada, "Arrival of Our Sister from Japan," 18 September 1940.
49   Hirayama, "Shōwa zenki Kagoshima no katoriku kōtō jogakkō appaku mondai no kenkyū," Part III, 23.
50   Ibid., 24.
51   *Sisters of Saint Maur in Japan 1872-1972,* 16.
52   Sister Mary Evangeline, *Four Centuries after Xavier,* 120.

2
Toward a History of Christian Scientists in Japan

James R. Bartholomew

It is with some trepidation that I write this chapter on the subject of Japan's Christian scientists. I have had misgivings not because the subject is uninteresting or inconsequential – quite the contrary – but because the topic poses serious intellectual challenges of definition and explanation and because gaining access to appropriate source material is equally difficult. What is a "Catholic" or "Protestant" scientist? Must the subject have merely been baptized? Should the individual have been faithful to God and the Church at the end of life? Might it be sufficient to proclaim adherence as a personal identity? Or what? For the sake of procedure, I define the subject partly as one known to have received baptism as a Catholic or Protestant Christian but also as anyone claiming a personal identity. Theologically, one could limit the operative definition to persons adhering to the faith at the end of life. But faithfulness at the end cannot always be ascertained and in any case is a matter of judgment for the historian. I do place more emphasis on individuals who were both baptized and adhered to the faith over a lifetime. But I also discuss one or two cases in which baptism was seemingly the only marker. And I insist that we consider the possibility that some Japanese may have asserted a Catholic or Protestant faith commitment as a matter of personal identity.

Access to source material is at least as big a challenge as formal definition. Standard reference materials relating to Japanese subjects only occasionally report anything relating to religious preference, though there are exceptions. And frequently, when they do refer to religion, one cannot always distinguish between Catholics and Protestants. I write as a historian, and the historian – as opposed to the social scientist working exclusively with living subjects – has to rely on full-length biographies and autobiographies. In the case of Japan, acquiring such materials is far more easily talked about than accomplished. In Japan, unlike in the United States or some other countries, biographies and autobiographies of scientists rarely have a commercial market. (There are technical reasons for this.) On the other hand, such biographies do exist – but most of the time they are published strictly as *hibaihin* (privately published items typically printed in very limited editions). Worse yet, book dealers do not recognize "scientists' biographies" as a meaningful category. Sometimes they will respond to queries about biographies of *hakushi* (holders of a doctorate in the Japanese system), but even that is not a sure thing. I will have more to say about source materials later on.

Importance of the Subject: Or, Do Numbers Matter?

Although an inquiry into the matter of Catholic (or Protestant) scientists can be defended on various grounds, the short – and the longer – answer to this question is that, yes, numbers do matter. It is a virtual certainty that the subject has attracted little attention up to now in part because the putative numbers of scientists professing Catholicism or some form of Protestant Christianity are few. But how reliable are any religious statistics for Japan? Most estimates report the number of all Christians in Japan at about 1 million or so; official Catholic statistics rarely claim more than 450,000 Church members.[1] One could say that observers of the Japanese scene who find Christianity in any form distasteful have a vested interest in continuing to report low estimates for the size of the Christian population. Moreover, such observers are fairly numerous. Less obvious is the fact that the supposedly "official" statistics generated by (in this case) the Catholic Church itself are not entirely believable. My contention is that, in a comparative context, these statistics are both misleading and nearly useless for my purposes. I am not interested here in how many people are likely to show up for Sunday Mass or make a financial commitment of support to a particular parish, topics of obvious importance for Church authorities. If these narrow definitions were operative in, for example, France, then we can be sure that estimates of the French Catholic population would be closer to 5 million than to the 50 million that is commonly reported.[2] In 1969, Father J.J. Spae's Oriens Institute for Religious Research in Tokyo found that about 2 percent (not 1 percent) of the Japanese population claimed to be Christian at that time. Moreover, 24 percent professed belief in "God" as understood in the Judaeo-Christian tradition, not in that of Shinto.[3]

What I am interested in here is the matter of Catholicism's impact (and that of the Christian tradition defined more broadly) on Japanese society as a whole. I strongly suspect that if one were to define "Catholic" in Japan the way it is defined in France (counting every living person who had ever claimed affiliation, even if lapsed), we would be talking about 1.5 to 2 million

Catholics, not half a million or fewer. If believers of non-Japanese ethnicity resident in Japan were included, we might have an estimate of 3 million Catholics. And if Protestants (active or lapsed) were then added in, we might reach a figure of close to 10 million people. I believe that such an estimate more accurately represents the impact of Christianity in Japan than does the very small number of 1 million adherents that one typically sees.

How to Approach the Subject

There are, of course, many reasonable strategies that one can adopt by way of investigating the complex relationship of Catholic (or of course Protestant) Christianity with modern Japanese society and history. I have personally drawn inspiration from a recently published study by Ronald Binzley that appeared in *ISIS,* the flagship journal of the (American) History of Science Society.[4] His focus is strictly on the modern (twentieth-century) US experience of Catholicism, and he frames the subject in reference to the famous 1955 critique of American Catholic anti-intellectualism and indifference to science prepared by Father John Tracy Ellis.[5] I do not believe that the particular perspective adopted by Father Ellis quite fits the post-World War II situation of Catholicism and science in Japan. For one thing, there is considerable evidence that "intellectuals," or at least people with higher levels of education, have been drawn to both Catholicism and Protestant Christianity with greater regularity than has been true of the general Japanese population. Moreover, this pattern would definitely include scientists as well as other well-educated Japanese. Nonetheless, Binzley's analysis is useful on four grounds. First, Binzley calls attention to the importance of changing religious statistics; in this case, we are talking about the numbers and changing proportions of Catholics who would be, and were, drawn to science and thus become active members of the scientific community. Second, he stresses the importance of organizations within the Catholic portion of the American scientific community. Third, he pays some attention to the nature and extent of science education in traditionally Catholic higher educational institutions. And fourth, Binzley brings into focus the matter of Catholic scientists' views of the proper relationship between science and religion.

Using this schema as a framework for discussing the Japanese situation, I will comment on each of these topics while warning the reader on two grounds. First, limited resources and time preclude any in-depth treatment of any of these matters. Second, most of the evidence that I can present is anecdotal, impressionistic, and frankly ad hoc. If some readers nonetheless find the chapter suggestive or stimulating, I will have accomplished my – albeit limited – purpose in writing it.

A Historical Survey of Christian Scientists in Japan

Other scholars have written about the general history of Christianity in Japan – the very successful but in some respects ultimately abortive Catholic mission of the sixteenth and seventeenth centuries, continuing with the energetic efforts by Protestant and Catholic missionaries to establish (or re-establish) the faith in the 1870s and beyond. The main point to underscore in this narrative is that Protestant Christianity was presented to the Japanese primarily through the filter of organized schooling. Catholics employed a similar strategy but for a considerable time concentrated on identifying and restoring to active communion with the Church those whose families had embraced Catholicism in the Tokugawa period or before. Protestant efforts had a less anti-nationalist taint than did those of Catholics. Protestant Christianity was also closely identified with Britain and the United States, the dominant (and emerging) powers of the late nineteenth century.

Apart from gleaning information from the autobiographies and biographies of individual scientists, we can draw some useful information from a five-volume set of materials assembled by a former employee of Japan's Ministry of Education. Sometime around 1920, Iseki Kurō sent detailed questionnaires to all 1,360 holders of the *hakushi* degree or doctorate in the natural sciences.[6] (In fact, he also solicited comparable information from holders of the doctorate in law, the humanities, and the social sciences, but this material does not concern us here.) Mori Arinori invented the *hakushi* system as minister of education in the late 1880s; by his own testimony, it had unique features.[7] Aspirants could either complete a graduate program at one of Japan's so-called imperial universities or seek the same degree by assembling a number of professional publications and submitting them for approval by a committee of professors at one of the same institutions. There were slightly different degree titles according to the specialty in question: *igaku hakushi* (doctorate in medicine), *rigaku hakushi* (doctorate in basic science), *nōgaku hakushi* (doctorate in agricultural science), *kōgaku hakushi* (doctorate in engineering), *yakugaku hakushi* (doctorate in pharmacology), *ringaku hakushi* (doctorate in dendrology or forestry science), and *jūigaku hakushi* (doctorate in veterinary medicine). One might pursue research in chemistry, for example, under almost any of these degree categories. Basic science, engineering, or even forestry science could encompass the subject matter of physics as an academic major; mathematics in this sense was available strictly in a basic science program.

Unfortunately, Iseki lost most of the material assembled before 1 September 1923 when the Great Kanto Earthquake struck Tokyo and Yokohama, and he had to do the project over again. Remarkably, he largely succeeded

– with one glaring exception. The crucial *rigaku hakushi* materials – covering physics, basic chemistry, mathematics, geology, and the non-medical biological sciences – had not been reassembled by the time he died. Some years ago, by consulting other reference works, I was able to fill in many of the gaps in his published material. But the original pre-1923 materials – available now for all of the categories except *rigaku hakushi* – do sometimes report information about religious matters, whereas the later reference works that I consulted about scientists in this category never say anything about religion. It is therefore possible to learn something about the interest in Christianity of some chemists, for example, but it is not possible when relying on these later works to learn anything about such interests among physicists or mathematicians.

To date, I have surveyed all of the entries for the engineering and pharmacology categories. Among the 400 or so individuals included, it is possible to demonstrate that at least six and likely eight were Christians. This would put the incidence of Christians in these groups at 1.5 to 2 percent, but the actual numbers were likely higher. From other sources, one can show that two of the six or eight were Catholic, but the Iseki material itself does not reveal this fact. The larger group includes Takamine Jōkichi, Nakajima Yosohachi, Shimomura Kōtarō, Yoshida Tarō, Tanaka Tatsuo, Satō Teikichi, and Nagai Nagayoshi. Takamine and Nagai were Catholics. Nakajima, Shimomura, Yoshida, Tanaka, and Satō were Protestants. This latter group of five included one mechanical engineer (Nakajima), one ordnance engineer (Yoshida), one electrical engineer (Tanaka), and two chemical engineers. Only the two chemical engineers were university professors (Satō and Shimomura); Satō was a member of both the Faculty of Engineering and the Faculty of Science at Tōhoku University. He studied the proteins of soda beans and their applications in industry. Shimomura in particular became nationally famous. He graduated from Worchester Polytechnique Institute in Massachusetts and took a graduate degree under Ira Remsen at Johns Hopkins University. Later in his career, he received a government decoration for developing the coke oven manufacture of ammonium sulfate as well as a low-temperature carbonization process useful in industry.[8]

If the numbers of Japanese who received the *hakushi* degree in "engineering" were typical of the larger community of *hakushi* recipients in pharmacology and medicine, then we should expect to find about ten Christians in the group. At present, I can identify only five as Christians. I strongly believe that there were substantially more, but the volumes that Iseki compiled do not identify anyone as Christian. It is possible that the categories he used in surveying medicine and pharmacology degree recipients worked against the recording of any information about religion. The word itself is mentioned only once in the entire volume. This is in an entry for a certain Takata Kōan. Iseki reports a few facts about Takata, in particular that he was an internist who had studied at the University of Berlin in 1911-12 and later directed a private hospital in Tokyo. However, the most interesting datum is his association with Dr. Aoyama Tanemichi, long-time dean of Tokyo University's Faculty of Medicine. In 1894, Aoyama headed a Faculty of Medicine delegation to Hong Kong because of an epidemic of bubonic plague in that city, and Takata was part of the delegation.[9]

Although not from Iseki's work, we do discover that Dean Aoyama "had a strong affinity for Christianity." His professional associates record elsewhere that he refused to consume alcoholic beverages due to his connection with Protestant Christianity.[10] From what we know of how this attitude affected his life and those of his close associates, it is virtually inconceivable that he was not a baptized Christian. Takata likely followed Aoyama's leadership in embracing Christianity. I should emphasize that Aoyama was one of the half dozen or so most influential leaders of the Japanese medical research community for the entire Meiji period. A close friend of Prime Minister Ōkuma Shigenobu (in office 1914-16) – the same Ōkuma who arrested Catholics in 1869 and the early 1870s – Aoyama dined with Ōkuma once a week for many years. Some observers believed at the time (1914) that Aoyama was the source of Ōkuma's decision to transfer control of Kitasato Shibasaburō's Institute of Infectious Diseases from the Ministry of Home Affairs to the Ministry of Education as a way of reining in the independent-minded Kitasato. What happened instead was that Kitasato resigned his laboratory directorship and founded a private facility, the Kitasato Institute, now expanded to include Kitasato University.[11]

Catholic Scientists

Although there were definitely many more, one can identify four Japanese scientists active in the past century and a quarter who were in any sense Catholic. More to the point, these four were very widely known. One was the bacteriologist Noguchi Hideyo (1876-1928), whose portrait now appears on Japan's 1,000-yen banknote. The reason is simply that Noguchi was the best-known Japanese scientist of the period. Born in a small village in Fukushima Prefecture, Noguchi was part of the small minority of scientists and academics who came from the peasantry. He injured his hand as a small child, and it became clear to the family that he could never become a successful farmer. Through a particular connection, he was referred in 1894 to a Japanese physician in Wakamatsu, Dr. Watanabe Kanae, a graduate of

Tokyo University and the University of California at Berkeley. According to some sources, young Noguchi became interested in medicine when Watanabe operated on his hand, slightly improving his ability to use his fingers. Noguchi's big break, at the age of sixteen, came when Watanabe agreed to accept him as a pupil in the study of medicine.

It was during his two years in Wakamatsu that Noguchi came into contact with the Catholic Church, and his desire to study foreign languages was a major source of his interest. Watanabe found him a teacher for German and English; the Wakamatsu parish church at the time was run by French priests, and they provided him with instruction in French. At the age of seventeen, Noguchi took instruction in the Catholic faith, received baptism, and joined the choir. He was also at this time much attracted to a young Japanese Catholic convert, Yamanouchi Yoneko. However, she rejected his attention – and this may well have been a turning point in his relationship with the Church. In the years immediately following, he enrolled in a proprietary medical school in Tokyo, the Zaisei Gakusha, and on graduation was accepted as a research student at Kitasato's Institute of Infectious Diseases.[12]

Calendar year 1899 was an important turning point in Noguchi's career because he met a rising star of American medicine, Simon Flexner, in Tokyo. Recently appointed professor at the University of Pennsylvania Medical School, Flexner visited Kitasato as part of a trip to the Philippines. Kitasato in turn sent Noguchi to escort Flexner to the institute, and that meeting marked the beginning of a close, lifelong relationship. The following year Noguchi arrived in Philadelphia, where he worked with Flexner until 1903, when Flexner moved to the newly founded Rockefeller Institute in New York as director and took Noguchi with him. For the next twenty-five years – minus one year in Copenhagen (1904) – Noguchi worked at the Rockefeller Institute, where he established a formidable, if controversial, reputation.[13] An indefatigable investigator, he published a long series of papers on syphilis, rabies, poliomyelitis, and other subjects, often with Flexner. For a time, he was believed to have isolated the causative organisms for each of these diseases, and these achievements won him more than a dozen nominations for the Nobel Prize in Physiology or Medicine. Ironically, the Nobel Committee believed that he and in some cases Flexner had actually succeeded.[14] In fact, they had not. A virus is the causative agent for each of these diseases, and until the development of the electron microscope in the 1930s no one could isolate these micro-organisms by following procedures deriving from the older field of bacteriology, which is what Noguchi and Flexner did.[15] Noguchi did have a lasting, major success during his Rockefeller years: demonstrating that paresis, a psychotic disorder often associated with advanced cases of syphilis, is caused by a micro-organism. But only one person proposed Noguchi for a Nobel award on the basis of this work.

In 1911, Noguchi married for the first and only time. As far as his relationship with the Catholic Church is concerned, this was ironic because his new wife, Mary Dardis Noguchi, was almost certainly a Catholic, at least nominally. Remarkably little is known about her life, but she was the daughter of Irish immigrants and grew up in Scranton, Pennsylvania. The family was poor, and two of her brothers worked in a local coal mine. It is not known how she and Noguchi met, but they were married on the spur of the moment, across the Hudson River from New York, by a justice of the peace. There is no indication that either of them ever attended church while they were married. Certainly, Noguchi himself was not buried in a Catholic graveyard after he died suddenly in Africa in 1928.

Two other prominent Catholic scientists active in this period also had foreign wives who were Catholic. However, compared to Noguchi, both men – Takamine Jōkichi (1854-1922) and Nagai Nagayoshi (1845-1929) – not only converted on marrying but also remained faithful Catholics for the rest of their lives. Takamine married Caroline Hitch, the daughter of a Confederate war veteran, in New Orleans in 1884. Nagai married Therese Schumacher, a native of the German Rhineland, in 1886. There were other similarities between Takamine and Nagai apart from their foreign-born wives and their conversions to Catholicism. Both were chemists of major stature. Both were active in the area of pharmacology. And both were unusually influential in the growth of chemistry in Japan.

Takamine was born in Kanazawa in 1854, the first son of a prominent domain physician who was also of samurai status.[16] Like Noguchi, Takamine was considered exceedingly bright and in 1872, at government expense, entered the Kōbu Daigakkō (Imperial College of Engineering), forerunner of Tokyo University's Faculty of Engineering. On graduation in 1880, he became one of a dozen engineering students to receive a government scholarship for study in Britain. Takamine then attended the Anderson College of the University of Glasgow for three years, graduating with a DSc degree in 1883. During summer vacations, he visited various factories, especially those that manufactured soda and chemical fertilizers, at Manchester, Liverpool, Newcastle, and other industrial centres. He then returned to Tokyo and took up a position in the Ministry of Agriculture and Commerce.

One of Takamine's major responsibilities was to study some of Japan's indigenous industries – indigo production, *washi* paper manufacturing, sake brewing – with a view to improving them and enhancing their future technical and market prospects. In this connection, Takamine travelled in 1884 for the first time to the United States to attend an international exposition held at New Orleans. Phosphate rock attracted his attention, partly because he was somewhat familiar with the mineral from his experience in Britain. He thus travelled to Charleston, South Carolina, and other locations where phosphate rock was mined, primarily with the aim of turning the phosphate into fertilizer. Takamine took a small quantity of phosphate fertilizer with him back to Japan and subsequently attracted the interest of several industrialists, who then organized the Tokyo Artificial Fertilizer Company with Takamine as chief executive officer.

He was the rare kind of scientist-entrepreneur often heralded in the United States. A highly creative chemist, Takamine also had an unusually thorough grasp of business affairs, including patent matters. In fact, in 1886 he served briefly as acting chief of Japan's Bureau of Patents. Moreover, his particular combination of scientific expertise, managerial talent, and business acumen made it possible for him to function equally well in Japan or the United States. In 1890, he was invited to assume a major role with a firm in Illinois whose directors had become interested in a new process that he had invented for producing alcohol. Viscount Shibusawa Eiichi, among others, urged Takamine to accept because this was the first time that a Western company had sought advice from anyone in Japan. In due course, Takamine himself established a company in Peoria, Illinois, to manufacture diastase, an enzyme found in the kernels of barley, with major applications in both brewing and medicine. The particular form of diastase that Takamine developed ultimately earned him a fortune.

His most notable scientific achievement was the isolation of adrenalin, the world's first known hormone. Through a major business connection with Parke, Davis Laboratories in Detroit, in 1900 Takamine travelled to the city to conduct research under the auspices of this firm, which was manufacturing the aforementioned diastase (known under the trade name of Taka-Diastase). Ultimately, Takamine moved his operations to New York City and the northern New Jersey area, where he established a private laboratory. He and his wife lived for about twenty-five years on Riverside Drive in Manhattan, where both were socially active. Despite his long-term American residence, Takamine retained both his Japanese citizenship and his ties to Japan. In 1913, on the cusp of World War I, he returned to Japan and undertook a lecture tour to promote the cause of a major research institution devoted to the physical sciences.[17] Although initial responses were skeptical – Japanese industrialists at that point were still wilfully dependent on foreign patents and inventions – a modest movement in favour of such a facility became a flood tide once the outbreak of war in Europe made Japanese access to European scientific and technical information difficult or impossible. Beginning in 1915, the Ōkuma cabinet responsible for Kitasato's departure from government service began planning to establish exactly the kind of large institution that Takamine had been advocating. In 1922, the Research Institute for Physics and Chemistry finally opened in Tokyo. During the interwar period, it was Japan's most important facility for both applied and basic research in physical science. Takamine continued to live and work in the United States. He remained faithful to the Catholic Church and died in July 1922. He was one of two major donors of the Japanese cherry trees given to the city of Washington in 1909.

An influential contemporary of Takamine, Nagai Nagayoshi was born in 1845 to a samurai family of the Tokushima domain.[18] After attending a local Confucian-style school, Nagai travelled to Nagasaki and was tutored by two European physicians, one German and one Dutchman. In 1858, he followed the latter to Tokyo (then Edo) for additional study. Germany's victory over France in the Franco-Prussian War of 1870-71 so enhanced the prestige of German medicine and science in Japan that Nagai decided on advanced studies in Germany. Accordingly, he spent the entire period from April 1871 to the spring of 1883 studying, assisting, and even lecturing in medicine, chemistry, and pharmacology at the University of Berlin.

While in Berlin, Nagai came under the influence of the renowned chemist August von Hofmann. This relationship strongly shaped the rest of Nagai's life. His original purpose in Germany was to study medicine. However, Nagai found Hofmann's lectures in chemistry so stimulating that he decided to shift his intellectual focus. Following Hofmann's leadership in part, Nagai became interested in the pharmacological side of chemistry, and a research project on the synthesis of acetic acid clinched the deal for him. The German chemist's influence on Nagai was not limited to academic matters. Nagai became personally close to Hofmann and his wife. He stayed a long time in Germany, and his German became fluent. At some point, Nagai decided to take Wilhelm as part of his name. Partly because of his extended sojourn and because he was now in his late thirties, the Hofmanns urged him to take a German wife, citing the well-known example of foreign minister Aoki Shūzō, who had done the same thing. Although initially skeptical of the suggestion, Nagai came to see the idea as having considerable merit, and shortly thereafter he was introduced through the Hofmanns to Therese Schumacher, whom he met in Munich. Two years later they were married in the cathedral at Andernach, and it was at this point that Nagai joined the Catholic Church.

In the 1880s, he and his German wife returned to Japan. Although he travelled extensively abroad, unlike Takamine, Nagai made his professional career in Japan. He was immediately named professor of chemistry at Tokyo University. However, the chemistry program in the university's Faculty of Science was under the control of chemists educated in Britain (especially Sakurai Jōji, 1858-1939), and in due course Nagai was obliged to transfer to the Faculty of Medicine. German speakers controlled this latter unit. Nagai was active in pharmacological chemistry from a research standpoint, in the context of administration, and in the often-heated politics of medicine, including its relationship with pharmacology and pharmacy. In 1887, he made his most important contribution to science by isolating ephedrine in a pure form. Ephedrine was the first natural sympathomimetic amine and gradually found its place in the standard armamentarium of Western – as well as East Asian – medicine. Nagai's 1929 funeral was held in the Kasumi-machi Catholic Church, presided over by a German priest, and was attended by a substantial number of dignitaries and high officials. His widow learned the Japanese language quite well and remained in Japan.

Mizushima San'ichirō (1899-1983) was one of the most important Japanese chemists of the past century.[19] A pioneer in the application of quantum mechanics to chemistry, he was equally at home in the domains of experimentation and theory. Even before studying in Europe, Mizushima provided the first experimental proof of Dutch chemist Peter Debye's theory of electric moments involving dielectric constants, a contribution that helped the latter to win a Nobel Prize in 1936.[20] While working at Debye's laboratory in Leipzig (1929-31), he used X-ray crystallography to study chemical bonding and produced results that forced a modification of J.H. van't Hoff's hitherto dominant theory of single bonds. As an experimentalist, Mizushima was adept in the use of both Raman and infrared spectroscopy and used these techniques to investigate molecular structures of 1,2-dichloroethane and other ethylene halides. In 1940, he and his research team showed that about 20 percent of 1,2-dichloroethane molecules exist in the "gauche" form of rotational isomers at room temperature. This study has been described as one of the "earliest examples of conformational analysis." During World War II, Mizushima conducted Raman spectroscopic analyses of "paraffin in petroleum and polymers as the material of radar," and after the war he worked primarily on the structure of proteins.

Born into a prosperous Tokyo merchant family in 1899, Mizushima became interested in chemistry in middle and high school. He attended Tokyo University, where he studied under Katayama Masao, a protege of Walter Nernst and Arnold Sommerfeld in Germany and himself a distinguished physical chemist. In 1938, Mizushima succeeded Katayama as full professor at Tokyo University and received the Imperial Academy Prize the same year. His aforementioned contributions to physical chemistry won him many additional honours. They included membership in the US National Academy of Sciences, the Indian Academy of Sciences, the Pontifical Academy of Sciences, and the National Academy of Spain and election as a fellow of the American Association for the Advancement of Science. In the 1950s, Mizushima was a visiting professor at Cornell University and the University of Notre Dame. Following his retirement from Tokyo University in 1959, he served ten years as director of the Research Institute of the Yahata Steel Manufacturing Company. In 1970, he was awarded the Order of the Sacred Treasure, First Class, by the government of Japan.

Because biographical essays and memoirs dealing with his life make no reference to any conversion experience, it seems likely that Mizushima was actually born into the Catholic faith. A Japanese Jesuit priest, Moriwaki Takao, who worked in Mizushima's laboratory and himself became professor of physical chemistry at Sophia University, writes of Mizushima's Catholicism as though it were a lifelong attribute, noting, moreover, that he was one of three full professors in Tokyo University's Department of Chemistry who were Catholic in the 1950s. (Minami Eiji and Nakagawa Ichirō were the other two.[21]) It also seems significant in a religious context that Mizushima's wife, Tokiko, came from the Shōda family, many of whose members were Catholic. In fact, her father was the brother of Count Shōda Hidesaburō, father of Empress Michiko. In later years, Mizushima spent considerable time at the University of Notre Dame, partly it seems because of its strong Catholic identity. In 1961, he became one of the first two Japanese scientists elected to membership in the Pontifical Academy of Sciences, noted above.

Organizations of Scientists

The article in *ISIS* by Binzley mentioned earlier focuses on two organizations of Catholic scientists in the United States: the Catholic Roundtable of Science, founded in 1928, and the equally unsuccessful Albertus Magnus Guild, founded in 1953. Despite its far larger Catholic population, the United States was only eighteen years ahead of Japan in witnessing the emergence of an organization of Catholic scientists. In 1948, Mizushima San'ichirō convened what he himself referred to in English as the Catholic Scientists' Association. Unfortunately, I have not been able to ascertain the Japanese name of this organization; Vatican archival documents refer to it as the Fédération des savants catholiques. To date, we know only that Mizushima himself served as its president and that the headquarters was located in his private residence in Den'enchōfu, Tokyo.[22] How many members did it have? Were there a few dozen? A couple of hundred? We do not know. And what was its agenda? The comparable American organizations began with fairly ambitious aims, but each was unable to maintain a substantial membership. Does the Catholic Scientists' Association still exist? If not, then when did it come to an end? If, as appears certain, Mizushima himself was the primary inspiration, then perhaps the organization expired on the occasion of his formal retirement or death.

And were there – or are there – comparable organizations of Protestant Christian scientists or perhaps associations that include both Catholics and Protestants? It seems likely that there are or have been. But perhaps there are not and never have been. One can readily imagine plausible circumstances that might have favoured such organizations; equally well can one imagine reasons why they may never have existed.

Science Education

There are two main questions to consider here. First, what distinctive features of science education can we identify in Japanese colleges and universities within a comparative international framework? Second, how, if at all, have historically Christian institutions differed from their secular Japanese counterparts? It is tempting to postulate that Japan's experience has been broadly similar to the experiences of major Western countries. But even if true, the Japanese experience cannot have been identical; in fact, it has not been. One can offer a twofold answer to why we should consider such questions at all. First, distinctive institutional patterns may have influenced the growth of Christian evangelization in Japan. Second, Christian evangelical efforts may have affected the nature, scope, and character of science education in Japanese institutions.

To begin with, science education in Japanese universities did have distinctive features vis-à-vis foreign institutions. Although an extended discussion lies beyond the scope of this chapter, I can mention three such features. First, engineering was established early in Japan, at essentially the same time as the basic science disciplines, and on a basis of full equality. The Japanese pattern contrasts with the history of science education in continental European and English institutions, where engineering and basic science were housed separately, with basic science invariably enjoying greater prestige.[23] Second, the Japanese pioneered in one important field, seismology. And third, genetics gained an earlier, more robust, intellectual, and institutional foothold in the Japanese academy than it did in any Western university system.

A few pertinent facts can be noted: Japan's technological challenge in the nineteenth century was so severe that the government rejected the social conceits of the European academy in favour of efficiency. Indeed, Japanese decision makers seem to have been influenced by the American land grant universities, in which engineering occupied a special position. As for seismology, this new field was an obvious focus of early interest in earthquake-prone Japan. By 1908, European countries were bringing in Japanese seismological experts for consultation.[24] Japan's experience with genetics was also distinctive because the Japanese were early practitioners. Of course, the Austrian monk Gregor Mendel was the first to formulate the basic laws of genetic inheritance (in the 1860s), but for various reasons his work was basically lost to science until 1900. Shortly afterward, it was a young Japanese agricultural geneticist, Toyama Kametarō, who then showed that Mendel's laws of genetic inheritance, based on experimentation with plants (peas), also applied to animals (in this case, silkworms). These Japanese animal studies commenced in 1900, almost immediately after the rediscovery of Mendel's work, and were published just six years later, in 1906.[25] Japan was also a genetics pioneer in another context. Because of a private benefaction, Tokyo Imperial University in 1917 became the world's first comprehensive research university to have an entire professorship dedicated strictly to the new field of genetics.[26]

Based on information currently available, it is difficult to say exactly how Japanese institutions with Christian roots might have differed from their counterparts in the state sector. Nonetheless, the case of the Harris School of Science at Dōshisha University, Kyoto, in the late nineteenth century and early twentieth century is instructive. In 1890, a wealthy American industrialist, J.N. Harris, who lived in New London, Connecticut, donated $100,000 to Dōshisha to establish the school named in his honour. Harris was a strong proponent of modern science education and a committed Christian; he also had close connections with Japanese Christians. He selected the aforementioned Shimomura Kōtarō to organize the Dōshisha program and oversee what became the Harris School. The new institution offered what for the time was a full program of courses in chemistry (Shimomura's specialty) but also physics, mathematics, geology, and biology. The Harris School operated about ten years, attracting a respectable number of students.

Unfortunately, the school ran afoul of the Ministry of Education in Tokyo and its effort to make education in the natural sciences a monopoly of government institutions, at least at the advanced level.[27] Medicine, as had been true during the Tokugawa period, was allowed a presence in non-state schools, but other scientific disciplines were much more restricted. A mix of motives might explain this policy: elitism, a desire to promote Tokyo Imperial University (and to a lesser degree its sister imperial universities), or perhaps some lingering defensiveness about the potential ability of natural science to influence social attitudes and policies. Government officials in the early twentieth century often referred to Tokyo Imperial University as Japan's *saikō gakufu* ("supreme institution of higher learning" serves as an awkward translation of this expression into English). Perhaps it is significant that Tokyo's campaign to shut down the Harris School by denying full accreditation followed in the wake of the Russo-Japanese War. And it seems a distinct possibility that the Ministry of Education's hostility toward the Harris School derived from a misdirected fear of Christian intellectual success in the culturally vital domain of the natural sciences. At present, however, I lack the evidence to establish this claim with full confidence. As for science education at other historically Christian institutions – Rikkyō, Aoyama Gakuin, Jōchi (Sophia), to cite a few cases – I do not know enough to proffer a reasoned opinion about official attitudes and the factors behind them. In even beginning to engage this subject, one needs to know much more about when particular science programs were established at these schools, what their intellectual orientations might have been, what sort of students they attracted, and what at least some of their students did professionally after graduation.

Scientists' Views on Religion and Science

Catholic and Protestant scientists' views about the relationship of science to religion in Japan comprise a topic of obvious strategic importance in the current discussion; they also comprise an aspect of the larger subject about which I know little. Certainly, Japanese scientists over the years have addressed the general topic of how religion and science are (or should be) connected. In the Meiji period, for example, Satō Teikichi, professor of chemistry at Tōhoku Imperial University, wrote several such works, among them a book called *Shizen kagaku to shūkyō* ("Natural Science and Religion").[28] We can assume that he and other Japanese scientists have commented not only on purely intellectual matters in the classic science/religion debate but also on ethical issues as they developed over the years. Such, at least, was the case historically in the United States. Binzley observes that the leaders of the Albertus Magnus Guild long insisted that there should be no difference at the laboratory level between science as conducted by Catholics and science as done by anyone else. At the same time, the AMG leadership also declared that Catholic philosophy should define the moral limits of which inquiries or procedures were acceptable in conducting research itself. In the absence of direct evidence, we can assume that the same distinction has been put forward in the case of Japan.

Conclusion

I cannot offer any substantive conclusion based on the limited evidence presented in this chapter. The most I can do is to offer a few suggestions – in no sense rank ordered – for future inquiries. There should be, first, an extensive historical survey of scientific education in Japanese research universities with roots in the Christian tradition. This should be a fairly straightforward procedure if one relies heavily on the published institutional histories of particular schools. Second, one could attempt a census of Catholic and Protestant scientists, whether these investigators were active in the relatively remote past or more recently. As a first approximation, it would be enough simply to compile a list of several hundred names without any particular concern for completeness or statistical representation of a larger population. Knowing an individual's field of specialization alone would permit the formulation of useful hypotheses about the relationship of (for example) chemistry to Catholicism or engineering to Protestantism. Third, one should develop a profile of the Catholic Scientists' Association, including the number and disciplinary range of its members, how large a following it had (or may still have), what particular agenda the membership sought to advance, and whether or not it enjoyed much success, however that term might be defined.

Beyond these specific proposals, I would simply urge that conventional wisdom about the history of science and religion in Japan be set aside in favour of a completely fresh approach. In so doing, future investigators might fulfill the promise of the present volume and further enrich our understanding of Japan's remarkable culture and history.

Notes
1 Katorikku Chūō Kyōgikai, comp., *Kyōkai jōzai chi '91*, 2.
2 See, for example, Levy, ed., *Time Almanac 2008*, 316-17.
3 Spae, *Japanese Religiosity*, 223-30.

4 Binzley, "American Catholicism's Science Crisis and the Albertus Magnus Guild, 1953-1969," 695-723.
5 See Ellis, "American Catholics and the Intellectual Life."
6 Iseki, comp., *Dai Nihon hakushi roku*. This work was compiled in both Japanese and English. The title in English is *Who's Who: Hakushi in Great Japan*.
7 Nihon Gakushiin, ed., *Nihon Gakushiin hachijūnen shi, shiryō*, 304-8.
8 See Iseki (note 6 above) for all biographical entries, arranged alphabetically and by degree category. In this case, see vol. 5, 229 (English), and 174 (Japanese).
9 Takagi, "Henrin no ni, san," 266-68.
10 Mitamura, "Tanemichi no sekai dōtoku," 165, 168-70.
11 See Bartholomew, *The Formation of Science in Japan*, 210, passim.
12 The secondary literature on Noguchi is enormous. I especially recommend Nakayama, *Noguchi Hideyo*, and Plesset, *Noguchi and His Patrons*. Regarding Noguchi and the Catholic Church, see Plesset, 41-42.
13 Flexner, *An American Saga*, passim.
14 The following Nobel referee report makes this clear: Sundberg, "Till Medicinska Nobelkommittén Angående Simon Flexners och Hideyo Noguchis arbeten rörande akut barnförlamling, syphilis och lyssa," especially 24.
15 Hughes, *The Virus*, 90, 96-98.
16 Shiobara, *Takamine Hakushi*, passim.
17 Kiyonobu and Eri, "The Japanese Research System and the Establishment of the Institute of Physical and Chemical Research," 181-82.
18 Kanao, *Nagai Nagayoshi den*, passim.
19 Kikuchi, "Mizushima, San'ichirō," 167-71. Quotations regarding Mizushima are from the Kikuchi essay.
20 Parker, "Peter Debye," 393-402. Parker does not mention Mizushima's contribution, but Kikuchi does and presents citations.
21 Moriwaki, "Mizushima Sensei to hitori no shisai kagakusha," 293-304.
22 See Mizushima's letter of 31 January 1949 to Dr. Pietro Salviucci, Mizushima File, Archives of the Pontificia Accademia delle Scienze, Citta del Vaticano. The French-language term appears in a letter of 13 December 1948 by Cardinal Paolo Marella, Apostolic Delegate to Japan, to Dr. Pietro Salviucci. From the archives listed above.
23 Bernal, *The Social Function of Science*, 95-96, passim. Also see Bartholomew, *The Formation of Science in Japan*, 97, 305; and Yuasa, *Kagaku shi*, 228.
24 Clancey, *Earthquake Nation*, 172-73.
25 Yuasa, comp., *Gendai kagaku gijutsu shi nempyō*, 96-97. See also Goldschmidt, *In and out of the Ivory Tower*, 108-10.
26 Yuasa, comp., *Gendai kagaku gijutsu shi nempyō*, 121.
27 Iseki, comp., *Dai Nihon hakushi roku*, vol. 5, 229 (English) and 174 (Japanese). The Japanese text refers to a "dispute" at Dōshisha "between foreigners and Japanese." Regarding the matter of educational monopoly, see Scheiner, *Christian Converts and Social Protest in Meiji Japan*, 184-85.
28 See Iseki, comp., *Dai Nihon hakushi roku*, vol. 5, 331 (English) and 261 (Japanese).

3
Tanaka Kōtarō and Natural Law
Kevin M. Doak

In his seminal study on modern Japanese Catholicism, Hanzawa Takamaro presents only two individuals as having made key contributions to the culture of Catholicism in modern Japan: Yoshimitsu Yoshihiko (1904-45), and Tanaka Kōtarō (1890-1974).[1] Of course, since both professors were indebted to the spiritual and intellectual influence of Father Iwashita Francis Xavier Sōichi (1889-1940), Hanzawa also presents a short chapter on Iwashita. But the centrality of Tanaka in modern Japanese Catholic thought can be understood from the major attention that he receives in Hanzawa's book: whereas Yoshimitsu is treated in one chapter (albeit a long one of 85 pages), Tanaka is discussed in the following two chapters (a total of 113 pages). Hanzawa then concludes with the sixty-page chapter on Iwashita and a slightly shorter chapter on the political thought of the Protestant Uchimura Kanzō (important since both Yoshimitsu and Tanaka began their Christian lives as Protestants under the influence of Uchimura). My point is not that the significance of Tanaka (or Yoshimitsu) should be measured by the number of pages devoted to him in this book. In fact, Hanzawa personally prefers Yoshimitsu's understanding of Catholicism to that of Tanaka, especially Yoshimitsu's more critical attitude toward modernity. But the fact that Hanzawa, even with a palpable bias against Tanaka, nonetheless gives so much attention to his thought does say something about the importance of Tanaka to the shaping of Catholic culture and thought in modern Japan. Perhaps one of the reasons for this attention is simply that, of all the Catholic intellectuals whom Hanzawa discusses, only Tanaka lived into the postwar period, even through the years of the Second Vatican Council. His longevity may be held up against him as an unfair yardstick (there is no way to know how Iwashita or Yoshimitsu would have reacted to the changes in postwar Japanese society or to the reforms of the Second

Vatican Council). But Tanaka at least provides us with an invaluable measure of how, in one important case, a vigorous Catholic theology from the prewar period was carried over into the new conditions of postwar Japan and the post-Vatican II Church.

From Protestantism to Catholicism: The Early Years

Tanaka was born in Kagoshima while his father was posted there as a judge. The Tanaka family did not come from the samurai class, as did many Meiji-era Protestants, but were farmers from the Saga region. Kōtarō's father had, by distinguishing himself in scholarship, been able to work his way to a judicial appointment. Education was highly valued in his household, and he emphasized the Confucian classics in the education of Kōtarō, lecturing him on *The Mencius* and *The Analects*. But he also had an interest in Christianity. Kōtarō's father and mother were known as local leaders in the movement to improve life *(seikatsu kaizen undō)* and thus were part of what were then considered the progressive elements in society.[2] Yet the overriding characteristic of young Kōtarō's life was a peripatetic experience that militated against his developing a parochial or traditional mindset. His father's judicial appointments took the family from Kagoshima to Nagoya and Matsue and then, during Kōtarō's middle school years, to Okayama, Niigata, Fukuoka, and elsewhere. During these years, the period between the late nineteenth century and the early twentieth century, Japan was forging a new sense of unified, national, and social identity under the Meiji Constitution, and Kōtarō's travels opened him up at the same time to a broader national sense of purpose that challenged the inherited traditions of local values with the transcendence of the nation-state. It was a heady time, when universal values were in the ascendancy and concerns with social reform often raised implicitly and explicitly the question of which values all people might share. Although one might discern the beginnings of an aptitude for natural law theory in this early life experience, more often Tanaka's early years have been described as drawing on the influence of the "spiritual individualism" of Abe Jirō (1883-1959), Abe Yoshishige (1883-1968), and Uozumi Setsuro (1883-1910).

This is one way of recognizing the impact of Protestant Christianity on young men of this generation; it is also a way of noting the sense they shared that traditional, parochial ways of understanding the world were not deemed sufficient for young Japanese of the time. Tanaka's own turn to Christianity did not happen until 1909, his second year at the elite Ichikō Higher School, when Tanaka miraculously recovered from a serious illness.

Around the same time, he read Uchimura's "Why I Became a Christian" and began a spiritual searching journey that lasted several years. Immediately after graduating from the School of Law of Tokyo Imperial University in 1915, he entered Uchimura's "churchless" *(mukyōkai)* Protestant group through the guidance of Tsukamoto Toraji, an older classmate who had studied at the Shūyūkan Confucian Academy.[3] From 1919 to 1922, Tanaka travelled throughout Europe and the United States on a government grant to study commercial law, his field of specialization. On his return from Europe, he got married and was appointed professor of law at Tokyo Imperial University, a position that he held until 1946. He had broken with Uchimura's Protestant group and become a Catholic in April 1926. In 1936, Tanaka was invited by the Instituto del Medio ed Extrem' Oriente in Italy to give lectures on commercial law and philosophy of law in Rome, Milan, Venice, Paris, Lyons, Lille, and Louvain. He was able to witness firsthand what fascism meant, and he immediately began publishing articles that rejected the fascist and national socialist programs.[4] Returning to his university that year, he was appointed dean of the Faculty of Law, a position that he held until 1939. In that year, Tanaka gave similar lectures on law at universities in Brazil, Peru, Panama, and Mexico. He was appointed chief of school administration in the Ministry of Education in 1945 and a member of the House of Peers in 1946. He was minister of education in the first Yoshida cabinet (May 1946-January 1947). From May 1947, he practised law with Matsumoto Jōji (his brother-in-law), specializing in the area of commercial law. Tanaka was appointed chief justice of the Supreme Court of Japan on 3 March 1950 and in the same year received honorary doctorates from Georgetown University, Fordham University, and Boston College. In 1960, he was awarded the Order of Cultural Merit. That year he stepped down from the Supreme Court and accepted a position as a justice of the International Court of Justice in The Hague, where he served until 1970. He passed away in 1974 at the age of eighty-four.

It was a long and rich life, one full of many lessons. In the first place, Tanaka's life forces a reconsideration of the commonly held notion that Christians were routinely persecuted during wartime. Although much attention has been focused on the Protestant Yanaihara Tadao, who was forced to resign his teaching post at Tokyo Imperial University in 1937 (he was kept on as a librarian), Tanaka – whose Catholicism was a matter of public record by then – was at that very time promoted to dean of the Faculty of Law at the same state-run university. Christians per se were not persecuted by the government (social attitudes of course are an entirely different matter, then and there as well as here and now). Rather, the key issue appears to be how one considered the state and its legitimacy. Many Protestant Christians had gradually become socialists and even Marxists, often leaving their faith behind in the process. For those who attacked the state during wartime (and Yanaihara's troubles stemmed from his critical articles on the state, not from his religion), there were consequences. Tanaka was hardly a statist. He in fact strongly condemned any effort to elevate a social or political identity above religion. As Hanzawa writes,

> Nothing was further from his mind than a nineteenth-century organic view of the state. He, influenced by [Wladimir] Solovjeff and [Jacques] Maritain, could not indulge any assertion of a particular cultural value that was offered in exclusivist terms – whether it be racism, ethnic nationalism, the dictatorship of the proletariat, or politics seen as the opposite of religion.[5]

Below we will take a closer look at the historical reasons for Tanaka's dismissal of such secular absolutes. Here it will suffice to note that Tanaka's life spanned the social transformations of Meiji Japan, when universal values were seen as trumping local particularities; to the 1930s, when particularism was raised in Fascist Italy, in Nazi Germany, and, in the form of class, in the Soviet Union; to postwar Japan, when once again many on the political right and left turned nostalgically to cultural particularism as a rejection of the universalism that seemed interchangeable with American values.

Tanaka's Catholicism, rooted in a neo-Thomist appreciation for natural law, provided him with a certain moral compass with which to navigate those troubled waters. Rather than judge his natural law theory from whatever intellectual trends happen to prevail today, it is important to situate his turn to natural law in his historical context to see why and how Tanaka turned to natural law in his effort to bring his Catholic faith and his social and political commitments into some form of unified action.

Hanzawa is probably right that Tanaka left Uchimura's "churchless" Protestantism because of what he had learned in Europe (that a common spirit underlay different artistic expressions) and because he did not find in the individualist, even anarchic, Protestantism of Uchimura's group a satisfactory answer to the social and political concerns that he, as a student of law, had always had.[6] In later years, Tanaka himself reflected on the differences that he felt from Uchimura's Protestantism:

> [What they were] mostly interested in were the problems of human life: faith, friendship, love, and marriage were the main themes ... At that time, the common characteristic was described as turning from the exterior to

the interior ... In general, they had no interest in politics ... It was not that they rejected the state, but they were indifferent to the state and society and sought immediate answers to the true, the good, and the beautiful as they grappled directly with the issues of life.[7]

Hanzawa points out that Tanaka, as a student of law, was likely drawn to Catholicism for its defence of the principle of knowledge as attainable, particularly as applicable to social problems, in contrast to the subjectivity of the Protestant tradition of individual interpretation of the Bible without the need to bring individual readings into the social whole through the Magisterium.[8]

In *Hō to shūkyō to shakai seikatsu* (1927), his first publication after joining the Catholic Church, Tanaka outlined a concept of Man as possessing a dual nature *(ningen no nigen-sei),* which he apparently had learned from Iwashita. This dualistic nature signified the irreducible gap that always exists in this life between Man as he is and Man as he ought to be. Existence and Ought, *Sein* and *Sollen,* always remain parallel lines in this world, and anyone who is not painfully conscious of this dualism is "either an angel or a beast."[9] Although, on the one hand, the only final resolution of this painful separa-tion is through the salvation of the gospel, on the other hand, Tanaka argues that this salvation must begin in this world by addressing the social problems that create greater propensity for evil. He expresses this point directly:

> The issue is not that the reform of institutions necessarily also restrains the external acts of human beings; rather, it comes down to the eradication of the evil that lurks in the human heart ... The spiritual salvation of an indi-vidual must be the first step toward the salvation of social life ... The exist-ence of dualism in social life is like that in the inner life of an individual. Thus, deliverance from the suffering of this dualism is exactly the same as in the case of an individual: it cannot be achieved through one's own power, efforts, but must rely on faith.[10]

Although Tanaka had yet to develop his theory of natural law, it is clear that, around the time he quit the Protestants and joined the Catholic Church, he was seeking a way to address both the sins of individual actions and the problem of evil in society as a general moral and social question.

Catholicism and Natural Law: Foundations in the Prewar Period

Hanzawa's philosophical approach helps us to understand the internal dynamics of Tanaka's thought on Catholicism as an adequate response to certain epistemological questions, particularly his quest for a coherent principle that could make sense of truth across time and culture. Ironically, it merely reproduces the logic of theoretical analysis inherent in his natural law theory more than it explains the significance of natural law for Tanaka at his time and place in history. This is not to overlook the "historicist" aspects of Hanzawa's analytic approach. Indeed, Hanzawa argues in a rather reductive mode that neo-Thomism and natural law theory can be attributed to a cultural crisis of the West and a reactionary effort by the West in the early twentieth century to reassert its own cultural universality. It is within that context of a cultural defence of Western modernity that he locates the "historicity" of Tanaka's theory of natural law and what for Hanzawa are its tragic limitations. It may seem a bit contradictory, or at least uncharitable, to adopt a historical mode of analysis to explain a mode of thinking that appeals to an ahistorical, universal natural law. At a minimum, I do not agree with Hanzawa that the whole appeal of natural law can be explained away in this manner. I do think that there is something to be gained from placing Tanaka and his theory of natural law in his own time and culture before looking at it from within the framework of natural law itself. I propose to do so, however, in more of a microhistorical fashion: not a theory that sees natural law ipso facto as a particular cultural ideology but an effort to look closely at Tanaka himself and the particular times in which he lived as a means of explaining not natural law theory but why he was attracted to natural law theory in the manner that he was.

His interest in natural law can be dated from the last years of the Taisho period (c. 1925) or roughly with his joining the Catholic Church. Tanaka himself has famously said that all of his vast corpus of writings can be reduced to efforts to explain this one idea: the theory of natural law.[11] There is no question that his interest in natural law was connected with his appreciation of the universality of the Catholic Church and the primacy that it put on known and knowable truth. Indeed, Hanzawa goes so far as to declare that Tanaka's discovery of Catholicism was identical with his discovery of natural law. Certainly, Tanaka read widely in Catholic natural law theorists, with Jacques Maritain and Viktor Cathrein being the most influential sources. How did Tanaka understand natural law? Here is what may be the best summary of his understanding of natural law, taken from his *General Principles of Jurisprudence:*

> In its basic meaning, the natural law ... refers to that which regulates the giving "to each what is his" ... "What is his" encompasses three elements in accordance with three categories of justice. As the point of departure for

a principle of natural law, in the first place, "what is his" carries the positive obligation that "you shall give to each what belongs to him." Second, there arises the negative obligation that "you shall not commit injustice toward anyone." As a logical and necessary conclusion of these two fundamental obligations, there arise the Ten Commandments that give us such orders as "thou shalt not kill," "thou shalt not steal," "thou shalt not commit adultery," and "thou shalt not bear false witness against thy neighbour," moral statements that have been substantially recognized by all ethnic groups in all times as is the obligation to repay one's debts. From the same source arise the injunctions to respect proper authorities and to honour contracts that have been legitimately made.

The natural law is based on our reason and is a self-evident universal principle that has become our common sense ... However, determining the precise details regarding how this principle shall be applied to particular cases is not as self-evident as the general principle of the natural law itself. It differs depending on each age and each place. As St. Thomas perceived, when it comes to matters of human actions, the truth does not always treat all people the same in every detail; rather, it is uniform only as a general principle. An adequate theory of natural law thus only recognizes universal applicability and immutability at the level of basic theory; it reserves flexibility when dealing with particulars.[12]

Tanaka's understanding of natural law is consistent with the definition of justice put forward in the most recent *Catechism of the Catholic Church*:

Justice is the moral virtue that consists in the constant and firm will to give their due to God and neighbor ... Justice toward men disposes one to respect the rights of each and to establish in human relationships the harmony that promotes equity with regard to persons and to the common good. The just man, often mentioned in the Sacred Scriptures, is distinguished by habitual right thinking ... "You shall not be partial to the poor or defer to the great, but in righteousness shall you judge your neighbor." (Leviticus 19:15)[13]

Not only is Tanaka's basic understanding of justice in his theory of natural law sound, but also his recognition that flexibility in application is necessary is an expression of the traditional Catholic emphasis on the virtue of prudence in matters of justice. It should not be interpreted as merely opening the door to a neo-Kantian emphasis on technique, as Hanzawa concludes.[14]

In fact, when Tanaka applied these thoughts to contemporary Japan, he strongly condemned the rise of a neo-Kantian intoxication with technique as an amoral philosophy (he seems to have had Miki Kiyoshi in mind). Tanaka worried that Japanese neo-Kantian philosophy underwrote a sweeping intellectual and cultural relativism during the 1930s. This reliance on natural science without a universal moral principle (such as Tanaka found in natural law) meant that technological absolutism was the default position among the Meiji intellectual elite. As Tanaka astutely observed, this positivism led to the view that "there is no science other than the recognition of the conventional morals and laws *(jittei-teki dōtoku mata wa jittei hō)* of a given society, [a view that is merely] a negation of the very idea of ethics or jurisprudence."[15] Tanaka saw such positivism as the greatest threat to the moral good of Japanese society, and he emphasized that this positivism informed movements on both extremes of the political spectrum.

These dangers were clearly identified by Tanaka, who was able to show from the vantage point of the early 1930s how the Japanese intellectuals' dalliance with neo-Kantianism during the Taisho period, albeit from a self-consciously liberal position at that early stage, ironically had led to a rejection of natural law theory and to a reactionary, extreme conservative politics. Tanaka's analysis revealed how neo-Kantianism, both in the specific case of legal theory and in its broader moral implications, led to a rejection of universal principles such as natural law in favour of a presumption of the subjective determination of values and norms. It was a retreat, in a sense, to a hypertechnical effort to transcend substantive politics, a position that left it implicated in the dominant political system of its time. What, then, would take the place of a universal standard of justice? Again it is best to listen directly to Tanaka:

Ultimately, this position [neo-Kantian moral relativism] makes it impossible for anyone to criticize another's acts as fundamentally immoral or unjust. One can only affirm or negate acts based on the established morals or established laws that a given society or state has enacted from necessities of social life in that society or state. As the place or time changes, what was unjust suddenly becomes just ... This discovery of a causal relationship between the social and economic conditions of a given society and its normative morals or laws also means there can be no science outside the perception of the established morals and established laws of a given society. This is a rejection of the very idea of jurisprudence or of the field of ethics.[16]

Tanaka ranked neo-Kantianism alongside Marxist materialism as the most popular mode of thinking among Japanese social scientists during the 1930s, and for much the same reason.[17] Both had surrendered moral and spiritual issues at best to the technical field of material and (pseudo-) scientific method. But there was an "at worst" as well.

The dark side of neo-Kantian philosophy was making itself known in the radical politics of relativism that was sweeping the world during the 1930s. Tanaka presented a powerful warning about the illiberal forces of cultural relativism on the rise in Japan. He knew something about these relativist radicals since he carefully monitored world political events, especially in Europe. Just one year earlier he had published a sharp rebuke of fascism from a Catholic position that held out the universality of human dignity and principles of human rights.[18] He was equally critical of Marxist movements that rejected universal principles of human rights and a sense of balance in their extreme political agendas. Indeed, by the early 1930s, Marxists frequently shared with rightists an embrace of the ethnic nation *(minzoku)* as the privileged agent of social and cultural identity. Extreme rightists did so from an organic belief in the primacy of the eternal folk that preceded political institutions such as the state; Marxists did so in light of Stalinist instrumental approaches to ethnic nationalism that sought to bring down capitalist imperialism. But in either case, liberal political values such as the universality of human rights were under attack from both sides, and Tanaka was one of the few who continued to speak out in their defence. And to defend human rights, it was necessary to defend the constitutional state from those who would replace it with a romantic concept of the nation as a natural, ethnic body.

The tensions between ethnic and political concepts of national loyalty are poignantly evident in Tanaka's prize-winning *Sekai hō no riron* (1932). Tanaka introduced the theory of natural law as a means of refuting radical conservatives who believed that law was a social construct that must reflect the specificities of Japanese social and cultural practice and Marxists who believed that law was merely a conventional tool in the struggle for world revolution. His main focus was to subordinate the claims of ethnic nationality within the constitutional, multi-ethnic Meiji state.[19] He began by addressing the thorny question of "what is a nation?" – recognizing that the concept of ethnic nationality *(minzoku)* developed out of race *(jinshu)* but was ultimately a distinct concept.[20] In addition to the element of race as a component in ethnic nationality, Tanaka drew attention to the usual litany of "cultural" elements in the nation (shared territory, spirit, language, religion, customs, etc.). A classical liberal who supported the Meiji constitutional state, Tanaka accepted the Marxist position that the nation was not the same thing as the state. Yet he believed that the constitutional state (where he enjoyed freedom to practise his Catholicism) was worth defending and that ethnic nationalism was a dangerous ideology, as contemporary events in Europe were showing.

Conceding the distinction between the ethnically determined nation and the political form of the state, Tanaka argued that what really mattered was the relationship between the state and ethnic nationality. What is the relationship between political sovereignty and ethnic consciousness? Does the state create the ethnic nation, or do distinctive ethnic features produce different forms of the state? In the end, Tanaka concluded that ethnic identity is not a mere invention of the state; rather, it assists in the formation of the state, though the state also helps to strengthen concepts of nationality. Ethnicity belongs to the realm of culture – literature, music, painting, and sculpture – and the state has little control over such cultural matters.[21] Indeed, ethnic culture is an inappropriate area for law, which is concerned with the more objective form of social life, the state.[22] Tanaka argued that a theory of natural law was an essential means of supporting the multi-ethnic Japanese state, pointing specifically to multi-ethnic states such as Great Britain and the United States to bolster his argument. He criticized historical legalists who opposed multi-ethnic states in favour of ethnic nation-states, and he traced their belief that law is merely a product of ethnic national spirit to the early nineteenth century (German) Romantic School.[23] Tanaka was willing to accept an ethnic definition of culture, but he argued that the ethnic group *(minzoku)* must be secured within a trans-ethnic, constitutional political order. Law transcends cultural attributes, and Tanaka thus concluded, "I do not hesitate in encouraging politicians to carry out the legislative policy of the state in a fundamentally different manner than national language policies: that is, in a purely rational technical spirit."[24] At stake in the rise of ethnic nationalism was not only a challenge to the constitutional state but also a deeper challenge to the very notion of a universally applicable natural law. It and the constitutional state were conjoined, as much by their common opposition to cultural particularism and fascism as by any inherent qualities they might have shared.[25]

Catholicism and Natural Law: A Legal Basis for Postwar Japanese Culture

We have already seen that Tanaka was able to move rather smoothly from prewar to wartime to postwar positions of influence in the Japanese legal and political world. It was a remarkable feat shared by few others. How could a brilliant legal scholar who had defended the Meiji Constitution from the position of natural law accommodate himself to the new Constitution of Japan announced on 3 December 1946? Quite well, it turns out. In fact, as Prime Minister Yoshida Shigeru's minister of education, Tanaka was listed along with other cabinet members in the official draft submitted to the emperor on 3 November. Furthermore, his own brother-in-law, Matsumoto Jōji, had played a key role in shaping the Constitution, giving his name to an early draft. So we should not be surprised to find that Tanaka was a strong defender of the postwar Constitution, as a member of the government, as chief justice of the Supreme Court, and in his constant stream of publications.[26] Nor did Tanaka feel any reason to change his strong commitment to natural law. As we have seen above, his approach to it recognized both its immutable character as a general principle and the necessity of prudence in its application. The postwar Japanese Constitution has been interpreted as just such a prudent application of natural law in light of changed times and circumstances.[27] And this interpretation was Tanaka's view as well.

Tanaka defended the postwar Constitution from the outset, once again interpreting it in light of the broader principle of natural law. In an article written in 1949, when Japan was still under occupation and Marxism was gaining legitimacy in the eyes of many who wanted to distance themselves from America, he argued for peace and internationalism, pointing to the new Constitution as the source of moral values in the new society. Whereas during wartime Tanaka upheld natural law against the particularism of statism *(kokkashugi)* and ethnic nationalism *(minzokushugi)*, his focus now was on cultural relativism and Marxism – both ideologies that rejected universal norms of morality and that were increasingly popular in the postwar period. In fighting these ideologies, he found a powerful ally in the Constitution:

> While the Constitution is the supreme law in relation to other actual laws, still ... as an actual law itself, there stands above, behind and under it as a base, the Natural Law which represents truth and order in the universe. This Natural Law is what defines the limits of actual [positive] laws. It demonstrates that even the will of the people, though having the supreme authority in the adoption of a constitution, nevertheless is not absolute but is relative to and governed by a higher principle. Whether sovereignty rests with the majority of the people [as in the postwar Constitution] or with the

emperor [as in the Meiji Constitution] makes no difference. The question was never raised under the Meiji Constitution, but it should be understood that even the supreme will of the emperor cannot be in conflict with the Natural Law.[28]

But Tanaka was not content simply to show that natural law underlay both constitutions. Nonetheless, he had made his point: there was no need for him to revise his legal theories simply because there was now a new Constitution.

Tanaka embraced the new Constitution as coming closer to a codification of the unwritten natural law:

The third article of the Preamble states that "the laws of political morality are universal," and the eleventh article asserts that "the basic rights of man are enduring and inviolable." Such laws – such natural laws – are not confined to one nation or one period of time. They endure, and they do so because they are founded on the true nature of man ... It is truth itself which governs social life. In truth itself rests true authority.[29]

So for Tanaka there was no dilemma, no reason to reassess his theory of law: he had never given the Meiji Constitution his unqualified support; he had supported it only to the extent that it reflected and encouraged the moral principles of natural law. His argument that natural law could be realized under monarchical sovereignty as well as popular sovereignty might be controversial in some quarters today, but it is fully consistent with the principles of natural law and the virtue of prudence in the application of those principles. It was not a specific law or constitution that would liberate a nation or an individual. Rather, Tanaka concluded, "the truth shall make you free *(Veritas vos liberabit)*."[30]

One lesson that Tanaka drew from his recognition that natural law and existing laws were never entirely identical was that education was most important in fostering a moral conscience. Laws did not shape morality, but morality informed the laws of a country and how closely those laws approximated natural law. Consequently, Tanaka happily accepted appointment as minister of education in the first Yoshida cabinet, and he defended the importance of education as a fundamental human right. One of his most influential postwar essays was "Nihon ni okeru daigaku no jichi" ("The Autonomy of Universities in Japan"), anthologized in a widely available collection on Japanese thought. He noted that one university had already given official recognition to "a communist party cell, other universities were following suit, and that cell's activities had upset the order on campus and had given rise to several scandalous events."[31]

Tanaka's argument was not simply the expression of anti-communist ideology. Tanaka drew on his personal experience during the war with extreme rightist professors who had tried to ideologize the university campuses in support of the Greater East Asia War, and he saw in this experience a warning of what can happen when university administrators and professors fail to defend academic freedom from abuses that arise within their communities. At all costs, universities must defend their autonomy so that the pursuit of the truth can take place freely:

> In freedom, we seek the truth, and this freedom must be politically guaranteed. Thus, the new Constitution guarantees this freedom. But this freedom is not absolute; we must recognize that it is limited by the very existence of truth. The freedom we enjoy is the freedom to search for the truth; we do not have the freedom to deny the very existence of truth or to distort the truth.[32]

Tanaka's defence of the university as an autonomous space for the pursuit of truth, and his defence of the very idea of truth, were both expressions of his belief in natural law. Natural law was a manifestation that the truth exists, is universal, and can be discovered through reason, even by those who do not share Tanaka's Catholic faith.

As a scholar of law, Tanaka recognized the importance of institutions such as universities as places where morality might be enhanced (or hindered). But his appeal was ultimately to the individual heart. The purpose of academic freedom and constitutional rights was to secure the dignity of the individual but also to allow the individual to discover the truth on his or her own. There was a spiritual dimension to education, for to discover the truth was to encounter God. In a similar vein, Tanaka's writings on natural law can be accepted merely as a professional argument within the field of legal philosophy even though he ultimately aimed at a higher, moral purpose: the conversion of the world, starting in Japan, to the Catholic faith. Perhaps it is best to listen directly to his own words:

> Japan possesses her own characteristic moral convictions and fine social traditions which are a legacy from Buddhism and Confucianism. Of these she must preserve all that is good. The Oriental peoples, including the Japanese, have always recognized the natural law. This Natural Law is

the common spiritual basis uniting the cultures of East and West. To raise this natural morality to the supernatural plane is the high mission of Catholicism. Faith in her own national moral virtues, as perfected by Christianity, could be for a reborn Japan her qualification as a member of the world community of peoples, giving us for the first time in our history a sense of Japan's place and mission in the world, and providing a spiritual bond between East and West, as well as a firm basis for world peace.[33]

This statement sums up best not only Tanaka's approach to natural law but also his role as a Catholic intellectual in Japan. If a European were to make this pronouncement, he or she could – and probably would – be quickly denounced for forcing "his/her own culture" on a different people. As a Japanese Catholic, Tanaka testifies to the limits of such a timid, if not relativistic, approach to faith and culture. In choosing Christianity and then finding the fullness of truth in the Catholic Church, he expressed in his own life story the significance of the natural law that he spent nearly half a century defending, explaining, and applying in cases that came before his court. And if the significance of natural law was that Japanese were not excluded from the truth because of their culture, then Tanaka himself provides the best example of how "the truth shall make you free."

Notes

1 Hanzawa, *Kindai nihon no katorishizumu.*
2 Ibid., 124.
3 Ibid., 125. The exact details of Tanaka's relationship with Tsukamoto elude me. The Shūyūkan, established in 1783 as the domainal school of Fukuoka, was closed in 1871, nearly two decades before Tanaka was born.
4 His reflection in later years that while in Italy in 1921 he never heard of Mussolini's name ("Ōbei yūgaku chū no omoide," n.d., included in *Ongaku to jinsei* [1953], cited in ibid., 127-28) needs to be balanced with the fact that even before his second trip in 1937 he clearly had become aware of Mussolini, as evidenced by his publications around that time. See his articles on "Fascism to katorikku no tachiba" and "Nazi-teki hō rinen no shisōshi-teki bunseki oyobi hihan"; both were republished in Tanaka, *Kyōyō to bunka no kiso.*
5 Hanzawa, *Kindai nihon no katorishizumu,* 162.
6 Ibid., 131-33.
7 Tanaka, *Watakushi no rirekisho* (1961), and "Kyōyō ni tsuite," in *Gendai seikatsu no ronri* (1951); cited in ibid., 126.
8 Ibid., 118.
9 Tanaka, *Hō to shūkyō to shakai seikatsu,* 37, 39, 271, cited in ibid., 146.
10 Tanaka, *Hō to shūkyō to shakai seikatsu,* 64, 291; cited in ibid., 147.
11 Tanaka, *Hō tetsugaku,* vol. 3, "josetsu"; cited in Hanzawa, *Kindai nihon no katorishizumu,* 176-77. Tanaka conveys the point through this humorous anecdote drawn from the painter Wilhelm von Kuegergen's autobiography. There was a painter famous for his paintings of church bells, but he would not paint any other subject matter. One

day a man ordered a painting of a knight from him. But when the painting was done,
lo and behold, it was not a knight but yet another church bell. When the customer
complained that it was a church bell, and not a knight as he had ordered, the painter
replied, "but it kind of looks like a knight, doesn't it?" Tanaka concedes that his
thirty-year-long obsession with natural law might lead some to compare him to this
painter.

12 Tanaka, *Hōritsugaku gairon*, 62-64, cited in ibid., 182-83.

13 *Catechism of the Catholic Church*, 1807, 444.

14 Hanzawa, *Kindai nihon no katorishizumu*, 192-97. Hanzawa's main critique of Tanaka
is that his natural law theory devolves into a technical, individualistic notion of
justice devoid of the concept of "common good." See ibid., 23. But his argument is
overly theoretical and not well supported by Tanaka's own writings. Tanaka does
incorporate the concept of the common good into his work (e.g., "Shin kenpō ni
okeru fuhen jinrui-teki genri," 289). When he says that "the common good ... is the
aim of government" ("In Search of Truth and Peace," 378), he implicitly argues that
all of his work for the Japanese government and for "world government" (as a judge
in the International Court of Justice in The Hague), along with all his writings on
law and justice, were devoted to the pursuit of this common good.

15 Tanaka, "Gendai no shisō-teki anākī to sono gen'in no kentō," 248.

16 Ibid.

17 Given these arguments by Tanaka, as cited above, it is difficult to accept Hanzawa's
view that there was still an element of neo-Kantian value consciousness in Tanaka
after his conversion from Protestantism. See Hanzawa, *Kindai nihon no katorishizumu*,
179. At best, it seems that by "an element of neo-Kantian value consciousness"
Hanzawa means that Tanaka still held "a positive appraisal of certain aspects of
modernity." But this argument, and his argument that "for Tanaka the norm of
natural law was to be found ultimately in the hearts and minds of the people *(minshū)*"
(23), strike me as overly polemical and reflective of Hanzawa's own time and concerns. Tanaka's attitude toward the people needs to be balanced with his concerns
discussed above on the dangers of the *minzoku* ("ethnic people," "ethnic nation").

18 Tanaka, "Fasshizumu to katorikku no tachiba," *Yomiuri Shimbun*, May 1932, reprinted
in Tanaka, *Kyōyō to bunka no kiso*.

19 Tanaka, *Sekai hō no riron*, vol. 1, 6. Volumes 2 and 3 were published in 1933 (reprinted
in 1950) and 1952.

20 Tanaka, *Sekai hō no riron*, vol. 1, 162-66. Compare Tanaka's distinction between the
ethnic nation *(minzoku)* as distinct from race *(jinshu)* with Anthony D. Smith's caution
that the *ethnie*, as the foundation for the modern concept of nation, "must be sharply
differentiated from a *race* in the sense of a social group that is held to possess unique
hereditary biological traits that allegedly determine the mental attributes of the
group." Smith, *National Identity*, 21.

21 Tanaka, *Sekai hō no riron*, vol. 1, 190-91, 193-95.

22 Ibid., 212-16.

23 Ibid., 268.

24 Ibid., 269.

25 Some parts of this section are taken from my earlier publications, "What Is a Nation
and Who Belongs?" and "Romanticism, Conservatism, and the Kyoto School of
Philosophy."

26 Sonoda Yoshiaki's recent book, *Kakusareta kōshitsu jimmyaku*, makes an argument
that is relevant here and nicely summarized in his subtitle: "Was Article Nine of the
Constitution Composed by Christians?"

27 See Inagaki, "The Constitution of Japan and the Natural Law."

28 Tanaka, "In Search of Truth and Peace," 380.
29 Ibid.
30 Ibid., 382.
31 Tanaka, "Nihon ni okeru daigaku no jichi," 270. It is interesting to note that this essay was published five years before the leftist student movements of 1968 closed down many universities in Japan.
32 Ibid., 281.
33 Tanaka, "In Search of Truth and Peace," 383. Bracketed words are as presented in *Sources of Japanese Tradition.*

4
Catholicism and Contemporary Man

Yoshimitsu Yoshihiko (translated and annotated
by Kevin M. Doak and Charles C. Campbell)

Editor's Note: Yoshimitsu Yoshihiko (1904-45) was one of the most influential Catholic intellectuals in prewar and wartime Japan. He was baptized in a Protestant community during his middle school years and did not enter the Catholic Church until 1927, when he came under the influence of Father Iwashita Sōichi. After graduation from Tokyo Imperial University's Department of Ethics in 1928, he went to Europe, where he studied under Jacques Maritain and Reginald Garrigou-Lagrange, OP (and corresponded with Erich Przywara, SJ), returning to Japan in 1930 and being appointed a professor of philosophy at Sophia University in the spring of the following year. Yoshimitsu also taught philosophy at the Tokyo Catholic Seminary and, from 1935 (on the recommendation of Watsuji Tetsurō), was appointed lecturer at Tokyo Imperial University. His mentor, Iwashita, died in 1940, leaving Yoshimitsu as the leading Catholic intellectual in Japan. He exercised considerable influence on a young Endō Shūsaku, who lodged in the Catholic dormitory San Felipe, where Yoshimitsu was master of the house. Yoshimitsu had contracted tuberculosis by the mid-1930s, and he struggled the rest of his life with the disease, succumbing on 23 October 1945. His essay "Catholicism and Contemporary Man," translated here for the first time, was originally given as a speech (presumably to the Catholic Student Association, which he led), published first in the November 1942 issue of *Shinkō Kirisutokyō* and then republished posthumously in 1947 in volume two of the *Yoshimitsu Yoshihiko chosakushū*. It provides an excellent window on how a leading Catholic philosopher of the early 1940s saw the relationship between Catholicism and modernity and may profitably be read together with his 1942 essay, "The Theological Grounds of Overcoming Modernity," which Richard Calichman has translated and published in his edited collection, *Overcoming Modernity: Cultural Identity in Wartime Japan*.

Part One

Let me state from the outset that, because Catholicism means Christianity in its fullest sense, I do not come from a position that opposes Catholicism to Protestantism. Even a cursory reading of the history of the Christian Church shows this to be true. Well before the rise of Protestantism, Catholicism was a religion that confronted all sectarian assertions, many of which are still with us today. Putting that aside for now, as I see things, there is not much need for an anti-Protestant attitude based on a Catholic confession of faith in Christ. Rather, the fundamental issue is the existential self-consciousness of religious Man as he confronts the atheism and secularism of the twentieth century. In that regard, in Newman's *Apologia Pro Vita Sua* and especially in his religio-philosophical reflection, *An Essay in Aid of a Grammar of Assent* (his life work), we find that the problem facing the Catholic comes down to the question of "atheism or Catholicism."[1] Once we have acknowledged the existence of God, inevitably we must agree with those who give reasons that affirm the truth of Catholicism. For a Catholic, the concepts of the true Lord, the true religion, the true Christianity, the true Church – they are all one and the same, and as such they become the grounds for a confession of faith in Catholicism.

There are probably many reasons and paths followed by those who have converted from Protestantism to Catholicism. But surely those converts who had been serious Protestants would all agree that they did not lose one iota of the truth of the Christianity they had believed in as Protestants. No one can go through that experience without some sense of heartbreak at leaving their old home and their brothers and sisters who had led them to the truth of God and Christianity. But once they find themselves in the Catholic Church, they pray for their friends of their former faith, and, from within the faith where the apostolic tradition lives, they confess and praise the complete and fundamental truth of the grace that they had previously known with gratitude and joy. It is often said, "people are most unforgiving of the errors they discover in themselves." Similarly, if the Catholic convert is overly critical of Protestantism as a philosophical system, then it only means that he is criticizing no one but his own former self.

Of course, each person has his own manner of confessing his faith. But we converts feel as if we are reading our own confession when we encounter this line from Newman's *Apologia Pro Vita Sua:* "It is not that we believe in some new doctrine upon our coming to Catholicism; it is only that we feel both the peace and certainty of having come into port from a rough sea."[2] Here our objective is not an apologia for Catholicism. It is merely to describe as plainly as possible from the Catholic position how the topics of Christian faith are conceived and received in response to specific historical periods. That is a matter of ecclesial history within the broader context of world history; it is really nothing more than the question of a Christian understanding of historical being as it is found in the world (what is frequently called "this world," in John's gospel). How does a Catholic find a Christian way of being in our times? How does he try to live it out? Here we can only reflect briefly on the main point from two or three perspectives.

Part Two

The problem of Catholicism today is a two-sided one. First, there is the question of how modern or contemporary Man can believe in the traditional, fundamental truth of Christianity. To put it in Kierkegaard's terms, it is the question of "how can Man become Christian?" *(Wie Man Christ wird?)*. Second, it is a question of what the apostolic mission of the Catholic is – no, of the Church ("what should the Church do?") – with regard to history, to our contemporary times. And it may be immediately noticed that these two issues are internally linked. It may be because the problem of faith, *the stumbling*[3] *of faith*, comes from the same historical conditions that affect one whether one is inside or outside of the Church. In the first case, we have a *stumbling* toward "the eternal" that occurs in time; in the second case, we have the *suffering* of the Eternal One in "time." As such, this suffering of the Church is the suffering that stems from the stumbling of brethren; it is a suffering of atonement that comes with the suffering of one's brethren's stumbling.

What is the stumbling of contemporary Man with regard to Christ and his Church? What is the particular stumbling of our time? From its onset, Christ's earthly Church essentially has been, and will always continue to be, the "Church Militant," fighting its way through the particular troubles and stumblings of every generation: the stumbling of the Jews, the stumbling of heresy, the stumbling of intellectual "culture," the stumbling of politicized *Volk*. Where is the particular difficulty for our own time, for modern society? Of course, in a fundamental sense, stumblings are always the same stumblings, and difficulties are always the same difficulties, and, at the point where eternity and time intersect, there has always been the same cross, really the same three crosses of Calvary. Thus, we cannot see ourselves as a special modern Man and boast of a greater sacrifice and spiritual heroism than our predecessors. To all who live in this world, the "here and now" *(hic et nunc)* is always the day of salvation, the place of the judgment, the greatest moment in eschatological time. Nothing has changed.

But I must hurry along, as I've already missed the deadline for this manu-
script. In the past, some have uttered, with an awareness of the pangs of
the modern intellect, "can we still be Christians?" Like the traveller who
has suddenly found himself in a dense wood or the hunter who sees the
trees but not the forest, the intellectual pursuit of modern Man suddenly
has become a prisoner of his own intellect. And when faced with the truth
of faith, it merely accumulates further intellectual difficulties.

Ultimately, both *the demand of the spirit* that still seeks to become a Christian
and *the intellectual self-satisfaction* that cross-examines the truth of God and
his Church in the court of the human intellect have remained separately
ensconced. Advances in biblical studies and general historiography have
demonstrated that, when confronted by the truth of Christianity's supernatural faith, the stumbling of the intellect (as found in the work of Renan
and Strauss[4]) was mainly the result of the "freedom to decide" of modern
biblical hermeneutics and the "equality of common sense" of a skeptical,
autonomous intellect – and not the inevitable result of developments in
philology and history. But by the time this was known, the century largely
had already lost "faith" itself.

When we ask "can we still be Christians?" as if the truth and authenticity
of Christianity were dependent on proof from us, when we allow for Christianity only through certain concepts that seem to be based on our own
spirit and intellect and seek God through humanist pragmatism, idealism,
modernism, or any other system that tailors itself to the measure of modern
Man, then we will find only spiritual nihilism, aggressive atheism, and the
like waiting at the door. When Nietzsche and Marx had washed away the
soft-hearted, conscientious Christian sentimentalism like a flood from
the highways of history, people began proclaiming the fall of the West,
not the fall of the Church. The first warning of the gradual collapse of the
foundation of humanity's spiritual value came as modern Western Man
started losing his ecclesiastic faith. Thus, Renan's declaration "there is no
supernatural" *(Il n'y a pas de surnaturel),* alongside the Nietzschean cry that
"God is dead," has even raised "the mythos of despair"[5] against personalist
human spirituality as modern Man has fallen into the Faustian fate: "And
thus I give myself up to sorcery" *(D'rum hab' ich mich zur Magie ergeben!).*
What this means is that the first intellectual stumbling against ecclesiastic
faith ultimately led to an aggressive atheism marked by a sense of Man as
hopeless, thus rendering ethics impossible and causing great suffering for
the children of this world.

We may say that the nineteenth century's intellectual difficulties with
faith are, for the most part, no longer with us. Down to the present day,

what stone from the great cathedral of the Church's apostolic tradition has been definitively removed in the name of science? If one could remove but a single rock of the Church's revealed doctrine, then the most splendid dome in the entire supernatural cosmos would come crumbling down in an instant. Nevertheless, even today scholarship has not been able to prove a single Catholic dogma to be lacking in apostolic foundation. Rather, with progress in historiography and biblical and ecclesial archaeology, the evidence for the historical and factual basis of traditional doctrine has only strengthened. Isn't it only that the problem of theological authority has become a psychological impossibility or obstacle?

We acknowledge the original apostolic foundation of Catholicism that conscientious historians such as Harnack have gradually strengthened.[6] Yet before long we brood over the mental drama of "I cannot believe," which we end up calling "the mistake of the apostles." Here one thinks of a good many canon lawyers in addition to countless ecclesiastic and doctrinal historians, representing a broad range of fields in religion, philosophy, and theology, covering both academic specialists and common-sense writers. At any rate, what we find today is that preachers who adopt a propaganda pose and lack all scholarly principles take uncritically what had been the product of high-minded criticism and apply it only as a critique of Catholicism, while brazenly indulging in the disgraceful behaviour of defending their own ideas of orthodox evangelical faith and never really touching on the real problems. Thus, they have found a way today to avoid the kind of intellectual anguish that others had felt when confronting the gap between an understanding of Christian traditional orthodox teaching and serious scholarly investigation. I guess that many people must be happy they were not born in nineteenth-century Europe. Yet, for all that, has it become any easier today for the "world" to come closer to Christ's "Church"? Just as in the past the chosen children of faith avoided intellectual stumblings and will probably be protected from the stumblings of our current times, will not the children of the world who have fallen intellectually before not fall again in the ethical practical difficulties of faith in today's new spiritual wasteland? We recall from among Karl Barth's keen insights his point that today's difficulty of faith in the gospel is a question of its practical possibility and that the difficulty of faith lies in the difficulty of its ethics. Yet we frequently fall into this trap over and over as if we had not heard him, and we still insist on pointing out that the difficulty of Christianity today lies in the general social-spiritual condition of an aggressive atheism that has inherited the legacies of the nineteenth century's intellectual anguish.

"Today, can we believe in Christianity?" is no longer the question we ask. The question for us is now "is Christianity a practical possibility?" I don't need to detail all the circumstances of the entire century that this question covers. We need only to think of those various symptoms of homesickness and homecoming in those who sought the absolute by turning to what they thought were "the Church" and "God's word" as they sought to escape from the spiritual desert of intellectual nihilism after World War I and, at the same time but in the other direction, with the gradually worsening tensions between social anxiety and political existence, of the modern phenomenon of Man's uprootedness that came from his increasingly disordered, barren faith – and how both were drawn into the spiritual and behavioural *catastrophe* that unfolded around the beginning of World War II. However, the *catastrophe* of the twentieth-century spirit – nay, of human nature – had already been anticipated through a deep groaning of the soul by those who suffered a prophetic faith in the spiritual conditions of the nineteenth century and who had defeated that *catastrophe* through their triumphant hymns of faith. We can point to someone like Péguy,[7] who followed men like Kierkegaard and Dostoevsky (though Péguy, as the last of the line, is himself a sign of victory in the twentieth century) in maintaining a strict silence while hiding all expressions of the holiness of the Church in the inner recesses of his soul. It was thanks to Dostoevsky's perspicacious insight that we understood that the problem of contemporary socialism is really the problem of "atheism," a problem of Man who, possessed by an "evil spirit," believes in the devil's existence but cannot bring himself to believe in God. The so-called mythos of the twentieth century is nothing but a new "aggressive atheism" that combines the anxiety of the intellectual self-consciousness of the "Godless mystics" with the despairing spirit and aesthetic priest consciousness of a "Catholicism without faith." Of course, as long as there is a deep consciousness of the disease and a "determination to be healthy," one may find therein not a self-abandonment to "sorcery" but a basic return to "nature" and thus a link to the road that will lead one toward that which is the foundation of the overall health of the human spirit. For we need to understand that what modern Man lost sight of was not just theological Being but this true, original nature. In this way, he who stumbles before faith today holds as a substitute for faith a certain kind of mystic or mythos consciousness that, in the context of this crisis of human nature, is itself no innocent humanism.

The reason for the ethical-practical difficulty of faith stems from certain conditions of social and historical existence. These conditions have made

Christian faith a difficulty not only in speculative matters but also in social life as it has been removed, first methodologically and then in principle, from social conditions. Finally, when those social conditions themselves took on the mystical character of a new religion, this difficulty and stumbling required a fundamental theological resolution that could also address deep, metaphysical issues. The spiritual salvation of contemporary Man can no longer be secured through humanism or idealism; rather, a theological resolution must be aimed not at the reasons that rationalist Man has lost all his innate certainties of "self-security" but at negative humanist radicalism.

Among possible candidates for a theological resolution, there are some, such as "dialectic theology," that adopt a modern position. But Catholicism does not hold that one can find true liberation from stumbling in the extreme dialectic opposition of an anti-humanist "only God" that is the "yes" established within a broader "no" to human nature, which is to say in the atheistic humanist mystic (or demonic) or in its essentially nihilistic character that arose in this crisis of the contemporary spirit. For Catholicism, the stumbling of our contemporary self-conscious, aggressive atheism, is itself something that calls for the supernatural consciousness of a heroic faith and as such signifies the struggle against what the Apostle Paul called "the evil spirit of the skies" and the Apostle John "the ruler of this world" (the devil that has power over human things). But because this dialectic theology does not liberate us to our true, ultimate, supernatural *telos*, we grasp it for what it is: something that tries to recover the created, original value of human nature that sought to "be like the gods." Only then can we comprehend how, outside of the Catholic faith, the place of supernatural God's own absolute truth, all other human spiritual solutions to modern Man's struggles of faith have already been rendered ineffective. We can also see here how all confessions of faith by religious Man in the contemporary spiritual conditions appear as "confessions of Catholicism" (we are not, however, saying here that this proves the truth of Catholicism). Yet, for contemporary Man, the existence of the Catholic Church, which has possessed the supernatural revealed faith throughout history and which has continued to insist down to the present day that it is the sole means of salvation (*Divina institutio*), is itself a stumbling block. Now, through his spiritual anguish, through his consciousness of Absolute Being, Man has come face to face with Catholicism. He cannot but be surprised by the life force of this Catholicism, which he thought had been defeated 400 years ago. What's going on here? Is the fact that Catholicism still exists in our day simply a matter of a reactionary or inert "historical phenomenon"? Or perhaps this thing that has survived all the storms of 2,000 years is a "miracle of history," a *supernatural phenomenon* that proves it was established by Christ himself? Today everyone has asked himself this question at least once – just as Christ asked, "Who do you say that I am?"

From a Catholic perspective, the emphasis on the absolute authority of the "Word of God" and the radical, negative, emotional, prophet-style "repentance" that the self-consciousness of faith in our contemporary crisis has achieved in the limited conditions of modern humanism has, insofar as it is an opportunity for a repentance that leads to Catholicism in the sense of John the Baptist (that is to say, a primary emphasis on faith in a supernatural being), a certain degree of truthfulness to it. And so long as the content of an active faith is a consciousness of a reprisal of orthodox doctrine (and it will be as long as the intent is toward the original, apostolic teachings), one may be confident that this will bring one back to Catholicism. But to the extent that it is a reconsciousness of a primitive Protestant emotionalism that only exists to reject Catholicism, it will not, in the end, liberate us from the polarized struggle of the modern spirit but should instead serve as a warning of a new intensification of that struggle. It is true that a supernatural heroism is required to overcome the stumblings of contemporary Man's faith, but that requires first a theological and metaphysical grasp of a healthy "nature" and the fundamental establishment of a "nature" that can be lived by a "humanity" that can be saved. This dual nature of the task that our stumbling sets before us is nothing less than the agenda for Catholicism to complete the work of the history of the Church in our time.

Part Three

The relationship of Catholicism to the world is well expressed by Christ, who is not of the world but who is the Saviour of the world *(Salvator mundi)*, the "one who was sent into the world" as "one who had already conquered the world." Similarly, the relationship of Catholicism to the world is a relationship that, in carrying out the business of the salvation of the world here in the midst of the world, leads us toward a realization of grace, of God in the world. In short, it is not a transcendental relationship of a dualistic opposition to the world, nor is it an immanent relationship of a monistic unity; rather, it may be called a relationship of, as it were, a transcendent immanence symbolized in the ideal of the blessing that surpasses all understanding: the hypostatic union of the human and divine natures of the Incarnate One. The relationship of the Church, the world of grace, and human nature must always be grasped as an expression of the strained efforts to realize the "Kingdom of God" in history.

The problem is that of "contemporary Man" and Catholicism. In our contemporary moment, the status of this battle for the "Kingdom of God" is shaped by a set of historical conditions unique in the history of the Christian Church. In the background are various conditions that, because of this essential "mission to the world" of the Church, are linked to far-too-human and far-too-historico-social things, such as debates over "the Church and society" and "the Church and culture," which have been shaped by European spiritual history. As for the so-called medieval order of Christianity in the formation of the emerging (ethnic-) nation-state societies of Europe, we find here that the Church in modern society has been forced to pay the price of sacrificing itself in a conservative context that has alienated it from modern society, modern people, and modern culture. Even if the sacrifice of the Church was something the Church itself wanted and hoped for in order to plant the seeds for a community of faith, the loss of the modern people who thus fell away from it must have been the greatest wound to the Church's supernatural heart of charity, in keeping with the heart we find in the gospels: "And Jesus took pity on the crowd."

In the enthusiasm with which in modern society the children of this world lose themselves night and day in an active interest in society as the place for "saving the world," yet stumble before the Church, and pour their passions down a road that leads outside the Church and denies the Church and denies God, a road where, lacking grace, they seek the impossible task of eliminating grace from the world, we find that, as noted above, this itself is the presence of "an evil spirit," and it calls out for a theological grasp of things. Be that as it may, however, we cannot say that it does not also indicate the new cross of a new active heroism that the Church places before us today.

The thousand years of the Church's work during the Middle Ages, its glories and its failures, may look different to different people: to some as expressions of a heroic, at times even titanic, strength of an active grasp of truth, and to others even the world's stumblings themselves may be taken as objects of wonder and admiration. (Here we can think of examples such as the heroic Pope Gregory VII, who grasped the Cluny Abbey reform movement in its spiritual context, and, in another sense, the very medieval crusades that were formed out of the entanglements of various political and religious factors.) Still, in the new conditions of modern society, we must know that, in order for the truth of grace to realize the Church's original mission, a new "mode of incarnation" is required.

From the beginning, the Church has been the same Church. The question is not how the Church can be one with the world but how the world can discover the Church. In other words, the problem lies in the realization of the "Kingdom of God" in history. Yet, if the modern spirit continues to reject God and to remain outside the Church, following its own internal path that has given its own particular values to nature and to a "human nature" that tries to fight against grace and truth, and if we do not see a practical and logos-centred outreach from the Church built on a heroic road to life that is ordered on the "priority of spirit," along with an acceptance of positive suffering, then there will be no salvation for the stumblings of faith in our time. In this sense, the Church, always remaining spiritually pure, must however act politically and, to that extent, has not been afraid to soil its ōwn angelic robes through the glories and failures of each and every age. The Church Militant must be both apostolic and political. We cannot cover all the details here. But I think that the Church's deep, mysterious relationship with "the world and the Christian," on which Christ preached at his last Pascal Feast as recorded in John's gospel, must be contemplated anew.

Christ's Church is in the world and becomes one not through human work but mysteriously in love; it must demonstrate to the world Christ's redemptive love. It must separate itself from the world and participate in all of Christ's own sufferings in order to bring the good news to a world that needs salvation. We, too, must through our practice of the cross love the world (note how many different meanings of the "world" are used in the gospels) that God loved so much that he gave his only Son.

Even so, the historical world is also the place of "the struggle of the soul" and thus cannot be equated fully with "the Church"; ecclesiastical existence is not political existence but a supernatural communion with the Holy Spirit. Stumbling continues throughout historical time, and thus the "Kingdom of God" does not come to us on Earth in its complete form. We cannot think about the salvation and stumblings of "ecclesial history and world history" only in reference to European Middle Ages and modernity. Already 400 years ago in the East, and especially in our fatherland Japan, ecclesial history in the form of the *kirishitan* brought its mission to a new "cosmos."[8] It is as if a new "Acts of the Apostles," set in the Indian Ocean and the Sea of China, has been added to our Bibles. The essential relationship of us modern Orientals to Catholicism as we deal with various cultural and ethical issues in the Oriental spiritual tradition does, I think, include a synchronic problematic with the Christian ancient world, the Christian medieval world, and Christian modernity. The Orient, these days, is an ambiguous thing. Do we not feel that ancient Man, medieval Man, and modern Man are living within us? This is surely what we mean by a traditional spirit. Moreover, as I noted at the outset, if the stumbling of "the Church and the world" is always the same, and if the cross that Christ's Church must carry is always the same cross, then we Christians find no difference between Orient and Occident but confront the same theological issues.

Still, the victory of the Church over all the stumblings of the world and all the temptations of history was prophesied by its founder to the head of the shepherds: "Simon, Simon, behold, Satan demanded to have you, that he might sift you like wheat, but I have prayed for you that your faith may not fail; and when you have turned again, strengthen your brethren" (Luke 22:32-33). This took place on the eve of the Church's stepping forth into history as the "Church Militant," but it was also the eve of the "Church Triumphant" over history.

Notes

1   Cardinal John Henry Newman (1801-90), the author of these two works, was received into the Catholic Church in 1845 and was a key figure in the mid-nineteenth-century Catholic renaissance in England known as the Oxford Movement.

2   Cf. "from the time I became a Catholic ... I have been in perfect peace and contentment ... I was not conscious to myself, on my conversion, of any difference of thought or of temper from what I had been before ... But it was like coming into port after a rough sea." Newman, *Apologia Pro Vita Sua,* 215.

3   The word that Yoshimitsu uses here and throughout the essay is *tsumazuki,* which we have translated literally as "stumbling." It may help to recognize that the fundamental meaning of stumbling in this Catholic context is "sin."

4   Ernest Renan (1823-92) and David Strauss (1808-74) are examples of the "historico-critical" method of biblical exegesis that sought to extract the "historical Jesus" from the "Christ of faith." Renan's most influential work in this vein was *Vie de Jésus;* Strauss's many works on these topics include *The Life of Jesus: Critically Examined.* For an authoritative Catholic critique of this "historico-critical" approach, see Ratzinger, *Truth and Tolerance.*

5   *Zetsubō no shinwa.* Yoshimitsu's use of the word *shinwa* here is that of Aristotle's concept of *mythos,* which connotes both the elements of tragedy itself and the idea of mimesis or "imitation of action." A few lines below he also employs the phonetic *myutosu.* The two should be understood as interchangeable and have been translated here in both instances as "mythos."

6   Adolf von Harnack (1851-1930). See his *Lehrbuch der Dogmengeschichte.*

7   Charles Péguy (1873-1914).

8   The term *kirishitan* refers to Catholic Japanese who lived between 1549 and 1865.

5
Kanayama Masahide: Catholicism and Mid-Twentieth-Century Japanese Diplomacy

Mariko Ikehara

Through the life and career of Kanayama Masahide (1909-97), a Japanese diplomat and a Catholic, we have a window onto the key role that Catholicism and the Catholic Church played in some of the central events of mid-twentieth-century Japanese diplomacy. The central and formative period of his eighty-eight years was during World War II, when Kanayama was stationed at the Vatican. There he became involved in what was ultimately a futile attempt to use the Vatican as a broker to end the war. Subsequent to his time in Rome, Kanayama had a number of significant diplomatic postings, notably in the Republic of Korea.

Kanayama was primarily a career diplomat who served where he was sent by the Japanese Ministry of Foreign Affairs. On graduation from Tokyo Imperial University in 1934, he immediately joined the ministry. His assignments thereafter included France (1934); Geneva, Switzerland (1935-39); Italy and the Vatican (1941-52; the Vatican from June 1942 to June 1952); councillor in the Philippines (1952-54); consul general in Hawaii (1954-57); director general of the European and Oceanic Bureau (1957-61); consul general in New York (1961-63); and then ambassador to Chile (1963-67), Poland (1967-68), and the Republic of Korea (1968-72).

Notably, over half of Kanayama's service outside Japan was in countries with sizable Catholic populations and powerful Catholic traditions. His Catholic faith seemed to play a special role in the decisions to post Kanayama at the Vatican and next in the Philippines and, perhaps, in his diplomatic endeavours in those postings.[1] In 1972, when Kanayama retired from the diplomatic service, he decided to dedicate the rest of his life to promoting better relations between Japan and South Korea.

In his 1980 book, *Dare mo kakanakatta bachikan* ("The Vatican Nobody Wrote About"), Kanayama writes that, because he had spent so many years at the Vatican, he became identified as "Kanayama of the Vatican," and his association with the Vatican benefited him greatly.[2] For this identification, he says, he cannot thank Rome enough. Precisely what he meant by this statement, and how his time in Rome was actually of benefit to him during the forty-five years of his diplomatic career and post-retirement life after his Vatican assignments, are not completely known. We can only surmise that his religious training and philosophy were useful to him during his postings to the Philippines, Chile, and Poland, countries with predominantly Catholic populations, as well as to South Korea, where the number of Christians grew rapidly in the postwar period.

Kanayama and Catholicism

Kanayama's parents were not Catholic; neither they nor his upbringing prepared him for Catholicism. Kanayama attended a public high school in Tokyo – Daiichi Kōkō – an elite school; its students, on graduation, almost invariably went to Tokyo Imperial University. In high school, he lived in a dormitory with a fellow student, Toshimitsu Yōichi, whom Kanayama later described as remarkably intelligent. Toshimitsu was president of the Catholic Club, which he invited Kanayama to join. Kanayama later wrote that, at that time, he was skeptical of religion due to his liberal tendencies and his attraction to Marxism.[3] Nonetheless, he accepted the invitation and started to attend meetings of the club. There Kanayama and Toshimitsu debated the topics of the day, including social issues.

Father Iwashita Sōichi, the highly prominent and influential Catholic, participated in the club's meetings as a lecturer. From 1925, the year when Iwashita returned from his postgraduate studies in Europe, until his death in 1940, he was instrumental in establishing Catholicism as a mainstream religion in twentieth-century Japan. During this period, the number of Catholics in Japan increased from 84,804 to 119,224.[4]

Kanayama says that, as he interacted with Iwashita, he came to realize the priest's sincerity. Iwashita spoke with Kanayama about current topics on a level that was principally secular; according to Kanayama, he refrained from any pronouncements that further discussion on a matter was foreclosed simply because "God thinks so and so." Ultimately, Iwashita's integrity and the openness of their discussions drew Kanayama to Catholicism. He then asked Iwashita to baptize him. The priest refused, telling Kanayama that he could not possibly baptize someone who had no understanding of Catholicism. Kōichi, Kanayama's eldest son, recalls his father telling him that he had once felt compelled to assert to Iwashita that "there is no difference between *benjo no kami* ['toilet paper'] and *kasorikku no kami* ['the God of

Catholics']," and perhaps it was this boldly provocative assertion that resulted in the rejection of Kanayama's request.[5]

For Kanayama, Iwashita's blunt refusal was a significant turning point. With Toshimitsu, he began to attend the father's weekly catechism classes held at Iwashita's home. Then, in the fall of 1930, Iwashita became president of the Kōyama Fukusei Byōin, the first hospital for leprosy patients in Japan, located in the town of Gotemba, in Shizuoka Prefecture, near Tokyo. The hospital had been established in 1887 by Father Germain Léger Testevuide, who belonged to the Paris Foreign Mission Society. Kanayama was deeply impressed by Iwashita's devotion in assuming a post that came with the substantial social stigma of an association with lepers.

One day, Kanayama writes in his memoir, a few years after he was refused baptism, Iwashita invited him to visit the leper hospital in Shizuoka to see for himself how patients were being saved by their love of God.[6] Kanayama accepted that invitation, and in December 1930 he spent over a week at the hospital. In his memoir, Kanayama relates that he observed the patients helping each other and singing Christmas carols in a chapel. He was profoundly moved by their deep love for one another and by their being united in their faith. For them, he recounts, religion was a way of life, beyond logic. Finally, on Christmas Eve of 1930, Kanayama, together with seven leprosy patients, was baptized by Iwashita and took the Christian name of Augustin.[7] This name reflected his respect for Iwashita because the priest's philosophy was deeply rooted in the writings of St. Augustine. So it happened that Kanayama became one of many Japanese influenced by Iwashita.

Kanayama's baptism took place while he was studying law at Tokyo Imperial University. On graduation, students of the university were expected to become eventually the leaders of Japan. Kanayama was no exception. After he graduated in 1934, he immediately joined the Ministry of Foreign Affairs. By joining Japan's diplomatic corps, he began to dedicate his life and career to working for peace. His dedication was consistent with the peace prayer of St. Francis of Assisi, "Lord, make me an instrument of your peace," which, according to his son Kōichi, was a guiding principle for his father. Kōichi read this prayer at his father's memorial service.[8] In 1936, after joining the ministry, Kanayama married Nagahama Yasuko, also Catholic. Based on his belief, rooted in Catholicism, that the birth of a life is guided by God's will, the couple had twelve children.[9] All were baptized as Catholic, and ten are still living.

Emperor Hirohito and Catholicism

After his first two diplomatic postings, in France and Switzerland, the ministry next stationed Kanayama at the Japanese Embassy in Italy for one year, and in June 1942 he was posted to the Vatican, where he spent the next ten years. How it transpired that he was posted to the Vatican must be understood in the broader context of the long history of relations between Japan and the Vatican as well as Emperor Hirohito's personal views of both Catholics and the potential for the Vatican to play a central diplomatic role during World War II.

Beginning with the visit of St. Francis Xavier, SJ, to Japan in 1549, Japan has had a long, if not close, relationship with Catholicism and the Vatican. In 1582, three daimyo from Kyushu sent a youth delegation to Rome. As is well known, Catholics and Christianity were repressed by the shoguns during the Edo era (1603-1867). During the Meiji period, Japan's attitude toward Christians and the Vatican itself warmed significantly. In the decades following the Meiji Restoration of 1868, the Vatican sent four envoys to Japan, including Archbishop (later Cardinal) Paulo Marella, who later served in Tokyo during World War II.

The Japanese government lifted the ban against Christians in 1873; however, the position of Japanese Christians was by no means secure thereafter. In 1885, the Vatican sent a special envoy to see the emperor to convey the request that Japanese Catholics and their possessions be protected. The emperor granted this request. In 1905, the Vatican again sent a special envoy to the emperor, this time to congratulate the emperor on restoring peace after the end of the Japan-Russia War, to thank him for protecting Catholic churches in Korea and Manchuria during the war, and to request further protection of Catholic churches in Japan. As relations thawed, in 1919 Pope Benedict XV sent the Vatican's first emissary to Japan, Archbishop Pietro Fumasoni Biondi, who was appointed apostolic delegate. In response, the Japanese government considered posting an emissary to the Vatican. Due to strong opposition from both Buddhist and Shinto circles, however, those plans were thwarted until 1942.

During the Second Sino-Japanese War, which began in 1937, prior to the attack on Pearl Harbor, contacts between Japanese officials and Catholic emissaries increased. For example, in November 1940, against the backdrop of Japan having signed the Tripartite Pact two months earlier with Germany and Italy, Bishop James Walsh and Father James Drought, both representatives from the US Maryknoll Foreign Mission Society, visited Japan. Their mission was to attempt to improve relations between Japan and the United States to avoid an imminent military confrontation. During their visit, Walsh and Drought met Japanese political and military leaders, including Foreign

Minister Matsuoka Yōsuke;[10] they became involved in drafting an unofficial Japan-US agreement to avoid war, which was to be taken up at a 16 April 1941 meeting between Japan's ambassador to the United States, Nomura Kichisaburō, and the US secretary of state, Cordell Hull. Despite these efforts, relations between the two countries deteriorated further, ultimately culminating in Japan's attack on Pearl Harbor on 7 December 1941.

In March 1942, Japan established its first-ever official diplomatic relations with the Vatican. Harada Ken (1892-1973), a Protestant (his wife was Catholic), was appointed Japan's emissary to the Holy See. He did not have the formal rank of ambassador, but he was treated as one. He arrived in Rome in March 1942, from Vichy, France, where he had been a counsellor. Kanayama, who was then serving as the third secretary in the Japanese Embassy in Rome, was sent to serve as the deputy of the mission to the Vatican. In selecting Harada and Kanayama, the Japanese government followed the example of Great Britain, which also had traditionally sent Protestants, with Catholic deputies, to the Vatican. What prompted the Japanese government to establish relations at this time over the vehement objections of Buddhist and Shinto influences?

Two fundamental drivers for this policy change, both an outgrowth of the exigencies of the Pacific War, were at play. First, the Japanese government understood that the United States itself was trying to use the Vatican for its own diplomatic advantage. Nazi Germany had invaded Poland in September 1939, followed immediately by the declaration of war by Great Britain and France. President Franklin D. Roosevelt determined that he would attempt to use the pope's moral influence to highlight the legitimacy of the Allied Forces for the world. To that end, in February 1940, he sent Myron C. Taylor, CEO and chairman of United States Steel Corporation and a Quaker, to the Holy See as an emissary (also not with the formal rank of ambassador) from the United States. In light of the Allies' efforts to use the pope's influence, and as a counterweight, Emperor Hirohito decided to establish relations with the Vatican and send an emissary to Rome.[11]

Second, and of no less importance, even before the attack on Pearl Harbor and, subsequently, the formal establishment of relations in March 1942, Hirohito came to understand that war with the United States now seemed unavoidable; he was looking ahead to how the conflict might end. The documentary record of the emperor's decided views with respect to the Vatican's potential role in bringing the war to a conclusion is substantial. Two months before the attack on Pearl Harbor, the emperor had instructed his closest adviser, Lord Keeper of the Privy Seal Kido Kōichi, "it looks like we will not be able to avoid this war, but once we enter the war, think now how to engage in peace negotiations ... For this purpose, it is necessary to establish diplomatic relations with the Vatican. Make necessary arrangements as soon as possible."[12] Then, on 2 November 1941, the emperor suggested to Prime Minister Tōjō that "we should think about relying on the pope to save the situation" (*jikyoku shūshū ni rōma hōō o kangaete mitewa ikaga to omou*).[13]

Some thirty years later, in 1972, Harada recalled:

What is more significant to me in looking back from now is that, before the outbreak of war, the Emperor ordered the Government to open diplomatic relations with the Vatican and to dispatch an envoy there in order to be ready for peace negotiations in case of war which he was most anxious to prevent. This fact was published later in the diary (on October 13, 1941) of Lord Keeper of the Privy Seal Kido, political advisor to His Imperial Majesty. It should be pointed out that there was decidedly no other single person in Japan then except the Emperor who foresaw the way of peacemaking even two months before Pearl Harbor.[14]

The emperor's prewar sentiments are further corroborated by his statements to his staff soon after the conclusion of the war. They record him as saying in 1946:

After the war started, I sent an envoy to the Vatican for the first time. This was my own initiative. Ever since I visited Rome, I had been thinking that we should be in contact with the Vatican. This was necessary regarding Japanese immigrants. During the first Prime Minister Konoe Fumimaro Cabinet, I raised the subject with [Foreign Minister] Hirota Kōki, and he concurred with me, but nothing was realized. After the war broke out, I requested Tōjō to send an envoy, thinking that it will be useful to have a communication channel with the Vatican to conclude the war, as well as to gather information from all over the world, and considering the fact that the Vatican has an immense psychological influence internationally. It turns out that the Vatican would have accepted an ambassador, so we should have sent an ambassador. [As noted, Harada was only an "emissary."] However, this being during the war, we were not able to send an able person from Japan, and because of the Japan-German Alliance it was regrettable that we could not be more active with the Vatican, which was estranged from Hitler.[15]

In hindsight, we might ask why the emperor thought that the Vatican might have been able to play such an important role in peacemaking. There are at least three possible explanations for this, though there may be several more. First, the emperor's mother, Empress Sadako, the wife of Emperor Taisho, was enormously interested in Christianity, though she remained a devout believer in Shintoism. She had been raised by a Quaker couple, had Christian teachers, and read the Bible every day. When she became empress in 1912, she surrounded herself with Quakers and patronized Christian charitable organizations.[16] She is quoted as saying, after the war, "what this country needs now is Christianity."[17]

Second, Kanayama himself speculates that the emperor was strongly influenced by his tutor, Yamamoto Shinjirō (1877-1942), a rear admiral in the Japanese Imperial Navy and a devout Catholic.[18] Kanayama writes that he believes that Yamamoto must have advised the emperor of the Vatican's influence internationally. Rear Admiral Yamamoto studied at Gyōsei Gakuen (Morning Star Academy) and was baptized Stephen at the age of sixteen. After his graduation in 1895, he joined the navy and, in 1915, was posted as a military attaché to the Japanese Embassy in Italy. On his return to Japan, he became a tutor to then Crown Prince Hirohito and served him for twenty years until his death in 1942. Yamamoto was familiar with the West, spoke both English and French, and in 1921 accompanied Hirohito during his visit to Europe, where Yamamoto arranged for him to meet with Pope Benedict XV. Yamamoto himself visited the Vatican six times and met four different popes – an unprecedented achievement for a Japanese national.

Third, practically speaking, as the "Greater East Asia Co-Prosperity Sphere" expanded, the number of Catholics under Japan's rule, in places such as China and the Philippines, increased. Kanayama speculates that, for this reason too, Japan needed to establish diplomatic relations with the Vatican.[19]

Having overcome objections within Japan to establishing diplomatic relations with the Vatican, the Ministry of Foreign Affairs commenced negotiations with the government of Italy. The Allies objected to these diplomatic efforts of the government of Japan, rightly suspecting that political motives underlay the Japanese initiative. According to Kanayama, the Vatican, for its part, was quite interested in establishing official diplomatic relations with Japan, principally because the Japanese military posed a threat to the missionary activities of Catholic priests in the territories occupied by Japan. In the end, the Allies' efforts to oppose formal relations between Japan and the Vatican were unsuccessful.[20]

The Japanese Mission to the Vatican: The Early Years

Japan's formal relations with the Vatican commenced when Harada submitted his credentials to Pope Pius XII on 9 May 1942. Kanayama remembers that, at the time, the pope thanked Harada for the Japanese military's humanitarian treatment of Catholic missionaries in the occupied territories.[21] With the mission having been established, in the absence of clear instruction or precedent, both Harada and Kanayama were somewhat unsure about what they were supposed to do. Kanayama thought to ask Father Antoine Candau, member of the Paris Foreign Mission Society, to serve as an adviser to the mission. Kanayama sought and obtained Harada's permission to do so. Since his high school days, had known Candau as one of the lecturers, along with Iwashita, at the Catholic Club. Candau was by then fluent in Japanese. He had travelled to Japan in 1925, at the age of twenty-seven; just two years later he was appointed the first president of the Tokyo Major Seminary.[22]

At the time of Kanayama's request for advice, Candau was at a hospital in Lausanne, Switzerland, for treatment of a serious injury that he had suffered as a captain in the French army just two years before. He agreed to Kanayama's proposal. Kanayama says that Candau seems to have thought that, by being close to the pope, he would be able to return to Japan to continue his missionary activities after the conclusion of the war rather than being caught in a power struggle between the Gaullists and the Pétainists. Kanayama relates that Candau ended up playing a crucial role on behalf of the Japanese mission in communicating with both the Italian government and the Vatican. He also facilitated Kanayama's connections in Rome, taking Kanayama to salon gatherings hosted by the French ambassador and by Italian aristocrats.[23]

Apart from being guided by Candau, Harada and Kanayama's first diplomatic assignment was to ensure the continued well-being of the Catholic priests in the Japanese-occupied territories. Their principal pragmatic task was to secure both communications and money transfers from the Vatican to those missionaries. The Vatican secured money transfers to Catholic priests in China by selling Japanese government bonds back to the Bank of Japan. In addition, the Japanese mission to the Vatican had to become involved in persuading the Japanese military of the need to protect priests from countries at war with Japan, such as the United States and Great Britain.[24]

Operation Vessel: Could the Vatican Be Used to Help End the War?

On 8 May 1945, Germany surrendered. With the emperor's clear instructions to make use of the Vatican as a peace broker, if and where possible, the

Japanese mission was hoping to launch peace negotiations with the Allies via the Vatican. Prospects for this effort looked slim, however. Kanayama himself does not cite any actual peacemaking overtures initiated by the mission. Then there was movement from the US side, which was surprising. In May 1945, Martin S. Quigley, an agent of the US Office of Special Services (OSS) stationed in Rome, launched an initiative, ultimately abortive, to use the Vatican and the Japanese mission – led by Harada and Kanayama – to propose a peaceful resolution to the war. Quigley was a Catholic and a graduate of Georgetown University, the Jesuit institution in Washington, DC. This endeavour, code-named "Vessel" by the United States, was pursued under the direction of General William J. Donovan, the OSS director and himself a Catholic.

Quigley had been assigned to Rome in late December 1944; his cover was as a representative of the Motion Picture Producers and Distributors of America. During his meeting with Donovan prior to his departure for Rome, the general specifically instructed him to "be alert at the right time to attempt to open up communications to Tokyo looking to the surrender of Japan. After all, the Vatican is one of the few possible points for such contact."[25] Quigley was fully aware that any approach to the government of Japan via the Vatican would not only have to be worked out with great care but also was rather unrealistic. Although Pope Pius XII himself "thought until the end that the contesting countries would turn to him as an official peacemaker," Quigley believed that "this aspiration was a completely idealistic dream, with no root of any kind in reality."[26] He nevertheless concluded that Donovan's directions were worth pursuing because unofficial support from the Vatican to end the war – before the impending invasion of Japan – ultimately might lessen the number of casualties.

To help him initiate an approach to the Japanese government, Quigley turned to Monsignor Egidio Vagnozzi, an experienced Vatican diplomat who, starting in 1932, had spent ten years in Washington, DC. Vagnozzi was well known to Reverend Tomizawa Benedict Takahiko, the ecclesiastical adviser to the Japanese mission to the Vatican. It so happened that Vagnozzi and Tomizawa lived in the same Vatican residence, Palazzo S. Marta, and had meals together – an ideal setting in which to broach the subject of whether and how the Vatican might be of assistance in brokering an end to the war.[27] On 26 May 1945, Quigley met with Vagnozzi. He revealed that he was an OSS undercover agent. He said that the German surrender presented an opportunity to make peace with Japan and pointed out that few communication channels were available to the government of Japan; the Vatican was one of them. Quigley told Vagnozzi that General Donovan had asked him to find ways of opening up communication with Japan, looking to the country's surrender; Quigley asked him to serve as a contact to the Japanese mission via Tomizawa.[28]

Vagnozzi agreed to take up the matter with Tomizawa. Quigley, concerned that the Japanese diplomats might mistakenly regard the overture as a trick, advised Vagnozzi not to mention the OSS and to tell them, instead, that the offer came from an American businessman in Rome who was well connected in Washington. He said to Vagnozzi that if the government of Japan would indeed be interested in negotiations leading to surrender, then the United States would make itself available for secret meetings on short notice.

Kanayama, in his memoir, provides a different perspective on this initiative and Vagnozzi's motivation and direction. He supposes that Vagnozzi must have come back from his posting in Washington, DC, with some sort of peace offer on behalf of the United States.[29] There is no evidence one way or another, however, to support Kanayama's speculation. In any event, the day after Vagnozzi's meeting with Quigley, the monsignor approached Tomizawa and asked him to play a personal role in opening the door to establishing peace between Japan and the United States and the Allies.[30] As Quigley reports it, Tomizawa responded to Vagnozzi that he was just a priest, not a diplomat, and that his connection to both Harada and Kanayama was strictly on Catholic Church matters. He said that Japan could charge him with defeatism and treason if he were to suggest that the country surrender. Vagnozzi told him that he himself was reluctant to undertake the proposal but that God had called on both of them to be his messengers of peace. Notwithstanding these concerns, the following day Tomizawa went to see Harada and told him that he had been approached by a monsignor of the Vatican's Secretariat of State with a request from an American for the opening of communication looking to peace.[31] On hearing this, Harada immediately asked Kanayama to join the meeting and take careful notes. Harada questioned Tomizawa about the bona fides of Vagnozzi. The next morning Harada and Kanayama met for three hours, during which time they drew up a list of pros and cons of sending a message to the Foreign Office reporting on Vagnozzi's conversation with Tomizawa. With an equal number of pros and cons, Harada adjourned the meeting. Kanayama says that he was of the view that they were obligated to convey to Japan any message they had received.[32]

The next day, after several hours of discussion, Harada confided in Kanayama that the emperor himself had instructed him to be alert to the possibility of making peace. He said that, "despite all its strangeness and its irregularity, this Vagnozzi initiative might well be the possibility foreseen by our august Emperor. Accordingly, I shall draft a cable to be encoded and sent tomorrow."[33] The message was finally sent from the Japanese mission in the Vatican to Tokyo on 3 June 1945.[34] No one in Tokyo responded to Harada's cable because the Japanese government had already determined to pursue an alternative diplomatic course – using the USSR – to end the war.[35] While Harada was waiting to hear from Tokyo, five days after the 3 June cable had been sent, he instructed Kanayama to summon Tomizawa and ask him to find out what more he could about the proposed peace terms. Kanayama did so, and Tomizawa immediately contacted Vagnozzi and requested that he ask "the American businessman" what those terms might be.

Vagnozzi contacted Quigley and reported that there had been no definite response from the Japanese side but that the Japanese mission was requesting additional information. Quigley thought that it was important to keep lines of communication open with the Japanese mission. So, without checking with Donovan or anyone in Washington, he listed the major terms of surrender: (1) occupation of Japan by American forces, (2) no permanent transfer of territory to the United States, and (3) no change in the status of the emperor, unless decided by the Japanese people.[36] Quigley's message to Vagnozzi was relayed to Tomizawa and then sent by cable back to Japan by Harada on 12 June.[37] Neither Harada nor Quigley received any response or further instruction from their home governments, so Operation Vessel came to an end in just over two weeks.[38]

Some, like Quigley and Vagnozzi, believed that had Japan responded to the Vessel initiative it might have been able to avoid the atomic bombings of Hiroshima and Nagasaki. The likelihood of Vessel being successful probably was never high. From the perspective of the Japanese side, we can assume that the emperor never learned of the overture. Given that he had initially thought of using the Vatican for peace negotiations to end the war, had he known of Vessel he might have asked the Supreme Council to pursue the possibility of enlisting the Vatican in addition to relying on the USSR to be the intermediary. But that did not happen. Moreover, there is little indication that any senior-level official in Washington was even aware of Vessel. This might not be all that surprising, as Donovan, who had had a personal relationship with President Roosevelt, was known to be disliked by President Truman.

Finally, with respect to the Vatican's reaction to Vessel, Kanayama himself speculated that Vagnozzi likely did bring it to the attention of Pope Pius XII and had his tacit consent to proceed. He noted that the pope frequently agonized over the catastrophe that Japan was facing. Officially, however, the pope had declared that unless the warring nations asked the Vatican to do so, it would not engage in peace negotiations; this was in accordance with Article 24 of the Lateran Pacts of 1929, which established Vatican City.[39] Because the proposal launched through Operation Vessel was not an official request to the Vatican from a combatant, the Vatican did not intervene.[40] So Vessel went nowhere, just like the other futile efforts to conclude the war, such as the Japanese approach via the OSS European director, Allen Dulles, in Bern, Switzerland, and another through the Swedish ambassador to Japan, Widar Bagge.

Kanayama himself mourned the lack of astuteness in Japan's diplomatic efforts to end the war. He watched helplessly as the Vessel initiative rapidly proved stillborn and, with the failure of peace initiatives, witnessed the dropping of atomic bombs on Hiroshima and Nagasaki, followed by Japan's unconditional surrender and the Allies' subsequent occupation of his country. Remarkably, he wrote that he doubted that Japan would have been better off had Vessel succeeded and Japan been able to end the war without being occupied. He thought that, because Japan went through what he considered the "valuable" experiences of unconditional surrender and subsequent occupation, the country itself could be reborn as an economic power.[41] Drawing parallels between the postwar political situation and a central element of his own faith, he supposed that the Japanese, in defeat, were like Christ on the cross, destined for resurrection.[42]

Kanayama's Postwar Years at the Vatican

Kanayama's efforts with the Japanese mission did not end with Japan's surrender. Harada's and Kanayama's main counterpart at the Vatican had been Giovanni Battista Montini, the number two official at the Secretariat of State, who later became Pope Paul VI (1963-78). In the wake of the bombing of Hiroshima and Nagasaki, and without any instructions from home or Harada, Kanayama, along with Candau, submitted to Montini a letter protesting the indiscriminate use by the United States of weapons of mass destruction.[43]

In January 1946, several months after the surrender of Japan, the Supreme Commander of the Allied Powers (SCAP) in Japan ordered all Japanese living in Europe to return to Japan. Harada did so. Kanayama had been planning to return to Japan, but he was not able to leave when his wife fell ill due to hard work associated with moving soon after the birth of their third child. The birth of their daughter Eriko was reported as "A Miracle at the Vatican."[44] They would have two more babies there. As the government of Japan did not send him any money, Kanayama was forced to support himself and his family by teaching Japanese at the Vatican, giving lectures, and reporting European news on RAI and Radio Vatican for broadcast in Japan.[45]

Kanayama became Japan's minister chargé d'affaires at the Vatican, remaining there until 1952. During his postwar years at the Vatican, he would, via Montini, ask for the Vatican's assistance in releasing Prime Minister Hirota Kōki, who had been arrested as a class A war criminal.[46] Hirota's son and Kanayama had been friends in junior high school. Kanayama questioned why Hirota had to pay for his political responsibilities with what he thought was the cruel punishment of death by hanging. In response to Kanayama's entreaties, the Vatican spent one month lobbying, on Hirota's behalf, the countries in charge of the International War Tribunal for the Far East (3 March 1946 to 12 November 1948). Their efforts were unsuccessful, and Hirota became the only Japanese civilian executed, in December 1948, as a result of the tribunal's proceedings.[47] In truth, Kanayama did not expect that Hirota would be able to avoid prosecution, because the victorious Allies were keen to punish those Japanese who had led the nation to war. He noted that he had even been surprised by Hirota's prosecution having been delayed for one month.[48] Kanayama's reaction to Hirota's fate might have been realistically tempered by having spent so much time in Europe during – and soon after – the war: Kanayama was keenly aware of the victors' views of Japan and the culpability of its political and military leaders.

In July 1952, Kanayama returned to Japan after twelve years in Europe. He brought Pope Pius XII's best wishes to the emperor.[49]

Kanayama in the Philippines

In 1952, after ten years at the Vatican, Kanayama was sent to the Philippines as counsellor. Coincidentally, since 1949 now Archbishop Vagnozzi had been posted to Manila as apostolic nuncio. On their reunion in September 1952, Vagnozzi remarked, "If the Japanese government had responded to the peace proposal by the United States back then, wouldn't it have avoided the tragic atomic bombings of Hiroshima and Nagasaki?"[50] In the Philippines, Kanayama's principal diplomatic tasks were to free Japanese war criminals imprisoned there. Once again he would be assisted by Vagnozzi. This effort was fraught with considerable delicacy and emotion. Filipinos remembered Japanese war atrocities, including the infamous Bataan death march and, in February 1945, the killing of about 40,000 Filipinos by the Japanese garrison in twenty days. Among those killed were the wife and three of the children of President Elpidio Quirino (1890-1956). In 1952, 108 Japanese war criminals were imprisoned at Muntinlupa prison, and just before Kanayama's arrival 14 had been executed. To ensure his security from possible Filipino hostility, Kanayama himself first lived in a hotel, protected by arms-carrying bodyguards. Even then, some seven years since the end of the war, Filipino antipathy toward Japan ran deep.

Kanayama was familiar with the circumstances of these war criminals because, while he was still in Rome, a delegation of members of the Japanese Diet had visited the Vatican to plead for their release, hoping that the Vatican would have influence over the Philippines. They had been unsuccessful. At that time, he did not expect that, just a few months later, he would be charged with the same mission.

During his first year in the Philippines, Kanayama visited President Quirino many times to appeal for the prisoners' release. Showing Kanayama his fingers, crooked as a result of Japanese torture, Quirino responded, "give me the names of Japanese prisoners who are worth releasing."[51] Beyond his own efforts, Kanayama says, he did not know what kinds of endeavours were also exerted by Archbishop Vagnozzi or others to secure the release of Japanese prisoners. He surmises that the nuncio appealed for mercy, in the name of the pope, to Quirino, a devout Catholic, on the bases that all human beings are members of one big family and that humanitarian consideration should be extended even to Japanese war criminals.[52]

In the summer of 1952, the song "Ah, the Night Is Deep in Monten Lupa" became popular in Japan. Its lyrics were written by Daida Gintarō, and the music was composed by Itō Masayasu, both of whom were Monten Lupa inmates sentenced to death. Through the prison chaplain, they introduced the song to Japan via Watanabe Hamako, a famous singer.[53] She would eventually perform for the Japanese inmates at the prison. Before President Quirino left in July 1953 for a cancer operation in the United States, Kanayama went to see him to make another appeal. He brought with him a music box and played the song as recorded by Watanabe. Although he did not understand the Japanese lyrics, Quirino listened to the song twice. When he was told that two prisoners had written the song, he promised to release them on the Filipino Independence Day, 4 July 1953.

President Quirino was good to his word. Fifty-six prisoners who had been sentenced to death were to be transferred to Sugamo Prison in Tokyo under a reduced sentence of life imprisonment; the others would be set free. Quirino said, "I do not want my children and my people to inherit from me hate for people who yet might be our friends ... After all, destiny has made us neighbors."[54] In July 1953, the prisoners were all repatriated to Japan. About 28,000 Japanese welcomed them as their ship arrived on 22 July. On 28 December that year, in an expression of Christian charity, Quirino granted amnesty to the fifty-two prisoners incarcerated in Sugamo Prison, and they were subsequently released summarily.[55]

Kanayama in South Korea

Japan and South Korea normalized their relations in December 1965, and Kanayama was Japan's second post-normalization ambassador, posted to Seoul from July 1968 to January 1972. During this period, bilateral relations and economic ties between the two countries deepened. In 1969, the Japan-Korea Cooperation Committee, a semi-official government binational group, was established. Members included elder statesmen and business leaders, and the Japanese side was chaired by former prime minister Kishi Nobusuke. While Kanayama was ambassador, the governments of Japan and South Korea and the committee negotiated for both a loan from Japan for construction of a subway in Seoul and funding to establish the Pohang iron mill (present-day Posco). Kanayama strongly advocated in favour of Japanese support for these projects because he believed that Japan should compensate Koreans for his country's past sins. Ultimately, these negotiations were concluded in the spring of 1972, shortly after he left Seoul. Growing out of his efforts to enlist Japan in the development of the Korean economy, Kanayama forged strong ties with President Park Chung Hee.

Alongside the steady improvement in economic ties between the two countries, Kanayama was involved in political matters, the most notable of which was the Yodo Hijacking of 31 March 1970. Nine members of the Japanese Communist League-Red Army Faction hijacked Japan Airlines Flight 351, headed for Fukuoka, and demanded asylum in South Korea. The plane landed in Seoul before ultimately flying to Pyongyang, where some of the hijackers still live today. Over a two-day period, Kanayama, together with the Japanese transportation minister, Yamamura Shinjirō, and the government of South Korea, successfully negotiated the release of all – more than 100 – passengers. Although Kanayama had offered to travel to Pyongyang with the hijackers, in exchange for the passengers' release, they demanded instead that Yamamura accompany them; he complied, resulting in a successful end to the incident.[56]

One of the major political decisions that confronted Kanayama while ambassador was whether to attend, on 1 March 1969, South Korea's annual Independence Day ceremony. It had always given Koreans an opportunity to denounce Japanese oppression during the occupation. Kanayama decided to attend – the first ambassador from Japan to do so – because he thought that Japan's official representative should endeavour not only to build bilateral relations but also to repent for past acts. To his surprise, his presence was appreciated, and during the ceremony Japan was not criticized for its occupation.[57]

Kanayama's Post-Diplomatic Career

Kanayama retired from the diplomatic service in 1972, intending to dedicate the rest of his life to promoting better relations between Japan and South Korea. He became director of the Joint Research Centre of International Relations, funded by the International Institute for Korean Studies in Tokyo, which in turn had funding from the government of South Korea ($200,000 for the institute and $100,000 for the centre).[58] These organizations were founded with the purpose of persuading Japan to become more favourably inclined toward South Korea, both politically and culturally. To further this objective, the organizations undertook various activities to shape public opinion. In 1974, for example, the institute arranged for two members of the Japan PEN Club, a chapter of the international writers' association, to visit Seoul. This visit became fraught with controversy when the visitors remarked that freedom of expression existed under the government of President Park and that, due to his political activities, not his literary works, Korean poet and philosopher Kim Chi Ha had been sentenced to death by the Park regime (he was not, in fact, executed).[59] Both the institute and the Centre would become subjects of controversy in the Diet in 1978-79, soon after the "Koreagate" scandal in the United States.[60] In Diet committee meetings, members of the Socialist Party pointed out that Japan's National Tax Agency had investigated allegations that both Kanayama's centre and the institute had evaded taxes and that the agency had found that expenditures of some ¥40 million were unaccounted for between 1974 and 1977.[61]

The implication is that these expenditures were used for illicit political purposes, but the Diet records on this matter are unclear. Based on the observations of Donald Ranard, then director of the Korea Desk at the US State Department, however, that may well have been the case. Ranard asserted that the Korean government practice of bribing Japanese Liberal Democratic Party (LDP) politicians was already well established around 1959-60, during the presidency of Syngman Rhee. Ranard, posted in the US Embassy in Seoul from 1959 to 1960, was in a position to read US intelligence reports that cited daily donations from the Rhee government to LDP politicians. According to Ranard, Rhee's representative in Japan would directly hand these politicians money to curry favour and to ensure that they would support reparations for South Korea.[62] Even if this was true, Kanayama's knowledge of such improprieties, or his role in them, is unknown.

Kanayama was close, however, to Choi Seo Myun, head of the institute, the centre's principal source of funds. Choi was a Catholic and a major political operator, with close ties to the Korean Central Intelligence Agency (KCIA) as well as to two former prime ministers of Japan, Kishi and Fukuda Takeo. Choi, called "Park Tong Sung of Japan," after the central figure of the Koreagate scandal, had been one of the founders of the Korea Democratic Party and was imprisoned on charges of assassinating Chung Dok Su, the party's political director in 1947. It was while in prison that he converted to Catholicism. During the Korean War, he escaped from prison and ultimately was smuggled into Japan on a US military plane in 1957, disguised as a Catholic nun.[63] Once in Japan, he met Tanaka Kōtarō, then chief justice of the Supreme Court of Japan and a prominent Catholic;[64] Choi asked Tanaka to help him in leaving Japan, having secured asylum from Portugal and Cuba – thanks to Catholic priests in South Korea. Given his position, Tanaka refused to assist Choi in this way, but he recommended that Choi report to the authorities and, with Tanaka as his sponsor, seek special permission to stay in Japan. Permission was granted, and Choi was able to stay in Japan legally. He established the institute in Tokyo in 1969.[65]

Kanayama himself also became associated with Choi, though it is not clear how they first met. They became so close, however, that Kanayama requested that some of his ashes be placed next to Choi's plot in South Korea. Kanayama's family fulfilled these wishes on his death.[66] In addition to promoting the cause of bilateral commercial and cultural relations via the centre, Kanayama once again became involved in political affairs. Most notably, he served as a secret envoy between the governments of Japan and South Korea in an effort to resolve the political crisis provoked by the kidnapping of Kim Dae Jung.[67] Kim, President Park's biggest political rival, was abducted from a hotel in Tokyo in August 1973. Five days later he was released in Seoul. The South Korean government's participation in the kidnapping seemed readily apparent when the fingerprints of Kim Dong Woon, the first secretary of the South Korean Embassy and believed to be the Tokyo-area director of the KCIA, were found in Kim Dae Jung's Tokyo hotel room. The South Korean government denied any involvement, however, and Kim Dong Woon quickly left Tokyo.

The Japanese public was offended by the South Korean government's violation of Japan's sovereignty and by its refusal to hand over Kim Dong Woon. Anti-Park sentiment increased. Leaders in the Japanese government, however, thought that the incident was largely one of internal Korean politics, albeit played out in Japan, and decided to send Kanayama to South

Korea to broker a political solution acceptable to both governments. Soon after Kim Dae Jung's abduction, Kanayama met the South Korean prime minister, Kim Jong-pil, and the KCIA director, Lee Hu Rak, in Seoul. In September 1973, the Japanese foreign minister, Ōhira Masayoshi (a member of the Anglican Church of Japan), asked Kanayama to deliver a letter from him to Prime Minister Kim. Kanayama engaged in secret shuttle diplomacy to calm the waters. Ultimately, three months after the kidnapping, on 2 November 1973, Prime Minister Kim visited Prime Minister Tanaka Kakuei, and they secretly agreed to close the case. In a postscript, some thirty years later, in October 2007, a report of the government of South Korea admitted that the KCIA, led by Director Lee Hu Rak, had carried out the abduction, but it was not able to find hard evidence to support the suggestion that President Park himself had tacitly approved the abduction.

There is an important religious and political backdrop to the kidnapping incident and to Kanayama's intervention. Kim Dae Jung was himself Catholic. The Korean Catholic Church was growing rapidly, with its membership roughly doubling every decade, from 285,000 in 1957 to 751,000 in 1968, 1,144,000 in 1978, and 2,009,194 in 1986.[68] Since the 1960s, Korean church organizations had become active in various social services, and Christian churches, particularly Catholic ones, in Korea were engaged in anti-government activities at the forefront of the democracy movement. Thus, Kim Dae Jung had strong support among the Korean Catholic Church. Some Japanese Catholics with close ties to the Korean Church were among his strongest sympathizers in Japan. They were critical of Kanayama's political expediency in attempting to assist the Japanese government in its efforts to resolve silently, and look past, the kidnapping.[69]

Criticism of Kanayama for his involvement in trying to influence Japanese public opinion favourably toward South Korea, or for his assistance in smoothing over the controversy arising from the Kim Dae Jung kidnapping, is offset somewhat by his charitable and social welfare activities. In 1973, he became chairman of the board of directors of Kyōsei Fukushi Zaidan, a social welfare organization that operates both an orphanage in Korea and an elder care service in Osaka and is headed by Yoon Kee, a Catholic.[70] Kanayama also served on the board of trustees of the Japan Family Life Association, a pro-life organization led by Father Anthony Zimmerman. Kanayama was well suited for this latter position as he was somewhat famous for having had twelve children. He felt blessed to have had so many offspring and wrote that his life had been made richer by their presence.

Kanayama was open minded. His daughter Kawasaki Yoshiko remembers that he had a liberal attitude toward other religions and that he would associate with adherents of Tenrikyō, a Japanese "new religion" founded in the nineteenth century; she also recalls that he would even attend gatherings of a cult known as Tenshōkōtaijingūkyō, popularly called *odoru shūkyō* ("dancing religion").[71] It might not be altogether surprising, therefore, that Kanayama also became associated with the South Korean-based Unification Church founded by Reverend Moon Sun Myung. Choi seems to have introduced Kanayama to Moon.[72] Choi was apparently close to the KCIA, and, given the South Korean government's support for his institute, it might have been natural that he also had ties with the Unification Church, which the Korean government employed for political activities in the United States and Japan.[73] Nonetheless, leaving aside these political and financial linkages, Kanayama might well have believed in Moon's message of world peace. In October 1982, he spoke at a Unification Church mass wedding ceremony, just as had former prime minister Kishi, who also had been a supporter of the Unification Church since its inception in Japan in 1959. In December 1982, Kanayama became president of the Association for Japan-Korea Cultural Exchange, which the Unification Church had founded. At the association, he was instrumental in building a free retirement home for the wives of the Korean men who had been forcibly relocated to Sakhalin by the Japanese military during the Pacific War. Kanayama embarked on this initiative as one way of expressing his personal regret for the atrocities committed by Japan during the war; he personally approached the Keidanren and Japanese corporations to solicit their donations.

Kanayama would also become involved in another project of the Unification Church. At the end of 1981, at the Church conference in Seoul, Moon proposed the International Highway Project, which would achieve world peace by promoting economic and cultural exchanges via highways that connect the world. The kick-off project was to be construction of a subsea tunnel between Japan and Korea. In 1982, the International Highway Construction Foundation was established by the president of Sekai Nippō, a Unification Church newspaper company in Japan; the following year the foundation's subsidiary, the Japan-Korea Tunnel Research Institute, was established, with Kanayama as its chairman of the board. The institute still exists today. Over the years, influential politicians, including Korean presidents and Japanese prime ministers, have supported the idea of building a tunnel to link the two countries.

Kanayama's Career: A Summing Up
At critical points in his career, Kanayama's diplomatic efforts were facilitated, if not motivated, by his Catholicism and close ties with the Vatican.

For Kanayama, Catholicism meant not merely attending church and praying but also endeavouring to be God's tool in the real world, following Christ's teaching about the final judgment:

> For I was hungry, and you gave me to eat. I was thirsty, and you gave me to drink. I was a stranger, and you took me in. Naked, and you covered me. Sick, and you visited me. I was in prison, and you came to me ... And the king answering shall say to them. Amen I say to you, as long as you did it to one of these my least brethren, you did it to me.[74]

Beyond the imperative of his personal philosophy, Kanayama, while serving as a diplomat who was also a Catholic, might have been effective due to Emperor Hirohito's own attitudes toward both Catholicism and the Vatican and the mid-century impetus for a closer relationship between the Vatican and Japan.

Kanayama's post-diplomatic career continued his decades-long service to building bridges between nations, in particular re-establishing and strengthening the relationship between South Korea and Japan. Given the historical complexities, challenges, and political dynamics of that relationship in the twentieth century, it was probably inevitable that he would be caught up in controversies. That said, though, his career and life, grounded in his Catholic faith, were devoted to the cause of peace.

Acknowledgments
I am grateful to the following people for their kind assistance in writing this chapter: Atsuta Miruko, the Diplomatic Record Office, Ministry of Foreign Affairs, Government of Japan; Roland Celette, Embassy of France to the United States of America; Jeffrey P. Cunard, Debevoise and Plimpton LLP; Jean Demange, retired, Ministry of Foreign Affairs, Government of France; Endo Toake, Hawaii Tokai International College; Father William Grimm, the *Catholic Weekly of Japan*; Kanayama Kōichi, Kanayama Masahide's eldest son; Karube Kensuke, Jiji Press; Kawasaki Yoshiko, Kanayama Masahide's eldest daughter; Kitano Mitsuru, Ministry of Foreign Affairs, Government of Japan; Komori Yoshihisa, *Sankei Shimbun*; Matsukuma Yasufumi, the *Catholic Weekly of Japan*; Mizuno Takaaki, *Asahi Shimbun*; Cardinal Peter Shirayanagi Seiichi; Tokuoka Takao, journalist; James Ulak, Freer Gallery of Art and the Arthur M. Sackler Gallery, Smithsonian Institution; Yamauchi Keisuke, Free Press; and Yoon Kee, Family of Heart. All translations from Japanese to English in the cited sources are by the author.

Notes
1 Eventually, Kanayama had twelve children, and the size of his family appeared to have played a role in where he was posted. In assigning him to foreign postings, the ministry considered that his salary overseas would be five to six times that in Japan;

foreign postings also entitled him to receive a special assessment for his children. In addition, in light of his family circumstances, the ministry decided that Kanayama should not be assigned to hardship postings.

2   Kanayama, *Dare mo kakanakatta bachikan,* 252.
3   Kanayama, *Dare mo kakanakatta bachikan,* 65.
4   Catholic Bishops' Conference of Japan Library.
5   Interview with Kanayama Kōichi, 9 November 2007.
6   Kanayama, *Dare mo kakanakatta bachikan,* 67.
7   Ibid., 65-68.
8   Interview with Kanayama Kōichi, 9 November 2007.
9   See Kanayama, "Kobukusha no tanoshimi," 241-45.
10 Editor's note: Matsuoka was baptized into the Catholic Church with the name Joseph on his deathbed in 1946. Sonoda, *Kakusareta kōshitsu jimmyaku,* 100.
11 Kanayama, *Dare mo kakanakatta bachikan,* 12-16.
12 Ibid., 13.
13 Kuroda and Hata, eds., *Shōwa tennō goroku,* 131; Sanbōhonbuhen, *Sugiyama memo,* vol. 1, 387.
14 Quigley, *Peace without Hiroshima,* 156.
15 See Terasaki, *Shōwa tennō dokuhakuroku.*
16 Shillony, "The Sons of Heaven and the Son of God," 6-7.
17 Ibid., 11; Woodard, *The Allied Occupation of Japan 1945-1952 and Japanese Religions,* 273.
18 Rear Admiral Yamamoto Shinjirō (1877-1942) is not related to Rear Admiral Yamamoto Isoroku (1884-1943), most remembered for his role in the attack on Pearl Harbor and the War in the Pacific.
19 Kanayama, *Dare mo kakanakatta bachikan,* 13.
20 Ibid.
21 Ibid.
22 Ibid., 69.
23 Ibid., 73-76.
24 Ibid., 17-18.
25 Quigley, *Peace without Hiroshima,* 80.
26 Ibid., 81.
27 Ibid., 82-85.
28 Ibid., 91-92.
29 Kanayama, *Dare mo kakanakatta bachikan,* 45.
30 Ibid., 110.
31 Quigley, *Peace without Hiroshima,* 114.
32 Kanayama, *Dare mo kakanakatta bachikan,* 47.
33 Quigley, *Peace without Hiroshima,* 118.
34 The Allies were able to decode Japanese diplomatic cable communications, and MAGIC summaries of these messages were distributed to a select group of American policy makers, with the president at the top of the list. (MAGIC was the code name for US cryptanalysis of Japan's diplomatic cryptographic codes. The term was coined by the US Army's chief signal officer, who called his code breakers "magicians" and their product "magic.") The MAGIC diplomatic summary of Harada's 3 June 1945 decoded message to Tokyo was as follows:

> In discussing the conditions that America would stipulate for an armistice, the American said that as a guess they might include the retrocessions of the oc-cupied territories, the disarmament of the Army and Navy, and the occupation

of Korea. He made no reference to the political structure of Japan and he said that he believed Japan proper would not be occupied.

From the point of view of relations with Russia, this matter is extremely delicate and should be handled with care.

The nature of the terms is patently absurd and ... we have various suspicions of his objectives ... Then Vagnozzi sent word that he would like some sort of an answer, and so I requested Tomizawa make this brief reply to him: "At this present time I believe that Japan does not seek to hasten the coming of peace. Moreover, needless to say, we cannot discuss such questions with a person whose official position and identity is unknown to us. Naturally, if it can be verified that he has an official background and America has any wishes to convey to Japan, they can be taken under consideration. However, any proposals limited to so-called unconditional surrender are entirely out of the question.

US WAR DEPARTMENT, "MAGIC" – DIPLOMATIC SUMMARY, No. 1167, 5 June 1945.

35 Hando, *Seidan,* 346-52, 398-405; Kajima Heiwa Kenkyūjo, ed., *Nihon gaikōshi,* vol. 25, 124-27; Kanayama, *Dare mo kakanakatta bachikan,* 49-52.
36 Quigley, *Peace without Hiroshima,* 135.
37 The MAGIC diplomatic summary of this cable states as follows:

Harada at first planned to disregard the matter but, when pressed by Vagnozzi for a reply, sent word that at the present time Japan was not seeking to hasten coming of peace, that no questions could be discussed with a person whose official standing and identity were unknown, and that in any case proposals limited to "so-called unconditional surrender" were entirely out of the question.

He [the American] apparently also stated that, while it would be extremely difficult to persuade the United States to change its demand for unconditional surrender at this time, the term "unconditional surrender" was open to various interpretations. However, I believe that this statement merely reflects an effort on his part to excuse himself.

US WAR DEPARTMENT, "MAGIC" – DIPLOMATIC SUMMARY No. 1177, 15 June 1945.

38 In February 1972, Quigley decided to find out what had happened to the peace initiative on the Japanese side. Nearly thirty years after the war, and for the first time, he wrote to Harada, revealing his identity as an OSS agent. Harada responded to Quigley that

Tokyo was already determined then to seek peace through the intermediary of Moscow, and it was considered to be a most difficult matter to persuade the Japanese Army to agree to terminate the war ... As you know, the Japanese Army was most firmly determined to fight to the very end and was strongly opposed to acceptance of "unconditional surrender" until the very last minute.

Quigley, *Peace without Hiroshima,* 195.
39 Article 24 of the Lateran Treaty states the following:

In regard to the sovereignty appertaining to it also in international matters, the Holy See declares that it desires to take, and shall take, no part in any temporal rivalries between other States, nor in any international congresses called to settle such matters, save and except in the event of such parties making a mutual appeal to the pacific mission of the Holy See, the latter reserving in any event the right of exercising its moral and spiritual power. The Vatican City shall, therefore, be invariably and in every event considered as neutral and inviolable territory.

40 Kanayama, *Dare mo kakanakatta bachikan*, 55.
41 Ibid., 54.
42 Ibid., 222.
43 Ibid., 62-63.
44 Ibid., 96.
45 Ibid., 102-4.
46 Hirota was prime minister from March 1936 to February 1937, then foreign minister from June 1937 until his resignation in January 1938, after which he remained a member of the House of Peers. In 1945, he led the Japanese peace negotiations with the Soviet Union. He instructed his lawyers not to offer any defence, and he was found guilty of count one (waging wars of aggression and war or wars in violation of international law), count twenty-seven (waging unprovoked war against the Republic of China), and count fifty-five (disregard for duty to prevent breaches of the laws of war). He was sentenced to death, and his sentence remains controversial to this day.
47 Martin S. Quigley, memorandum dated 25 June 1963 on the meeting with Kanayama Masahide, Consul General in New York.
48 Kanayama, *Dare mo kakanakatta bachikan*, 224.
49 See "Jūninen buri bachikan kara kikoku, Kanayama dairi kōshi, niji tomonatte," *Asahi Shimbun*, 5 July 1952, 3.
50 Ibid.
51 Kanayama, *Dare mo kakanakatta bachikan*, 56.
52 Ibid., 58.
53 Ibid., 59; Dower, *Embracing Defeat*, 514-15.
54 TIME: *Sequels, Forgiving Neighbor*, 27 July 1953. http://www.time.com/.
55 See "Kesa natsukashi no kokoku jōriku," *Asahi Shimbun*, 22 July 1953, 3. An interesting postscript involving 700 other war prisoners incarcerated in Sugamo demonstrates further connections between Japan and Catholicism. In 1953, Crown Prince Akihito (now Emperor Akihito) met Pope Pius XII in Rome; this meeting was followed up by a visit to the pope in 1954 by Prime Minister Yoshida Shigeru. (His wife, Yukiko, was a devout Catholic, and Yoshida himself, on his deathbed in 1967, was christened Joseph Thomas More by Cardinal Hamao Stephen Fumio.) The prime minister stated that continuing to incarcerate these prisoners would only prolong the war memories and would be harmful. Pius XII concurred with Yoshida and promised his support to free them. Sonoda, *Kakusareta kōshitsu jimmyaku*, 21.
56 By coincidence, among the passengers was future Cardinal Hamao Stephen Fumio (1930-2007). His elder brother Minoru, also a Catholic, was a chamberlain at the crown prince's palace and served as a governor for Naruhito, the crown prince. Another prominent passenger was Hinohara Shigeaki (b. 1911), a Christian who was the director of St. Luke's International Hospital; the imperial family financed its buildings, and many of its members rely on it when ill.
57 Hamanaka, "Nikkan yukō no kakehashi, Kanayama Masahide-shi no kiseki to gyōseki."
58 Committee on Cabinet, 30 March 1978, Committee on Foreign Affairs, 14 June 1978, House of Representatives, Japan.

59 Committee on Foreign Affairs, 14 June 1978, House of Representatives, Japan.
60 Koreagate refers to a 1976 political scandal in the United States involving the KCIA's alleged efforts to influence over 100 members of the US Congress through Korean businessman Park Tong Sun. Ultimately, several members of Congress were forced to resign or were censured. The KCIA also used Reverend Moon Sun Myung to try to influence US public opinion.
61 Committee on Budget, 2 March 1979, House of Representatives, Japan.
62 Committee on Budget, 25 April 1979, House of Representatives, Japan.
63 Choi had sought asylum in the United States through the US ambassador to the Republic of Korea, Walter C. Dowling; because Choi was from South Korea, an ally of the United States, and not from North Korea, asylum was not granted.
64 Editor's note: see the chapter in this volume on Tanaka by Doak.
65 Interview with Choi Seo Myun, *Gekkan Chōsen*, June 2002.
66 Interview with Kanayama Kōichi, 9 November 2007.
67 Kim Dae Jung was abducted after a meeting with the leader of the Democratic Unification Party at the Hotel Grand Palace in Tokyo on 8 August 1973. He was moved to Osaka and then was put on a boat heading to Seoul. A weight had been attached to his feet, indicating the kidnappers' intention to throw him into the sea. The US ambassador to the Republic of Korea, Philip Habib, and Donald Ranard, the director of the Korea Desk at the US State Department, are said to have intervened, resulting in a pursuit of the boat by the Japan Maritime Self-Defence Force.
68 Andrew E. Kim, *A History of Christianity in Korea: From Its Troubled Beginning to Its Contemporary Success.* Source: Korea Overseas Information Service. http://www.tparents.org/.
69 Indeed, after the kidnapping, Japanese Catholics continued to find Kim appealing. Cardinal Shirayanagi Peter Seiichi visited Seoul in 1976 and tried to free Kim, who was under house arrest at the time. Interview with Cardinal Peter Shirayanagi Seiichi, 5 November 2007.
70 Interview with Yoon Kee, Director, Family of Heart, 9 November 2007.
71 Tenshōkōtaijingūkyō was established by Kitamura Sayo in 1945. It teaches its followers to attain a spiritual state by dancing and forgetting themselves. It appears as if this group is no longer very active. Interview with Kawasaki Yoshiko, 7 November 2007.
72 Interview with Yamauchi Keisuke, President and CEO, Free Press, 5 November 2007.
73 Committee on Cabinet, 30 March 1978, Committee on Foreign Affairs, 14 June 1978, House of Representatives, Japan; *Investigation of Korean-American Relations*, report of the Subcommittee on International Organizations of the Committee on International Relations, US House of Representatives, 31 October 1978, 351.
74 Matthew 25:35-40; cited in Kanayama, *Dare mo kakanakatta bachikan*, 71.

6

Crossing the Deep River: Endō Shūsaku and the Problem of Religious Pluralism

Mark Williams

Mention the name of the author Endō Shūsaku in Japan even today, some ten years after his death, and chances are that the initial response will include some allusion to Endō as "Christian author," followed, increasingly in my recent experience, by some reference to *korian-sensei*, the "light-hearted," "other" side of his personality that he was at such pains to nurture throughout his career. Pursued through composition of a series of "entertainment" novels to complement the "serious" *(junbungaku)* texts on which his international reputation was initially established, as well as through careful cultivation of a laid-back media image (his self-deprecatory Nescafe ads spring readily to mind) designed to appeal to a mainstream readership who sought in their literary pursuits something other than heavy theological discussion, this determination to draw attention to the complexity of the human composite has long been recognized as lying at the core of Endō's art.

Despite his baptism into the Catholic Church at the age of twelve, albeit largely at the behest of his devout mother and aunt, and his subsequent insistence on the strength of his faith, Endō was occasionally embroiled in well-publicized controversies with the institutionalized Church (notably following publication of *Chinmoku* [1966; *Silence*, 1969]). It is hardly surprising, however, to see the two issues conflated, with the resulting all-too-frequent portrayals of Endō as an author engaged in a somewhat lonely pursuit of an "other" form of Christianity better suited to the Japanese spiritual climate – one that, to borrow the pervading imagery of *Silence*, possessed "roots" that were not "destined to wither and die" in the "mud-swamp" of Japan – than that "Western" version of the faith that he saw himself as having inherited with his baptism and that he struggled with so painfully during the three years he spent studying in France in the early 1950s. The following passage is often cited as evidence of his determination to effect a wholesale reconfiguration of his reading of the gospels:

> Throughout my career, I have sought in my writing to see if I couldn't re-shape [Christianity], the Western dress that my mother had given me, and make it something that I could call my own. After a while, certain parts began to fit. But other parts remain too long or too heavy for me. And I have to confess that I do have this sense that it is this that renders my literature into something unique to me.[1]

These and similar comments have long been cited as keys to the narrative focus of novels such as *Silence* and *The Samurai*. My aim in this chapter, however, is to consider them rather as precursors to the approach adopted in Endō's final works – and, in so doing, to position *Fukai kawa* (1993; *Deep River*, 1994), the work completed just before his death, as a logical extension to his spiritual questioning. More specifically, I consider the later novel as a literary embodiment of the attitude of religious pluralism that Endō openly espoused during the latter half of his career but that can, in retrospect, be clearly seen germinating in his earlier works. In so doing, I call into question the all-too-convenient portrayals of Endō as an author intent on locating an inculturated form of Christianity, better suited to the spiritual climate of Japan. At the same time, as we consider the legacy of St. Francis Xavier, SJ, in Japan, I attempt to highlight Endō's contribution to the post-Vatican II debate on interfaith dialogue, albeit with the important caveat that we must approach Endō as artist rather than theologian and thus look in his work not so much for fresh theological insights as for literary representations of elements of this debate.[2]

Hick and Religious Pluralism

From his earliest forays into the literary scene, Endō made much of his determination, following his return to Japan, "to locate God on the streets of Shinjuku and Shibuya, districts that seem so far removed from him."[3] Drawing heavily on the image of Christ as the key element in this process, the early Endō positioned himself, in both his critical essays and his works of fiction, alongside those who portrayed themselves as engaged in the process of the global enculturation of Christianity. In this, his understanding of the process reflects that of critics such as Karl-Josef Kuschel, who viewed it as a process of the acceptance and transformation of the various cultures of peoples and nations which cannot be concluded in history – as a counter-concept to the way in which, over the centuries, missions have made Christianity with an exclusively Western stamp a foreign body within non-Western cultures. The accommodation, indigenization and contextual-ization of the gospel are parallel concepts. This kind of enculturation is deliberately focused on the development of new types of Christianity.[4]

To readers of *Silence,* and perhaps most strikingly of the later work *The Samurai,* Kuschel's portrayal will find resonance. In many ways, however, publication of *The Samurai* marked the end of an era for Endō; during the ensuing decade, he came increasingly to view the process through the prism of the burgeoning dialogue on religious pluralism. His thoughts on the subject were first given serious airing in *Watashi no aishita shōsetsu* (1985; "A Novel I Have Loved"), a fascinating study of Mauriac's novel *Thérèse Des-queyroux,* which Endō had always cited as having first piqued his interest in the challenges confronting the Catholic author,[5] but which he here con-siders from the perspective of religious syncretism and as a literary exercise in interfaith dialogue. This study was followed by a series of discussions with various theologians and philosophers engaged in pursuit of interfaith reconciliation, discussions that were subsequently incorporated into the study *Fukai kawa o saguru* (1994). At the same time, Endō was to stress the influence derived from his readings of several Western Christian philoso-phers working in this area, and he was subsequently to acknowledge his debt to three in particular: John Hick, Ninian Smart, and G. Houston.[6] Of the three, it was Hick's 1985 study, *The Problems of Religious Pluralism,* which Endō read shortly after its appearance in Japanese in the late 1980s, that he mentioned as a source of many of the issues addressed in *Deep River.*[7] Before continuing with a reading of *Deep River* as a literary consideration of religious pluralism, therefore, let us briefly consider the approach, advocated by Hick, to which Endō found himself drawn.

In attempting to account for his attraction to the theological stance advo-cated by Hick, Endō cites his vision of humanity as "naturally religious" as a powerful introit.[8] Within the human faculty, suggests Hick, is a religious awareness, which, in deference to Wittgenstein's notion of "seeing-as," he labels "experiencing-as" and which offers an interpretive element to all human experience.[9] Hick deploys the term to draw attention to the fact that our awareness of the world is both multifaceted and multidimensional, and he draws from this the logical corollary: "There is not just one form of 'experiencing-as,' with its own superstructure of theological theories, but a plurality, which we call the different religions" (26). The focus for Hick, then, was on that "something of vital religious significance" that, while "taking different forms all over the world within the contexts of the different historical traditions" (329), can nevertheless be subsumed under the rubric of "faith." Each world religion thus represents an "alternative soteriological 'space' with which, or a 'way' along which, men and women can find salvation/liberation/fulfillment" (47). As such, each comprises an "inner skeletal framework of beliefs," which "giv[es] shape to a distinctive form of religious life, wrapped in a thick institutional skin which divides it from the other religions and from the secular world within which [each] exists" (28).

The depiction had an immediate resonance for Endō as he continued to consider the issue of religious acculturation, especially when it was supported by Hick's portrayal of all religious experience as the transformation of human existence from "self-centredness" to "reality-centredness," a process that Hick sees as the "event ... which one can see occurring in individuals all over the world, taking different forms within the contexts of the ... various religious traditions" (29-30), yet with each in its own way offering a "way" to salvation/enlightenment/fulfillment. Endō found himself drawn to this image of the various traditions as representing not static entities but living movements, and it led him to seek a literary consideration of religious pluralism, the third of the three approaches to religious tradition considered by Hick and the one to which both found themselves inexorably drawn.

In keeping with the emerging consensus, Hick was happy to go along with the depiction of the first two approaches as "exclusivist" (whereby "salvation is restricted to one group, the rest of mankind being either left out of account or explicitly excluded from the sphere of salvation" [31]) and "inclusivist" (whereby Christ's atonement can be seen to cover all human sinfulness, with each individual open to God's mercy, but which nevertheless retains the concept of all salvation, "wherever it happens, as the work of God" [33]). Arguing in contrast that if salvation is seen as occurring in all traditions there is a need "frankly to acknowledge that there is a plurality of saving human responses to the ultimate divine Reality" (34), Hick is vehement in his advocacy of this third approach, that of

the great world faiths as embodying different perceptions and conceptions of, and correspondingly different responses to, the Real or the Ultimate from within the major variant cultural ways of being human; within each of them the transformation of human existence from self-centredness to Reality-centredness is manifestly taking place – and taking place, so far as human observation can tell, to much the same extent. (36)

Following years of struggling to come to terms with his innate dissatisfaction with the first two approaches, Endō admitted to feelings of relief when he encountered Hick's affirmation of a pluralist position.[10] More specifically, Hick's ability to account for the manifold differences within the various traditions – for so long a stumbling block to acceptance of this view – persuaded Endō to pursue the issue in his own literature. The following passage in particular was a source of considerable reassurance:

Each of the great world traditions affirms that in addition to the social and natural world of our ordinary human experience, there is a limitlessly greater and higher Reality beyond or within us ... and to give oneself freely and totally to this One is our final salvation/liberation/enlightenment/fulfilment. Further, each tradition is conscious that the divine Reality exceeds the reach of our earthly speech and thought ... and [each offers] the distinction between the Real an sich (in him/her/itself) and the Real as humanly experienced and thought. (39)[11]

According to this view, the "real in itself" could be but one – a single entity that is "nevertheless capable of being humanly expressed in a variety of ways" (40). At the same time, the various divinities come to be seen not as rivals but as "different concrete historical personae, in terms of which the ultimate divine Reality is present and responded to by different large historical communities within different strands of the human story." Each represents, in short, a distinct way in terms of which "the one divine noumenon is humanly experienced" (42).

On occasion, Endō might well have found himself trapped in what Hick describes as the "ecumenical Catholic dilemma": the desire to "engage in authentic dialogue with people of other faiths on an equal footing, and yet also to retain [one's] belief in the unique superiority of Christianity."[12] But there was greater comfort to be drawn from the explicit focus on such concerns and from the response of those, like Houston, who argued thus: "If a Christian dialogues with a Buddhist, he need not lose his faith, nor must he convert. He must first try to understand. There must be an arena of openness and expression. Once this takes place, one can rediscover one's own roots. This of all things modern civilization needs to do. We are all eroding at the roots."[13] The result was the projection of a more syncretic vision onto his literature, a radical shift from the earlier essentialized contrast between the "monotheistic West" (with its "absolute division between God, angels and man") and the "pantheistic" East, in which "everything represents an amalgam and extension of the individual and in which the individual remains but part of the whole."[14] In its stead lies a more sophisticated approach, one premised on an acknowledgment that "I no longer perceive a conflict between 'Gods and God' ... as I am inclined to religious pluralism" and indebted in equal measure to the Buddhist preoccupation with knowing the self and the Christian focus on redemption.[15] At the same time, in discussion with William Johnston, an authority on Christian-Buddhist dialogue, Endō acknowledged his fascination with "the search, not for Christianity, not for Buddhism, but for a third religion, ... one that is divorced from institutionalized religion such as Christianity, Buddhism, or Islam," for a religion that "transcends sectarianism, ... a great life force."[16]

As suggested earlier, with the benefit of such hindsight, it is possible to discern in some of Endō's earlier pronouncements, and indeed in his early fictional scenarios, hints of such an engagement with the discourse of religious syncretism, of a "search ... for a third religion." Critics have been quick to draw parallels, as corroborative evidence, between the widely discussed image of the maternal, compassionate God of novels such as *Silence* and *The Samurai* and the Bodhisattva, Amida of Jōdo (Pure Land) Buddhism, who preaches that all who invoke the name of Amida with sincerity will be redeemed and brought to the Pure Land after death.[17] Discerning in the statue of Amida an expression of eternal compassion redolent of that offered by a crucified Christ on the *fumie* that had inspired Endō to engage with the history of the Christian missions to Japan in the first place, the critic Tokunaga Michio, for example, suggested that, "in Endō, God always exists as a mother who forgives any evils people commit and who never gives them any punishment whatsoever. This is Amida."[18]

It is tempting – but not particularly helpful – to attribute this superimposition of images to some vague notion of the "Japanese spiritual context" in which Endō was working. For Endō himself, the aim seemed to be explicitly acknowledged: in an interview published shortly after completion of *Silence,* he recognized that he sought "a kind of reconciliation of Catholicism and Jōdo-shū Buddhism."[19] As Mase-Hasegawa has suggested in her insightful study of the theology implicit in Endō's literary corpus,[20] however, the image of the young Endō as an author with a single-minded focus on

the burgeoning interfaith discourse is not entirely convincing: equally significant in contributing to his image of the maternal Christ was his oft-cited
devotion to his own mother and his concerted study of the history of the
Hidden Christians *(kakure kirishitan)* of Japan, who for centuries had been
obliged to disguise their statues of Mary as icons of Kannon, the maternal
Bodhisattva of mercy and compassion, and whose faith Endō described in
the following syncretic terms: "I consider that the *Kirishitan* believed in
Western Christianity without realizing that they have Japanized it. In other
words, without realizing the fact, they believed their own form of Christianity. Their subconscious absorption of Shinto and Buddhism secretly dis-
solved Christianity."[21] As noted earlier, however, it was only in the 1980s
that Endō's study of interfaith issues became more formalized – and it is
thus to his later works that one must turn for a more comprehensive literary
embodiment of the discourse of religious pluralism. Let us move, then, to
a consideration of the extent to which this discourse – and more specifically
the perspective offered by Hick – is treated in *Deep River*, a novel described
by more than one critic as a "full reckoning *(sōkessan)* on Endō's entire
oeuvre," but that can equally be viewed, more particularly, as "Endō's interpretation of Christianity and a mediology of his theology."[22]

Toward Pluralism

In many ways, *Deep River* represents a logical progression for Endō. The
empty lives and absence of hopes and dreams betrayed by the protagonists
struggling to come to terms with life in the "mudswamp" were painfully
exposed in *Sukyandaru* (1986; *Scandal*, 1988), a novel in which Endō's closest
examination to date of the complexity of the composite individual prompted
this comment from the critic Moriuchi Toshio:

> The "Christian author," [Endō], should be done with delving into the dark
> recesses of his soul, the scene of carnage in his heart. He should know that
> faith brings not only peace but also fear and terror to the heart ... I am
> fascinated to discover whether, in the future, [Endō] will intone the music
> of destruction or of rebirth.[23]

Implicit in this comment is a reading of the Endō narratives to date that sees
the protagonists embroiled in a series of journeys of self-discovery that
ultimately prove inconclusive. To be sure, these journeys might have brought
the protagonists face to face with aspects of their previous suppression into
their unconscious. However, to Moriuchi – and indeed to several others

who expressed dissatisfaction with this work (e.g., Satō Yasumasa) – there were still questions about the extent to which these fictional creations had assimilated, and subsequently availed themselves of, such newly acquired self-knowledge. What was needed now, they suggested, was a work that would delve deeper into the spiritual elements of these various journeys – and could thereby provide a fresh perspective on the concerted search for identity that had pervaded the author's oeuvre. What was required, in short, was a novel that would give more explicit voice to the issue of religious plurality with which Endō had long been fascinated.

The first indication in *Deep River* of the significance of this particular focus on inter-faith issues lies in the decision to locate the action in India, a place depicted by Endō as "unfathomable, where everything co-exists chaotically, where both good and evil are accepted as existing in a symbiotic relationship ... Going to India, you come to sense the existence of another great world of a different dimension that co-exists with our own."[24] The attraction of India is depicted by the tour guide, Enami, at the pre-departure orientation, as lying precisely in its status as symbol of religious syncretism: "In India today, adherents of the Hindu religion make up an overwhelming majority, followed by Muslims, while Buddhism has all but disappeared ... To put it another way, the people at the lowest level of society, those who do not fit into any of the social classifications, have sought salvation in Buddhism."[25] More specifically, as he prepared to write *Deep River*, Endō found himself drawn to Varanasi, a city with religious significance for those of various faiths, lying at the confluence of the Ganges and Yamuna Rivers. Here Endō discerned a location rich in symbolism, an echo of the collective unconscious in which the lives of all humans, regardless of background, religious affiliation, and life experience, were brought together into the flow of the great river. It is Mitsuko, toward the end of the novel, who points out to her fellow travellers that "the Hindus apparently call the Ganges the river of rebirth" (200).

In the preceding narrative, however, much has been made of the significance of the river, not just to the Hindus (and, as Endō is at pains to point out, those of other indigenous faiths for whom the river holds a spiritual significance), but also to the protagonist, Ōtsu, who until recently was studying in a Christian seminary in Europe:

Every time I look at the River Ganges, I think of my God. The Ganges swallows up the ashes of every person as it flows along, rejecting neither the beggar woman who stretches out her fingerless hands nor the murdered prime minister, Gandhi. The river of love that is my God flows past, accepting all, rejecting neither the ugliest of men nor the filthiest. (185)

Here in this convergence Endō detected a fusion of life and death, of beauty and ugliness, of hope and despair, that can be seen as a perfect symbolic endpoint for the searches embodied in so many of the earlier Endō protagonists.

Moreover, in using the Ganges as a metaphor for divinity and in drawing an explicit comparison between the river and the concept of the "great life force" *(ōki na inochi)*, which is how Ōtsu (who has now turned his back on the institutionalized Church of the West and has chosen to serve the needy from a Hindu *ashram* beside the great river) chooses to give expression to the divine, Endō can here be seen drawing heavily on Hick's vision of a

> divine Reality which is in itself limitless, exceeding the scope of human conceptuality and language, but which is humanly thought and experienced in various conditioned and limited ways ... Around these different ways of conceiving, experiencing and responding to the Real, there have grown up the various religious traditions of the world, with their myths and symbols, their philosophies and theologies, their liturgies and arts, their ethics and life-styles. (104)

Further indication of the determination to address, in *Deep River*, many of the issues raised by Endō's consideration of religious pluralism lies in the decision to subsume the narrative structure of the novel in the guise of a travelogue. The drama centres on a tour of Indian religious sites, with each chapter devoted to the experiences of one of the members of the tour party. Significantly, each member embarks on the tour alone, each with a very different agenda; as the narrator reminds us, "they all seem to be going to India with very different feelings" (32). They are portrayed, in short, as oblivious to each other, each engaged in a personal search for lost love – for a light that can envelop even the "world of ugliness" in which each has become embroiled (the depiction is that of Endō).[26] As the tour proceeds, however, the narrative focus comes to rest increasingly – and in typical Endō fashion – on the process of rapprochement between the various actors, as one by one the distinctions between the total strangers are shown to mask a crucial link. Increasingly, therefore, each participant comes to focus not only on the successful accomplishment of his or her respective mission but also on assisting others in the pursuit of their goals. Thus, Numada accompanies Mitsuko in her search for Ōtsu, Mitsuko involves herself closely both with Isobe's search for his reincarnated wife and with Kiguchi's determination to perform an appropriate memorial ritual for his fallen war comrades, and Enami, the tour leader, identifies more and more with the individual concerns of his clients. The various missions are valorized until, by the end, each comes to assume the aspect of a spiritual journey, one that serves to locate each of them squarely in a shared humanity.

The framework is carefully constructed, and the more the various personalities become enmeshed in each other's life the more the tour itself can be seen as a literary consideration of the three great themes that Hick sees as shared, albeit in different forms, by all the major religious traditions. He defines these three strands as (1) the "immense potentialities of the human spirit"; (2) a "realizing of the deeper human potential [as] a matter not of perpetuating but rather of transcending our present self-enclosed individual existence"; and (3) a state in which individual ego-boundaries have been transcended, yet to attain [it] the present conscious ego must voluntarily relinquish its own self-centred existence" (135-37). As the drama unfolds, the core characters are drawn to the banks of the Ganges, where they find themselves confronted by previously ignored aspects of their inner selves. To be sure, each places a very different interpretation on this experience, but in each case it is presented in terms of heightened self-awareness, of spiritual awakening or rebirth. And in each case, the portrayal incorporates an element of Hick's depiction of salvation as a casting off of the shackles of self-centredness in favour of something that can transcend these "individual ego-boundaries," what Hick portrays as reality-centredness. Let us turn, then, to a consideration of the respective processes of self-awakening as evidenced by the various protagonists in *Deep River*.

In Search of Renewal

During the course of the novel, the various individual searches are portrayed as variants of the concept of *tenshō,* a notion of rebirth that, for all its clear Buddhist connotations, is nevertheless fused with parallel concepts from other traditions. Initial indication of this intent is provided by the title of the novel itself, with its overt reference to the eponymous Negro spiritual as a prologue. The spiritual, born of decades of slavery in the American South and replete with its dreams of freedom from persecution in the promised "campground," focuses on the River Jordan, the "deep river" that represents the final obstacle separating the Jews from the promised land of Israel. Here was a river symbolizing not so much removal of the memories of slavery as slaves' desire to take this burden with them to the promised land. So near and yet so far, before their eyes lay the land of renewed hope and new beginnings – the vision of rebirth that Endō discerned in the Ganges and that he adopts as his central metaphor.

Much of the subsequent narrative focus is on the interior monologues of the various protagonists, and here the process of attainment of heightened self-awareness – of rebirth – is removed from any specific denominational interpretation and replaced with the depiction of a series of characters with a heightened sense of reality-centredness, one that is overtly attributed to increased ability and willingness of the characters to acknowledge greater complexity to their being than they had formerly countenanced.

First to sense this heightened awareness in the novel is the war veteran, Kiguchi, whose trip to India has been motivated by the desire to commemorate his former colleagues, who perished in the infamous "death march" through the Burmese jungle at the end of the Pacific War. He knows that his own survival was thanks, in no small measure, to the selfless care of his friend, Tsukada, and his recollection of those days, "as they dragged their legs along in utter exhaustion" (86), incorporates a hazy differentiation between his physical self and "an exact replica of himself walking alongside him":

"Walk! You must keep walking!" His double, or perhaps the Kiguchi who was about to collapse physically, had bellowed at him. "Walk! Keep walking!" ... He was certain that his exact duplicate had stood at his side, berating him. (87)

The "exact replica of himself," "his double," or "his exact duplicate" – all translations of the same *mō hitori no jibun* in the original – continues to haunt Kiguchi. But it is only with the passage of time, after decades of struggling to come to terms with his past, that Kiguchi is finally able to recognize this doppelgänger as an integral part of his being, acceptance of which is essential to the process of transition to reality-centredness in which he is engaged. Yet release from its clutches is ultimately achieved only as he stands beside the Ganges intoning the Sutras and concluding that, like good and evil, the two aspects of his being are linked in a symbiotic relationship: they stand "back to back with each other, and they can't be separated the way you can cut things apart with a knife" (200).

Another character who is ultimately portrayed as engaged in a similar quest for rebirth/salvation is Isobe, a "typical" salaryman whose life has been transformed by his dying wife's comment that she would "be reborn *(umare-kawaru)* somewhere in the world" and her injunction that he look for and find her (19). The words continue to haunt Isobe following her death, inducing him to make contact with those involved in a research project at the University of Virginia in which specific instances of "reincarnation" are being examined. The trail leads him to northern India, to the village of Kamloji near Varanasi, to investigate the claim made by a five-year-old girl, Rajini Puniral, that she had spent a previous life as a Japanese. In this case, the object of Isobe's search is both specific and concrete, and at one level his is a classic case of pursuit of the Buddhist concept of karmic reincarnation of his wife. Significantly, however, though Isobe fails in his search for a physical reincarnation (he quickly abandons all attempts to track down Rajini), there is a sense of heightened spiritual awareness attributed to him as he too stands alone beside the Ganges at the end of the novel. This awareness elevates the entire process to transcend denominational interests and consequently accords more closely with Hick's consideration of the issue of mortality: "A realistic conception of resurrection would have to postulate the divine re-creation of psycho-physical beings in another world or worlds" (133). Isobe's response to the purported "failure" of his quest is thus of considerable interest:

> He had finally come to understand that there is a fundamental difference between being alive and truly living ... "Darling!" Once again he called out towards the river. "Where have you gone?"
>
> The river took in his silent cry and silently flowed away. But he felt a power of some kind in that silvery silence. Just as the river had embraced the deaths of countless people over the centuries and carried them to the next world, so too it picked up and carried away the cry of life from this man sitting on a rock on its bank. (189)

Here Isobe appears to have moved beyond the historical process of reincarnation as preached in Buddhism and Hinduism; he has come, instead, to realize that his wife has been reborn within him – and to have approximated, instead, the vision of a "vertical, or perhaps better a diagonal, series of many lives in many worlds, moving nearer to the divine heart of reality" as postulated by Hick (144).

Of all the participants on the tour, however, the one whose journey toward salvation/rebirth/discovery of self emerges as the narrative focus is Mitsuko. She stands in many ways as the living embodiment of the seemingly conflicting and contradictory qualities symbolized by the Ganges. From the outset, she is aware of conflicting impulses within her being – the one drawing her to devote much of her free time to care of the sick and elderly as a hospital volunteer, the other attracted, in spite of herself, to the "freshly severed head and blood flecked lips" of the Hindu goddess Kali. The narrative makes no attempt to call into question the satisfaction that Mitsuko derives from her job as a volunteer. Yet there is an alternative life force that she comes increasingly to discern within these sacred Hindu images that leads her initially to question which is the "real Mitsuko" but eventually to acknowledge that "both images were herself" (115). Increasingly, moreover, she comes to view these conflicting voices as the source not so much of concern as of acceptance of a greater complexity to her being than she had previously countenanced: "On ... occasions, she heard another voice identical to hers saying: *"This invalid isn't going to get better ... "* None of the nurses or doctors was aware of her two faces ... *Ōtsu wrote that God has many faces,* she suddenly thought ... *And so do I"* (124-25; emphasis in original). This heightened perception induces Mitsuko to travel to India "to search out the darkness in her own heart" (58). Once there, as she comes to discern in the Hindu icons symbols of the "real love" for which she thirsts, she finds herself increasingly juxtaposing such images onto that of Ōtsu, for whom such love has come to assume the form of an unwavering commitment to selfless acts of care and concern for those in greatest need.

The transformation effected in Mitsuko is depicted in restrained terms as she increasingly perceives herself as part of the great "river of humanity":

> *I have learned, though, that there is a river of humanity. Though I still don't know what lies at the end of that flowing river. But I feel as though I've started to understand what I was yearning for through all the many mistakes of my past ... What I can believe in now is the sight of all these people, each carrying his or her own individual burdens, praying at this deep river.* At some point, the words Mitsuko muttered to herself were transmuted into the words of a prayer. *I believe that the river embraces these people and carries them away. A river of humanity. The sorrows of this deep river of humanity. And I am part of it.* (210-11; emphasis in original)

As Mitsuko stands beside the Ganges in an attitude of prayer, her renewal is complete. Only now can she begin to empathize with her fellow travellers, whose own intensely personal searches earlier failed to arouse her interest. And only now is she in a position to acknowledge the presence of a divine reality, which in deference to her earlier antipathy toward specifically Christian terminology Ōtsu agreed to call his "Onion."[27] Here, for the first time, she experiences the presence of this "Onion ... reborn in the lives of other people, ... reborn in Ōtsu" (215).

The passage is crucial to an understanding of the distance travelled by Mitsuko during the course of the novel.[28] Of even greater significance, perhaps, is how she, more than any other character in the novel, embodies a shift in focus from the image of Christ to a wider divine image.[29] On arrival in India, her search for love and meaning to her life smacked of desperation. However, with her interest piqued by the sense of the *ōki na inochi* ("great life [force]") that she discerns with growing conviction in the religious iconography that she encounters there, increasingly it comes to be superimposed onto a more specific search for God. Only at this point, therefore, as she stands beside the Ganges, can she "start to understand" the nature of the process in which she has long been engaged. Only now can her private musings evolve into "the words of a prayer."

The examples are by no means exhaustive: there are occasions in the lives of all but one of the tourists when they experience a sense of spiritual awakening. The one exception is Sanjō, whose attachment to the self-centred pursuit of worldly success is highlighted to the end but whose lack of any transformation toward reality-centredness only serves to underscore the force of the process experienced by the others. In terms of narrative intensity, however, all these experiences pale in comparison with the experience of Ōtsu, who is initially depicted as the caricature of the weak and ineffective victim of circumstances but whose quest for spiritual fulfillment leads to his elevation nearly to the figure of the "mediator," a being seen by Hick as present in all world religions and "who opens up a new, exciting and commanding vision of reality in terms of which people feel called to live." In Hick's analysis, this figure "may be theistic ... or it may be a non-theistic vision." The important attribute, however, is that as this figure is embraced, the individuals concerned "feel called to transcend the empirical ego which obscures their true nature" (77).

From the outset, the sense that, for all his lack of social graces, Ōtsu is not alone is crucial. He has a vision of a powerless yet compassionate God to which he constantly alludes. On the one hand, as he struggles in vain to comprehend the harsh criticism that he receives for his "heretical" views in the theological tradition espoused in the French seminary to which he initially turns, he finds himself confronted by the image of a seemingly unfathomable divide between East and West, one that readers of Endō's earlier works will immediately recognize:

After nearly five years of living in a foreign country, I can't help but be struck by the clarity and logic of the way Europeans think, but it seems to me as an Asian that there's something they have lost sight of with their excessive clarity and their overabundance of logic, and I just can't go along with it. Their lucid logic and their way of explaining everything in such clear-cut terms sometimes even causes me pain ... An Asian like me just can't make sharp distinctions and pass judgement on everything the way they do. (117-18)

For all his struggles, however, Ōtsu clings to the vision of a divine reality that represents the ultimate influence behind all of his decisions. This is the being – and, as he readily admits, whether he be called God, Tomato, or even Onion is of no concern – who offers him the absolute reassurance that he seeks:

Just as my Onion is always beside me, he is always within you and beside you, too. He is the only one who can understand your pain and your loneliness. One day he will transport you to another realm. We cannot have any idea when that will be, or how it will happen, or what form it will take. He makes use of every means. (120)

Already there is evidence of a pluralistic perspective denied to the earlier protagonists – and of Ōtsu as a man who seeks to live out Hick's rejoinder that "what is important is not the conventional organizations and their official formulations, but the religious way of experiencing and participating in human existence and the forms of life in which this is expressed" (18). And it is not long before Ōtsu is openly acknowledging his conviction that "God has many faces. I don't think God exists exclusively in the churches and chapels of Europe. I think He is also among the Jews and Buddhists and the Hindus" (121).

Seen in this light, Ōtsu's decision to move to India and seek refuge in a Hindu *ashram* is a logical sequitur. It is there, as Ōtsu works among the dying beside the Ganges, that he awakens to the vision of God not as some supernatural, omnipotent being but as a "great life force," analogous to Hick's "reality an sich," which envelops not just the individual but also the whole natural world. Here is an image of divinity that Ōtsu identifies as "not so much an existence *(sonzai)* as a force *(hataraki*; lit. work)" and that he does not so much "believe in" *(shinkō ja nai)* as "depend upon" and "trust" *(shinrai shite imasu)*(66); here is "an entity that performs the labours of love," an "entity of unbounded gentleness and love," that can be seen as the narrative embodiment of the author's determination, cited in his composition notes, to "clarify the relationship between the 'great life force' and Christ."[30]

There are occasions when Ōtsu may appear too much as an authorial mouthpiece. Where the real force of this literary creation lies, I suggest, is less in the ideas that he espouses and more in the extent to which the narrative portrayal of Ōtsu comes to be fused with this image of the "great life force" – to the extent that he ultimately appears as a literary personification of Hick's concept of the divine or real. In his study, Hick cites three qualities shared by the central figures of all religious traditions: (1) that "the life of the mediator of the Divine or Real was such that the ordinary moral sense of humanity could recognize him to be good rather than evil"; (2) that he offers a "vision of Reality ... such that a new and better existence is possible within or in relation to it"; and (3) that, "as people have taken the step of living in terms of this vision, they [are] in fact transformed (whether suddenly or gradually)" (78).

In helping those in need – in striving for their salvation, not in a physical sense or even in an orthodox Christian sense, but in reconciling them with their own inner beings – Ōtsu's conduct closely embodies all three of these qualities. Seen thus, the image appears to be all embracing – and it is here that Endō appears to have heeded the caveat spelled out by Hick, who, despite his advocacy of religious pluralism, was nevertheless at pains to assert his position as "*Christian* philosopher" and who thus vehemently denied the charge that his was a "non-judgemental inclusivism" that, in the interests of harmony and goodwill, denies that the different religions make any conflicting truth claims.[31] The issue was important for Endō and is addressed in the novel in Ōtsu's response to Mitsuko's innocent query about whether he has converted to Hinduism: "No, I'm ... I'm just like I've always been. Even what you see here now is a Christian priest. But the Hindu *sâdhus* have welcomed me warmly" (180-81). Despite his outward appearance, Ōtsu remains wedded to the ideals, born of his Catholic heritage, that earlier led him to pursue his studies in France. His conviction of the centrality of selfless love at the core of all religious schema has been hardened in the light of confrontation with European orthodoxy. And at the heart of this conviction lies the example that he attributes to the Onion:

> If the Onion came to this city, he of all people would carry the fallen on his back and take them to the cremation grounds. Just as he bore the cross on his back while he was alive ... In the end, I've decided that my Onion doesn't live only within European Christianity. He can be found in Hinduism and

in Buddhism as well. This is no longer just an idea in my head, it's a way of life I've chosen for myself. (184)

The man to emerge from this drama is one who conforms closely to Hick's image of Christ not as "God incarnate" but as "a man who was startlingly open to God" (14), of whom Endō had no hesitation in admitting: "Christ Himself takes the form of ... Ōtsu in this novel. Perhaps I should call it an imitation of Christ, but I have tried to juxtapose the life of Ōtsu onto that of Christ, the failure."[32]

Conclusion

The central character to emerge from this drama – one who at the end of the novel is left struggling for his life following a lynching at the hands of a party of mourners angered by the insensitivity of Sanjō, who, despite frequent warnings, has continued to take photographs of the funerals held beside the river – represents the most complete consideration in Endō's oeuvre of an individual on the journey that Hick describes as transporting the individual from self-centredness to reality-centredness. As a result of his quiet care and concern, Ōtsu succeeds in touching the lives, whether directly or indirectly, of each of the tourists. And as his presence and example come increasingly to confront each character with his or her own doppel-gänger, so the initial portrayal of a group of unspectacular individuals is subverted, the seeds of spiritual transformation subtly planted. Significantly, none of those to whom Ōtsu offers help is cured in the conventional sense; by the end, none has achieved the object of the quest that led him or her to participate in the tour in the first place, and there is no guarantee that all will be well following the return to Japan. The tourists travelled to India very much alone, and they will be leaving it equally alone. Their eyes have been opened, however, and, in encountering the spiritual and mystical power of the river, each now has the potential for salvation/liberation in the Hick-ian sense of "a new and limitlessly better quality of existence that comes about in the transition from self-centredness to Reality-centredness" (69).

In retrospect, the process is reminiscent of that hinted at in the portrayal of Rodrigues in *Silence*, whose faith is paradoxically rendered stronger and more personal following his act of apostasy; of Hasekura, the "weak" samu-rai in *The Samurai*, who ends up willingly embracing death for a faith that he never formally espoused; of Suguro, in *Scandal*, who gains inner strength as he confronts the reality of his unseemly double – indeed of a whole raft of earlier Endō protagonists who can now all be seen as engaged in a similar journey from self-centredness to reality-centredness. Nowhere more so than in *Deep River*, however, is this process linked so explicitly to the discourse of religious pluralism, and nowhere does Endō explore more closely the full ramifications of Hick's ultimate claim that, "by attending to other traditions than one's own, one may become aware of other aspects or dimensions of the Real, which had not been made effectively available by one's own tradition" (44).

As noted earlier, more than one critic was moved to portray the novel as a "full reckoning on Endō's entire œuvre." Such comments might have been prompted, in part at least, by the knowledge that the novel had been written, literally, on Endō's deathbed. When viewed in the context of the process of religious enculturation to which Endō had been committed from the outset of his career, however, this assessment assumes a greater significance. With the earlier works, most memorably with *Silence*, it is hard to escape the sense of an author exploring the possibilities of Christianity enculturated within Japan. The discourse of globalization that was to emerge as an ever more powerful voice in the ensuing decades was, however, one to which Endō was finely attuned: the evolution from his earlier focus on the *kakure kirishitan* within Japan to a broader interest in religious pluralism testifies, I suggest, to a move beyond the earlier perceived national divides. In many ways, the evolution evidenced in these texts is that outlined by David Bosch in his seminal work of the early 1990s, *Transforming Mission*. Endō surely would have been at ease with the latter's portrayal of enculturation in Asia as assuming the form of "the search for identity amid the density of religious pluralism."[33] The scope of inquiry had been considerably expanded – with the novel *Deep River* for the first time overtly addressing the notion of Japan enculturated within the context of global culture. It was an issue to which Endō was unfortunately unable to return before his death in 1996; but, when assessing the legacy of this "Japanese Christian author," we would do well to recall this emphasis on the single, global context – an emphasis that, in retrospect, is evident even in the earliest Endō texts.

Notes

1 *Endō Shūsaku bungaku zenshū* (hereafter *ESbz*), 12: 396.
2 Here I share the vision, espoused by critics such as David Jasper (see *The Study of Literature and Religion*), of the writings of Endō, Graham Greene, Mauriac, and so on as encompassing two levels: that of storytelling and that of implicit theology.
3 *ESbz* (2000), 12: 380.
4 Kuschel, *The Poet as Mirror*, 21.
5 See, for example, Endō's "Katorikku sakka no mondai."
6 Personal conversation, 7 July 1991.
7 Endō, *Fukai kawa o saguru*, 12.

8 Ibid.
9 Hick, *Problems of Religious Pluralism,* 18. All subsequent references to this text are cited as page number only in parentheses.
10 See Endō, *Watakushi no aishita shōsetsu.*
11 Endō admitted the significance that he attached to this passage in personal conversation, 7 July 1991.
12 Hick, "Notice: The Latest Vatican Statement on Christianity and Other Religions," 5.
13 Houston, *The Cross and the Lotus,* 7.
14 *ESbz* (1975), 10: 18-19.
15 *ESbz* (2000), 13: 416.
16 Endō, *Fukai kawa o saguru,* 181-82.
17 This focus on the maternal aspects of the Christian God was widely discussed following publication of *Silence* – and rendered more explicit in several of Endō's subsequent short stories, notably "Haha naru mono" (1969).
18 Tokunaga, "A Japanese Transformation of Christianity," 149.
19 Mathy, "Shūsaku Endō," 608.
20 See Mase-Hasegawa, *Christ in Japanese Culture.*
21 *ESbz* (2000), 13: 361.
22 Tsuji, "Iesu no medioroji," 5. See, e.g., Inoue in Endō, Inoue, and Yasuoka, "'Shin' to 'katachi,'" 209; and Satō in Yasuoka et al., "Tsuitō," in *Shinchō,* 199.
23 Moriuchi Toshio, *Tosho Shimbun,* 12 April 1986.
24 Endō, *Fukai kawa o saguru,* 11, 19.
25 Endō, *Deep River,* 30. All subsequent references to this text are cited by page number only in parentheses.
26 Cited in Kawashima, "*Fukai kawa* no jikken," 13.
27 "If you don't like the word [God], we can change it to another name. We can call him Tomato, or even Onion, if you prefer" (63).
28 In this regard, we should remember that much of the groundwork for this complex character was effected in the earlier novel *Scandal* in the form of Mitsuko Naruse: the significance that Endō attached to this character is evidenced by the fact that, for several years after completing *Scandal,* he worked on a draft of *Deep River* in which Mitsuko was clearly identified as the main protagonist. See Endō, "Fukai kawa sōsaku nikki."
29 See Mase-Hasegawa, *Christ in Japanese Culture,* for further discussion of this aspect of the novel.
30 Endō, "Fukai kawa sōsaku nikki," 54.
31 See Hick's riposte to this charge made by Paul Griffiths and Delmas Lewis in Hick, ed., *The Myth of Christian Uniqueness,* 88ff.
32 Endō, in Endō and Kaga, "Taidan," 11.
33 Bosch, *Transforming Mission,* 454.

7
An Essay on Sono Ayako

Toshiko Sunami

(translated and annotated by Kevin M. Doak)

Sono Ayako's Debut: "Enrai no kyakutachi" ["Guests from Afar"]

Sono Ayako's debut on the literary stage came with her short story "Enrai no kyakutachi" that appeared in the April 1954 issue of *Mita Bungaku*. Within months, this work was nominated for the Akutagawa Prize and reprinted in the September issue of *Bungei Shunjū*. Then, the very next year, in the May 1955 issue of *Shinchō,* "A Special Collection of Novelists in the Third Generation of the New Man," she was considered a member of "the Third Generation of the New Man," alongside Kojima Nobuo, Yoshiyuki Junnosuke, Shōno Junzō, Onuma Tan, Hasegawa Shirō, Matsumoto Seichō, and Yasuoka Shōtarō.[1] Sono was all of twenty-four years old. Perhaps it is said too often that an author's entire life-work can be found in his first work, but with "Enrai no kyakutachi" this is truly the case.

"Enrai no kyakutachi" is about an eighteen-year-old girl named Namiko who works as a concierge at a hotel in Hakone that, in the immediate aftermath of the war, serves the American military. Namiko has decided that victory or defeat in war is no more than a result of the vicissitudes of time, so she adopts a singular attitude of treating the occupation force as "guests from faraway" America. Through Namiko's interactions with the soldiers as equal human beings, the narrative gives us a penetrating insight into the arrogance and baseness that afflict the victors and the loss of self-confidence and servility that afflict the losers. At the same time, it reveals the author's acute political sensibility that, providing us with multiple opportunities to see the pride and magnanimity of those from the victorious country and the helplessness of those from the defeated country, seems quite prophetic about the subsequent future of postwar Japan. It is said that the original title of this short story was "Autumn, 1947."

The girl Namiko, who serves as the protagonist of this story, is two years older than Sono, who was sixteen in 1947. She is quite fluent in English, which until a few years prior was forbidden as the language of the enemy, and a real internationalist who has a good grasp of the moral backbone of the occupying nation, America. We may consider her the alter ego of Sono herself, who was a student at the Catholic Sacred Heart Women's Academy from kindergarten through university and who was baptized a Catholic when she was seventeen. What surprises readers about Namiko is that she is completely free from any of the emotions that the defeated nation has embraced: bitterness, resentment, sense of inferiority, or humiliation. Girls like that were not exactly commonplace in Japan at that time. Miyoshi Yukio is now deceased, but someone like him would say that Sono, along with Endō Shūsaku, Tsuji Kunio, and Okawa Kunio, start from the assumption that "the West" is also their homeland. Okuno Takeo has recorded his impression of his first encounter with "Enrai no kyakutachi" as follows:

It made me feel refreshed, as if my long-standing way of feeling about things had been swept away. I guess I had to say to myself, "well, this girl can really write! What's your problem?" And the next thing I knew, I found myself a bit attracted to this saucy young girl named Namiko, and then I even felt a bit of envy, jealousy, and a nostalgic sense of affinity with this new writer called Sono Ayako who, I feared, was out of my league. The reason was that we Japanese had felt, since the end of the war, a sense of irritation and inferiority toward the American occupation forces. You see, they were the winners, and their physique and nutrition were all excellent, and they swaggered all around town with their material wealth and sense of entitlement, whereas we suffered from hunger and malnourishment, having nothing to eat or wear.[2]

During a period of transition, it is more often the young intellectuals who arrive on the scene with much clearer eyes than their elders. We saw this with the 1907 Elementary School Ordinance that brought to an end the common phenomenon of children not attending elementary schools, and the children then got a much better view of the needs of their day than their uneducated and illiterate parents. In any event, we must not forget that Namiko – really Sono herself – was clearly one of the wartime generation and shared with Okuno the bitter taste of the sorrow and misery of a defeated nation. But having tasted deeply and intensely what war had to offer, Sono herself, like her protagonist, had "become a reflective adult" who was "well beyond her actual years." What kind of reflective adult had she become? One who recognized that war was misery, regardless of whether one wins or loses, and that it was not only those who lost the war who were its unfortunate victims. She saw nuns thrown in jail simply on the basis of allegations that they were enemy aliens, and she knew of those, like the protagonist of "Umi no ohaka" [November 1954; "Buried at Sea"], who originally were English and thus technically victors in the war but who had come to Japan during the war under the auspices of international law and the encouragement of Japan and, charged later as collaborators with Japan, had been stripped of their citizenship. And how could she not consider herself responsible for the evils of the war, since she had been mobilized at the age of thirteen to work in a munitions plant making weapons as a female factory worker? Sono Ayako was forced to recognize that, "in the final analysis, I assisted in war and murder." Tsuruha Nobuko has suggested that the war "was good material in helping Ayako understand what Christianity is all about."[3] What she means is that Sono was able to understand that war is a trial that God gives equally to all those involved in it, a grace that encourages one to examine one's conscience. That is why Sono felt she could not wallow in the feelings of shame and inferiority of a defeated nation and really had no choice but to come to her senses and get on with life.

Given her values, how did Sono, at a time when the majority of Japanese were cowering in the postwar despondency and shame of collective repentance, regard a Japan that was rushing headlong toward democracy under the guidance of the General Headquarters of the Allied Army? It must have caused her no end of irritation that Japan did not have the wisdom to sense immediately that it had a responsibility and obligation for having started the war. On that point, we may gain insight from Namiko in "Enrai no kyakutachi." Namiko whispers in the ear of a military doctor, her "honourable friend," that "(America) has an obligation here. Because of the war, the Japanese have perverted their destiny. Thus, as victors, the Americans have an obligation to help the Japanese through any means and at every opportunity."[4] Implicit is a kind of passive-aggressive decision that Japan's reconstruction cannot be done without the help of the occupying country, that the kindness of America in planting democracy along with its military occupation should be regarded as a necessary means for moving on, and that for the time being the best thing would be to hop on board. Of course, this way of thinking should not be confused with a naive belief that because America is a Christian country it would never do anything bad to Japan.

Namiko thinks that Japan's reconstruction is something that ought to be done by Japanese finding the courage to do it with their own hands, so she seeks the key to this reconstruction by pointing out that, "without trying to destroy certain institutions and morals, one would never know whether claims that they were provisionally and temporally constructed by humans are right or wrong."[5] (This is what the character of Dr. Diulio calls "the strength of defeat."[6]) To the extent that defeat in the war gave the Japanese an opportunity to assess the morality of prewar Japan, the war cannot be said to be a total loss. If reflecting on Japan's loss in the war could become the cornerstone of a new construction of the state, then defeat in the war might cease to be merely grief and sorrow. Namiko is deeply struck by the thought that, since in the Japanese oracles [*omikuji*] good and bad fortune are the front and back of the same stick, depending on how you receive the oracle stick you can convert misfortune into good fortune. Thus, it is not from any intent to deceive the victorious nation but as a reflection of Namiko's own sense of reality that she has no qualms about giving a humorous, incorrect interpretation of the oracle: "There is concern that your desires will be smashed by an unexpected event: Unlucky." According to Namiko, "it says you may face some small obstacle, like a flat tire on your car, or your refrigerator may break down. But afterward it seems that what you are planning now will certainly come true."[7]

Sono did not completely express her view of life that is rooted in her faith in an unconditional God until 1969, when she published *Ikenie no shima* ["Sacrificial Island"] and "Mumeihi" ["An Anonymous Marker"], or 1970, when "Kizutsuita ashi" ["The Wounded Reed"] came out. Her greatest literary achievement is thought to be either *Aru shinwa no haikei* [1971-72; "The Background of a Certain Myth"] or *Chi o uruosu mono* [1974; "What Waters the Land"], which deal with the Pacific War. But the outline of her thinking that was shaped by the war and the Bible can be found already at the time of "Enrai no kyakutachi."

> Yes, this world is filled with contradictions, but it is those contradictions that give humans the power to think. If there were no contradictions and everything ran according to plan, we human beings would be rotten to the core. At the very least, I would stop thinking and become utilitarian, and faith and philosophy would disappear. A world where justice was fully realized certainly would not be as good a thing as we think. It may seem paradoxical, but what makes it possible for humans to possess human dignity is the randomness of this world. Where the law of the jungle prevails over justice, everyone can easily fall under the sway of power and money, and that is precisely where we have the freedom to continue to be human by resisting those temptations.[8]

Sono is a writer who had this kind of mature way of thinking when she was barely over twenty years old. As readers, we would be wrong to read either Namiko or the author of "Enrai no kyakutachi" in a naive manner. Certainly, one finds in the margins of this novel a satire of the way in which Helen Keller was received – hallelujah chorus and all – as a kind of flattery of the nation that had won the war. Was this merely an exposé of the servility of a defeated nation? Sono's philosophy recognizes that a "holy woman" who sees light in the midst of darkness and who appears covered in the ugliness of old age will not be welcomed in any fashion other than the insincere one of flattery. Actually, for most of the Japanese people, as a defeated nation, Christianity was nothing more than the religion of the victorious country, a religion that was stationed in Japan along with the occupying army. Still, it is a historical fact that, when Helen Keller came to Japan the second time in August of 1948 as a blind evangelist, she gave great hope and courage to the visually and hearing impaired, regardless of whether they were on the winning or losing side of the war. Naturally, Sono must have been moved by the event and must have hoped that Japan not consider defeat as an ultimate disaster but learn from Helen Keller (who had overcome the loss of sight, hearing, and speech) and strive to accept the grace of the ordeal. When we understand this, then we can see that, while there is no question that the occupying army certainly are "guests from afar," the most eagerly awaited "guest from afar" is this holy woman suffering her triple handicap.

Literature, the Bible, and the War

Sono was born in the year of the Marco Polo Bridge Incident (1931), experienced the Tokyo air raids of 1945, and lived through the immediate aftermath of defeat when Japan was awash with poverty and disease. For her, it was certainly a case of "war as the decisive experience." Under the weight of all the lies of the state and the ugliness of mankind that flooded the world once Pandora's box was opened, Sono was deeply affected by the question "why do people so easily jump into war and get swallowed up by it?" While aware that "the prototype of human society is war," she wanted to know who is happy to see wars expand out of control. What drives people and states to throw themselves into the raging flames of war? It seems as though, while she sought the meaning of war and the mystery of Man's simultaneous attraction to both life and death, her continued focus on the reality of the wartime was her way of resisting the daily temptation to conclude that death might have been a better alternative.

Because Sono had wandered mercilessly amid the ravages of war, inequality, and on the edges of life and death, she sought answers from the Bible as to why Man must experience such things. So she was drawn to the world of novels built on evidence and reasoning. She was greatly influenced by the Bible, particularly the Old Testament books such as Job and Ecclesiastes (aka "The Words of Qoheleth [the Preacher]"). "For everything there is a season, and a time for every matter under heaven: a time to kill, and a time to heal; a time to tear down, and a time to build; a time to love, and a time to hate; a time for war, and a time for peace" (Ecclesiastes 3:1-8). She found a firmly grounded hope and an accurate perception of reality in the philosophy of eternity that holds God's immeasurable grace is available to us at all times. In addition, even her method as a novelist in terms of psychological understanding and perception of human beings was drawn from Paul's letters. To Sono, a novelist must "become a slave to all in order to win [understand] more people" (1 Corinthians 9:19). In other words, we can say that the young Sono compared the reality of war with the stories of the Bible and, in order to understand the limits of Man, who is unable to avoid the worst of human calamities, drew on the harsh Old Testament and found salvation in God the Father.

In addition, this stance and method that Sono learned from the Bible, which holds that one must empty out oneself and grasp things in as pluralistic a manner as possible (which in reality was a kind of self-mortification for her), allowed her to develop an objective human panorama that gave away no hint of its underlying penitential nature. In the climate of contemporary Japanese literature, which tends to evaluate highly novels that strongly push the author's self-assertion on readers, we have to say that, in constructing a clear-sighted world where one finds the "vanity of vanities, all things are vanity" (Ecclesiastes 1:2), Sono is a female writer of unusual gravitas.

Consider this:

I think it is precisely the way of thinking that will not allow a man his own reasons that is characteristic of fascism. A child falls in the street. Why did he fall? A simplistic answer that it was merely because there was a rock in his way is not something I find satisfactory. Why was the rock there? Why did the child's mother let go of his hand so he could fall? Only by asking such questions can we arrive at an insight from a different perspective that sees, to the extent that conception allows, a deep, surprising interrelationship of all things. This is really what human understanding is all about.[9]

This kind of nuanced, modest position on human understanding lies at the basis of Sono's production of novels.

But this point should not be interpreted only in literary terms as a thoroughness in taking the high road of literary composition. Every author tries to construct a reality from multiple viewpoints through the various perspectives of his characters. The key is whether an author considers the reality of a carefully prepared, thoughtfully constructed novel as complete or not. Sono writes from an awareness that the end result of all her efforts is always incomplete. In any event, this means that she writes fully aware that it is impossible for Man, who never really understands his own self, to approximate the eyes of God. On this point, she resembles Endō Shūsaku, another member of the "Third New Man" group of writers who was conscious of the eyes of God in "the margins of the novel." Like Endō, she also excluded from the world of novels the "grand theory" of politics that tries to make a final judgment of right and wrong. "Politically tone-deaf" was one nickname for the "Third New Man" writers, but for writers who sought to develop the novel by centring it on the relationship of Man to God, political ideology naturally was understood to be something that had to be overcome.

This kind of authorial position of Sono is most clearly manifested in those works that pursue the true nature of the tragedy of the war, which was Sono's lifelong topic. She modestly described the actual nature of the war as it came to the fore through her painstaking reading of and listening to the voluminous source material and testimonials she collected. Representative works include *Ikenie no shima: Okinawa joseito no kiroku* ["Sacrificial Island: Notes from Okinawan Schoolgirls"]; *Aru shinwa no haikei,* which deals with the collective suicide of the residents of Tokashiki Island; *Chi o uruosu mono,* which records the reminiscences of the older brother of an innocent soldier who died as a war criminal for things that happened during the Malay Singapore battle; and of course "Kōbai hakubai" ["Red and White Plum Blossoms"], which depicts the cruel fate of the Fifth Brigade of the Imperial Guard infantry in the Malay Singapore battle. Of these works, the one where Sono most clearly presents her own position as a writer and her view of the war, while destroying the scapegoat myth that had been fabricated by anti-war ideology after the war, is *Aru shinwa no haikei.*

In the last days of the war on the island of Tokashiki in Okinawa, 300 residents attempted collective suicide with a grenade that had been given to them by the military (draftees). The anti-war journalism of the postwar period wrote this event up as an indictment of an actual group massacre that was carried out on the orders of the highest commanding officer of the military (i.e., the special attack, or "kamikaze," squad) to the villagers to commit suicide. This was because they saw the perpetrators as having survived the war, living on in the postwar without any punishment, while Okinawa was forced to continue being sacrificed for the "mainland" in the postwar, just as in the prewar.

It was this grudge that claimed that Okinawa is always right and the "mainland" is bad and hateful that passed off the idea of the collective suicide of innocent people as a self-evident fact. But Sono pointed out that significant doubts about the event were simply glossed over. As a general rule, the military does not have the authority to issue orders to civilians, and it is simply impossible for regular troops to do something like arbitrarily hand out grenades to civilians (families). And there is the difficulty – impossibility – of understanding what kind of abnormal psychology might have driven 300 people to collective suicide. Sono's conclusion, after painstaking investigation into the records and memories of those involved, is that, "the more I researched, the more complicated and impossible it became to understand it. Almost all of the eyewitnesses each had different memories and thoughts about it ... Rather, what I found most perplexing is that, like the myth, they all seemed a bit too precise about what they believed had happened."[10] So, ultimately, Sono came to this general conclusion about the incident:

> I do not claim that Captain Akamatsu did nothing wrong, nor do I slight the fact that more than 300 people died. But 300 people do not just die. I feel as certain as if I were there that, even if a captain did order suicide, people do not just die without being killed unless there is some kind of psychology involved. That is just human nature.[11]

In short, the matter cannot be dispensed with as merely a question of whether military authorities issued an order for suicide. Rather, she surmises that collective suicide was a result of the exceptional conditions of the battlefield that she describes as "a collective insanity in the broader sense ... in which both the Japanese army and the American army had no fear of human death."[12] She goes further to declare that collective suicide itself was nothing more than the result of a tragic, foolish, deplorable evil of "non-personhood." Having said that, however, she asks whether one who has never killed anyone can really ever understand the brazen killing that takes place on the battlefield or the collective suicide of 300 people. She concludes by saying that the only thing she does understand is that "war is meaningless! They all died for no reason."[13]

A Storyteller

When a writer tries to write about war from a humbled stance that lacks the eyes of God and maintains silence in the face of a reality that supersedes all understanding, he can at best become a storyteller (a recorder of rumours) who finds human truth among contradictory testimonies and written records.[14] The riddle of war, a riddle that only deepens the more one digs exhaustively into research, cannot be easily solved, and there is nothing to do but adopt the method of narrating it for readers as evidence of the larger riddle of Man. In the afterword to *Ikenie no shima*, Sono notes the following: "Because I wanted to give people the truth of the war ... I completed this work with the co-operation of nearly 200 people. They were the ones who wrote it; I was merely a storyteller. But it brings me great joy that we were able to record one aspect of history in this way."[15] Still, it was due to Sono's spirit that she found an appropriate style for a method that would tell facts as facts, and in the process Sono's war stories found success. That success stemmed from the fact that she built that structure (i.e., style) of her novels on her philosophy that, for a storyteller with a limited perspective, only the tragedy of war is visible: it is difficult for anyone to see God's plan that lies hidden behind a war.

Fundamentally, Sono's literature depicts the limitations and destiny of Man, the existence of Man premised on the existence of God. Because Man is "the image of God," even the protagonist of a novel is only a provisional protagonist. Because she sees everything concerning Man as being in God's hands, she is really depicting God (his hands) when she is describing an individual or society. In short, a writer is essentially nothing more than a storyteller who narrates, as she finds it, the reality (absurdity) of Man as given to us by God. She does not struggle against the silence of God, as does Endō Shūsaku, who, faced with unjust fate and absurdity, wrote in *The Sea and the Poison*, "is there really such a thing as God?"[16] Sono says to us that "without having killed a person, you cannot understand anything [about the war]" (i.e., if you had killed, you would have understood [what it was like]). But those very words betray a failure to imagine that there could be someone who, even after killing a person, still does not understand anything. One wonders what Sono would make of a person who is outside of God's hands, like Toda in *The Sea and the Poison*, who said, "nothing is changed. My heart is tranquil. The pangs of conscience, the stabs of guilt that I've waited for so long haven't come at all."[17]

Sono's Catholic faith has influenced the structure of her novels and has yielded excellent results. Adopting the stance of a storyteller who merely narrates has brought about success in other works besides her war stories, works such as "Umi no ohaka," "Waga koi no bohyō" ["The Gravemarker of My Love"], "Ochiba no koe" ["The Voice of Fallen Leaves"], and *Kiseki* ["Miracles"].[18] But we should bear in mind that strong faith does not always lead to such strong writing.

Notes

1 The first New Man Society *(Shinjinkai)* was founded in 1918 at Tokyo Imperial University and centred on the Christian intellectual Yoshino Sakuzō. The name New Man seems to have been inspired by the Christian journal of the same name, founded by the Christian intellectual Ebina Danjō in 1900. That journal, *Shinjin* ("New Man"), took its name from Ephesians 4:22-24: "You are to put off the old man, which is being corrupted through its deceptive lusts. But be renewed in the spirit of your mind, and put on the new man, which has been created according to God in justice and holiness of truth" (revised Challoner-Rheims Version of the New Testament). The New Man Society remained active until 1928. The term "Third Generation of New Man" *(dai-san no shinjin)* was coined by Yamamoto Kenkichi in his January 1953 article in *Bungakukai* by the same title. Yamamoto's term was in response to Usui Yoshimi's introduction of the concept of a "Second Generation of New Man" in the same journal one year earlier. In addition to Yasuoka and Kojima (listed above), the Third Generation of New Man included Sono, her husband Miura Shumon, and Shimao Toshio, all five of whom were Catholic. See the broader discussion on the Third Generation of New Man, the theme of the February 2006 issue of *Kokubungaku kaishaku to kanshō,* where Sunami's article originally appeared. There appears to be no significant difference between the second and third generations. Striking, however, is the disproportionate influence that Christian intellectuals had in both prewar and postwar New Man groups.
2 Okuno, *Joryū sakkaron,* 202.
3 Cf. "What is Christianity? What does it mean to believe in God? Ayako, from a tender age, came to these questions not from theories and book learning but from how the Sisters [who taught her] lived a life that transcended their time or, perhaps we should say, how they lived in eternal time. The war taught her all sorts of things." Tsuruha, *Kami no deku Sono Ayako no tamashii no sekai,* 52-53. Translator's note: Sono (at the time known by her birth name Machida Chizuko) entered Sacred Heart Women's Academy in 1938 at the age of six as a kindergarten student. She graduated from Sacred Heart (Seishin) University in 1954, with a degree in English. She was baptized in the school's chapel in 1948, taking the baptismal name Maria Elizabeth.
4 Sono, "Enrai no kyakutachi," reprinted in *Enrai no kyakutachi,* 89.
5 Ibid., 97.
6 Ibid., 98.
7 Ibid., 110.
8 Sono, "Kurayami no naka no kami" ["God amidst the Darkness"], in *Watakushi no naka no seisho,* 164-65.
9 Sono, *Aru shinwa no haikei,* 250-51.
10 Ibid., 252-53.
11 Ibid., 254.
12 Ibid., 266.
13 Sono, *Chi o uruosu mono,* 143.

14 Translator's note: The word that Sono uses for "storyteller" is *kataribe,* an evocative word derived from the ancient *Kojiki* that referred to clans who specialized in transmitting oral legends prior to the introduction of writing in Japan.

15 Sono, *Ikenie no shima,* 244.

16 Endō, *Umi to dokuyaku,* in *Endō Shūsaku bungaku zenshū,* vol. 1, 130. Cf. Endō, *The Sea and the Poison,* 79.

17 Endō, *Umi to dokuyaku,* 172-73; cf. Endō, *The Sea and the Poison,* 154. Translation here is Gallagher's.

18 Translator's note: None of these works has been translated into English. There is, however, an extensive discussion of *Kiseki* ("Miracles") in Gabriel, *Spirit Matters,* 48-62.

8

The Theory and Practice of Inculturation by Father Inoue Yōji: From Panentheism to *Namu Abba*

Yoshihisa Yamamoto

I want to begin this chapter with the words of the Jewish German philosopher Karl Löwith (1897-1973), who taught in Tōhoku Imperial University in Japan from 1936 to 1941, after the Nazi regime had come to power in Germany. Having taught many Japanese students for several years, he criticized their mental climate as follows: "They live on two stories, as it were: a lower, fundamental one in which they feel and think in the Japanese manner and ... an upper one in which they line up with European knowledge from Plato to Heidegger, and the European teacher wonders: Where is the staircase, to take them from the one to the other?"[1] When the Japanese people opened their country in the midst of the nineteenth century, they felt it necessary to modernize Japan to avoid colonization. So they introduced European institutions and cultures in Japan and made the modern university system. To modernize Japan was, in many respects, the same as to Westernize Japan. On the other hand, it was very difficult for them to change their traditional ways of feeling and thinking immediately. So the Japanese people, especially the intellectuals, continued to be faced with a split within themselves.

The situation was complicated. To keep Japan independent, it was necessary for Japanese to modernize/Westernize their country. But if they succeeded in doing this, they had to lose their traditional national (cultural) identity. But since the concept of modernity itself included the concept of national identity as the basis of a national state, Japanese continued to feel some ambivalence in the modern period toward their traditional culture. Ironically, success in modernizing the country strengthened this tension within them. To keep their independence, they had to transform their traditional ways of life and thinking. But at the same time, to give political independence true meaning, it was necessary to retain the traditional ways of life and thinking. This was the fundamental problem with which Japanese intellectuals were faced after the Meiji Restoration of 1868.

We find the same situation in the case of the reception of Christianity in Japan. On the one hand, many Japanese people (especially the intellectuals) went to church because they had a yearning for European culture. On the other hand, however, many of them left the churches because they found it difficult to assimilate European Christianity. Thus, in some sense, the inferiority complex toward the West, sometimes compensated by the sense of spiritual superiority of traditional Japanese culture over the materialistic culture of Europe and America, was both the driving force toward and the repelling force from Christianity.

To cope with the situation, several Catholic intellectuals tackled the problem of the inculturation of Christianity in Japan. The most famous attempt was by the Japanese Catholic novelist Endō Shūsaku (1923-96). His work is discussed in Chapter 6. But Endō was not alone in this attempt. Other novelists and priests were part of his circle and developed their own approaches to resolving this problem. Among them, the theory and practice of inculturation by Father Inoue Yōji (b. 1927) is most important. Although his name is not widely known outside Japan, he is one of the most important Japanese Catholic figures of the postwar period.

Basic Characteristics of the Thought of Inoue

Inoue's project needs to be placed in context. There are several Catholic priests in Japan who have been tackling the problem of inculturation: Father Kadowaki Kakichi (b. 1926), Father Okumura Ichirō (b. 1923), and Father Oshida Shigeto (1922-2003).[2] These advocates of inculturation of Catholicism in Japan are all of the same generation. They grew up before World War II and were shocked by Japan's defeat. The shock of defeat and the spiritual vacuum that followed were the main reasons that led them to convert to Catholicism. Among this group, however, Inoue enjoys a unique position. All the other advocates of inculturation practised Zen Buddhism, whereas Inoue never practised it. His theological theory and practice are based on the everyday feelings of ordinary Japanese people. His books are not academic books. They are written in an easy-to-read Japanese. And they are based on his own everyday experiences. He never writes anything that is not based on his own experience. To grasp the importance of his approach, consider that most of the Japanese books on Christianity are translations and adaptations of European and American theologians.

Inoue started his study of theology by reading Aquinas, as was the case with most Catholic seminarians before the Second Vatican Council. But after having studied Aquinas for several years, he found it almost impossible to accept the European type of Christianity that Aquinas represented. So he left the Carmelites, went back to Japan, and became a parish priest in Tokyo. Then he started to construct a Japanese-flavoured Christianity that could be accepted by ordinary Japanese people not acquainted with European culture. For them, he formed a small Catholic community, Kaze no Ie (The House of Pneuma).

Although Inoue has written more than twenty books, all are in Japanese, and only one has been translated into English. We can find most of his important ideas in the translation of his maiden work, *The Face of Jesus in Japan.* Thirty years after his first book was published, Inoue described the key features of his thinking in the following terms: "I wrote *The Face of Jesus in Japan* because I felt that 'Oriental nothingness,' 'the body of Christ,' and 'the God as *Abba,*' which has a strong maternal principle, became overlapped more or less, however dimly. It was in 1976. I was forty-nine years old. It was seventeen years since I had returned to Japan."[3] He developed his original ideas on inculturation as a reaction to the sense of discomfort that he had felt toward Christianity when he was young.

One aspect of Christianity that Inoue found difficult to accept was the austere image of God in the Old Testament. After some period of struggle, he came across the autobiography of St. Thérèse of Lisieux.[4] He was fascinated by the unconditional trust in the compassionate God that was manifested in the way of the spiritual infant. He often cites the following episode, as reported by her sister:

> She [St. Thérèse] loved God as a child loves his father with outbursts of incredible tenderness. One day during her illness, when referring to Him, she said "Papa" when she had meant to say "God." It seemed to her that we were smiling over her slip, and with much feeling she told us: "Nevertheless, He is indeed my 'Papa,' and it is a consolation for my heart to be able to call Him by that name!"[5]

Inoue realized by reading this episode how to liberate himself from the image of the austere God. He was so fascinated by the spirituality of St. Thérèse that he was baptized soon after reading her autobiography.[6]

Inoue then went to France to enter the Carmelite order because he wanted to share in the same spirituality as St. Thérèse. But he met with two other difficulties there: one of them was the intellectualism of Thomism, and the other was the individualism of Europe. Before Inoue went to France, he did not have much interest in Japanese culture. One of the triggers of his interest was the encounter with Professor Henri de Lubac (1896-1991), whose lectures he attended in France. De Lubac was familiar with Hōnen (1133-1212) and Shinran (1173-1262), both founders of major schools of Japanese Buddhism, and the title of one of de Lubac's books was *Amida: Aspects du Bouddhisme*. That one of the best Christian theologians in France was publishing his research on Amida Buddhism amazed Inoue. In his book *Catholicisme*, de Lubac claimed that to spread the Christian gospel must not be to Hellenize and Latinize all cultures. Universality must not mean uniformity. Rather, Catholicism should be a unity in diversity, for each nation has its own proper culture. These positions of de Lubac influenced Inoue greatly. He had been trying to become French and was hurt because he always ended up not being French. But he gradually became convinced that he could be a good Christian even if he remained Japanese.[7] The professors in France encouraged him to become a kind of Japanese "Church Father." They told him that it was not necessary for him to imitate them. He wanted to integrate Christianity and Japanese culture just as the ancient Church Fathers had integrated Christianity and Greek thought.

Returning to Japan, Inoue continued his study of theology at Sophia University and was surprised to find that there were no required courses on the history of Japanese thought or Japanese culture in the curriculum of the Department of Philosophy, let alone in the curriculum of the Department of Theology. So most Japanese who finished the seminary curriculum and became priests were almost completely ignorant of Japanese cultural heritage, even though they had acquired enough knowledge of European culture. Inoue was convinced that the educational structure of theology was one of the biggest reasons that most Japanese people deemed Christianity to be a foreign religion and continued to reject it as outlandish for Japanese. He found it difficult to find a single person among the priests and seminarians in Japan to talk with about the idea of Jesus in Japanese culture, as it was being discussed in France.[8] So Inoue decided to read the works by Watsuji Tetsurō (1889-1960), Suzuki Daisetsu (1870-1966), and Kobayashi Hideo (1902-83). He says that there was no deep reason for choosing these three writers. He thought vaguely and intuitively that, if he followed these writers, he could grasp the essence of Japanese culture. All three were acquainted both with Japanese culture and with European culture. They were not ones to neglect Western culture and blindly follow traditional Japanese culture. In a word, they represented the self-expression of Japanese traditional culture in the global context of the modern world. They got deeper insights into traditional Japanese culture through the medium of Western culture. And I think that this characteristic applies to Inoue himself.

Panentheism is one of the key concepts of his thinking. He adopted this concept as an integration of European theism and Oriental (Japanese) panentheism. He states:

> Christianity is neither a panentheism that identifies nature and God nor a transcendental theism that grasps God as existing transcendentally apart from nature. It is a panentheism in which nature never exists without the action of God and in which God and nature are neither the same nor separate.[9]

Inoue is not a systematic writer. He does not try to construct a rigid theological system. His emphasis on the practical character of religion makes his thought somewhat fragmentary and difficult to summarize. But below I will try to construct a systematic explanation of his thought as far as possible and offer a critical evaluation of it by posing it in a broader, global context.

The Practical Character of Religion as an Alternative to Intellectualism

Inoue does not refer to God as an object separate from human beings. He always speaks of the relationship between God and Man or between God and himself. So his thinking tends to be experiential, concrete, and psychological. He contrasts the experiential way of knowing with an intellectual way of knowing, and he assigns the latter way to Europeans and the former way to Japanese:

> In the main current of the Greek and European way of thinking, the confrontation of subject and object is presupposed. And the subject tries to know *about* the object. On the other hand, the Japanese approach, which has been alive deep in Japanese culture since the ancient *Kojiki* [712 AD], seems clearly to have put emphasis on knowing things themselves. Maybe this is because what Japanese people have had interest in and cared most about was not the world as an object that confronts the subject but something like a fundamental life force that embraces both subject and object.[10]

To know *about* something is to acquire knowledge by forming concepts. It is apprehension from outside a thing by placing it before the intellect as an object. Similarly, to know Jesus and to know about Jesus are two different things. To know God and to know about God are thus two different things. Inoue maintains that it is necessary for us to jump into the life of something to know it.

Although Inoue contrasts the European way and the Japanese way of knowing in the passage cited above, he received the first insight concerning this distinction between knowing things and knowing about things from a European, Henri Bergson.[11] I want to emphasize that Inoue got many of his basic insights from European saints and scholars. He then transformed them into a kind of Japanese theology. He has emphasized on many occasions that he is not a scholar. But his knowledge of European theology, philosophy, psychology, and literature is amazing. Inoue cites many Western philosophers, theologians, biblical scholars, and even psychologists.[12] So we must understand that what he calls "the Japanese way" is not limited only to Japanese people. He is responding to the Christianity that he encountered in France before the Second Vatican Council. So his response has an appeal not only for Japanese people but also for European and American people today who have been struggling to understand the gospel in the intellectual climate of contemporary global society after the council.

Religion, for Inoue, is not a matter of thinking but a matter of practice.[13] He understands the New Testament not merely as a book that conveys objective truth to humans but also as a practical guidebook that requires action and shows us the way to eternal life.[14] So we cannot understand the teachings of Jesus in a true sense unless we make up our minds to obey his teachings and start to act as he taught us.[15] We can know about Jesus without acting as he taught, but we can never know Jesus without acting as he taught. However much one is acquainted with the Bible, unless one has an attitude of prayer, by which one tries to respond to the Word of God, one cannot know the joy of the gospel. What is necessary for us is not to understand the guidebook intellectually but to act according to it. The scientific inquiry and historical study of the New Testament perform only supplementary functions for knowing and living out the gospel of Christ.[16]

This emphasis on the practical character of religion gives us an important insight into the debate on religious pluralism and exclusivism.[17] According to Inoue, we cannot have a bird's-eye view of religion because we are not the absolute being. All we can do is believe that the way in which we are walking will lead us to the summit of the mountain. No one is qualified to speak on whether other ways lead people to the same destination or not. We can think about two ways simultaneously, but we cannot follow two ways at the same time. So both the religious pluralism that states that every religion leads people to the same destination and the religious exclusivism that states that other religions do not lead to the same destination are wrong because they overlook the limited human condition. Religious truth is not a universal truth in thinking but a subjective truth in practice.[18]

According to Inoue, we cannot know God if we try to know about him scientifically or objectively. We know God only by experience. So how can we experience God? According to Inoue, we can do so only by practising the teachings of Jesus. And those teachings can be epitomized by three words: *abba, agape,* and *pneuma.*[19] The theology of Inoue is based on his deep insight into these key concepts of the New Testament. I will outline these concepts below.

Namu Abba: An Alternative to the Severe Image of God in the Old Testament

The three aspects of Christianity that were difficult for Father Inoue to accept (the austere Old Testament image of God, intellectualism, and European individualism) seem at first glance to be three completely separate problems. But the solution to the first two problems is integrated in his doctrine of *abba,* an Aramaic word for "father" used by an infant, like the English word *papa* (or *daddy*). Jesus is said to have always used this term when he addressed God. Inoue cites the words of Joachim Jeremias, a renowned biblical scholar:

> We do not have a single example of God being addressed as *Abba* in Judaism, but Jesus always addressed God in this way in his prayers ... *Abba* was a children's word, used in everyday talk, an expression of courtesy. It would have seemed disrespectful, indeed unthinkable, to the sensibilities of Jesus's contemporaries to address God with this familiar word.[20]

When Inoue read books by Jeremias after he had returned to Japan, he was very surprised because the conclusion of the renowned biblical scholar was the same as the way of the spiritual infant of St. Thérèse of Lisieux, who did not have any theological education. From that time on, *abba* became one of the most important concepts of Inoue's theology: "In the Epistle to the Galatians (4:6-7), St. Paul mentions as follows: 'And because you are sons, God has sent forth the Spirit *(pneuma)* of His Son into our hearts, crying, "*Abba!* Father!" Therefore you are no longer a slave, but a son; and if a son, then an heir through God.'"[21] As Inoue notes, the feeling that a slave has toward his master is one of fear of judgment and punishment. The God of the Old Testament is like such a master. He is a God of fatherly principle, full of anger, judgment, and terror. To the contrary, the feeling that an infant has in the arms of his or her father is one of peace, joy, and trust. The God of Jesus is like this father, who embraces all living things in his arms.[22] *Abba* is not a fatherly principle that represents order and might. Rather, it is something that embraces us and exists prior to the distinction of father and mother in the human sense.[23] And Jesus tried to teach us that the God who was *abba* for him is also *abba* for us all.[24]

Inoue developed this theme by combining it with another insight, concerning ontology and language. When a father embraces his child with his big arms, the father is not an object for the subject-child. Rather, the father embraces the child from behind.[25] Inoue divides words into two categories: words as labels by which one distinguishes an object from other objects (e.g., tree, rock, mountain, etc.), and words as cries of experience (e.g., Hurray! Alas! Ouch! etc.). When a child says *abba* to his or her father, it is more a cry of experience than a label. The main intention of the child is not to distinguish the father from other beings. Rather, the child is expressing the experience of union with the father in love and trust.[26] A child can enjoy a lively sense of fulfillment in such a situation because he or she has an unshakable sense of being protected. It is because the child thinks that he or she will never be forsaken by the father that he or she can play in peace and have self-confidence.[27] The sense of being watched over by a gentle gaze gives the child a sense of freedom.

The relationship between Jesus and God the Father was similar. When Jesus called God *abba*, it was not a mere label to distinguish him from other objects while Jesus stood outside God. It was not an abstract and objective concept to distinguish things. Rather, it was an expression of lively experience that could not be verbalized otherwise. Every experience is both an experience of the one who experiences it and an experience of something else. When Jesus called God *abba*, it was an invocation of something fundamental without which he could not be himself any longer.[28] *Abba* is not a word by which Jesus talks about God while he stands outside God but a verbalization of the lively experience of unity with God that Jesus experienced as his son.[29] God can never be objectified or conceptualized. In this sense, we can say that God is nothingness, beyond being and non-being in the ordinary sense.

Jesus expressed this joy of unity, saying, "All things have been handed over to Me by My Father; and no one knows the Son, except the Father; nor does anyone know the Father, except the Son, and anyone to whom the Son wills to reveal Him" (Matthew 11:27). In the Greek text, the word *epiginosko* is used for "to know." According to the article which Bultmann wrote in the *Theological Dictionary of the New Testament*, it is necessary for us to understand this word in the context of the Hebrew usage of the word *yada'* (to know). The connotation of the word *yada'* was not a mere objective cognition but a deep experiential cognition, just as when we usually say, "He does not know the real world yet."[30]

Elsewhere, Inoue writes that "religious cognition is not *theorein* ('objective cognition') but *yada'* ('experiential and subjective deep cognition')."[31]

According to Inoue, Jesus' move away from Judaism is expressed best by the fact that his prayers always began with the word *abba*.[32] The God in the Old Testament is a God of fatherly principle who is too holy to approach and who confronts people in a thundercloud as the God of hosts. In Judaism, people prayed using solemn and stiff prayers such as "Father, Lord of Heaven and Earth," "Our Shield," "The Shield of Our Ancestors," and so on. The Gospel of Matthew reports that Jesus followed the convention of Judaism and taught his disciples to start the prayer using "Our Father Who Art in Heaven." But according to Inoue, the people of the community of Matthew, who edited this gospel for the Jewish people, dared to adopt the Jewish convention lest the Jews were tripped up by the simple expression of *abba* and hindered from converting to Christianity. Although *abba* means "papa" or "daddy," it does not represent an authoritative, manly, fatherly papa but a papa with a motherly principle who cares even for the lilies of the field and the birds of the air. Such an understanding of God the Father as *abba* is the fundamental difference between the Old Testament and the New Testament.

The difference in the image of God between the Old Testament and the New Testament is very important in understanding the theology of Inoue.[33] He relates this difference to the climates under which these images of God were formed. He read the famous book *Climate and Culture* by Watsuji Tetsurō and applied his insight to his theory of the differences between the testaments. *Climate and Culture* was written as a critical response to Heidegger's *Sein und Zeit*. Watsuji thought that Heidegger overemphasized the temporality of human beings and underestimated spatiality. So he emphasized the influence of geography and climate on human culture. Inoue was inspired by Watsuji, especially by the idea of the receptivity of Japanese people to nature, which was very important to him. In Watsuji's scheme of things, Judaism, Christianity, and Islam belonged to the same category as religions of the desert. Inoue, however, made one important correction. He thought it necessary to distinguish Christianity from the other two religions.[34] Most of the prophets in the Old Testament were from the desert, wilderness, and rocky mountains. In these areas, nature was very severe, and life was under constant threat. There were no trees or plants in the desert. In the Dead Sea, there were no fish because of its dense salt.

Here nature overwhelms and rejects human beings. So, to protect the people from such severe nature, the God of Israel had to be so strong and so severe as to overwhelm it. On the other hand, Nazareth, where Jesus grew up, and the surrounding area of the Sea of Galilee, where he was engaged in his activities with his disciples, had a pastoral climate full of water and vegetation. And his disciples were fishermen in Galilee. This climate had a big influence on the image of the God of Jesus, who embraces everything with love and tenderness.[35] Although one should not over-emphasize the relationship between climates and cultures,[36] if Jesus was a full human being, it would be natural that his thought was influenced by the climate in which he grew up.

In accordance with his understanding of the New Testament God, Inoue composed a prayer called "The Prayer of the House of Pneuma":

Abba,
Our souls are stained by egoism,
Please wash and purify them by your *Pneuma* of *agape,*
The clouds in the sky, a small stream, and a single flower in the field, they are praying together,
Please make our prayers purified before you in line with their prayers,
Your Son Jesus started with accepting the weakness, imperfection, and sins of people without becoming judgmental,
Please bring our heart closer to his heart full of *agape,*
Your Son Jesus reflected and accepted the mind of the people who were trudging along their way of life full of burden and became friends with them,
Grant us a friendly mind by which we can reflect the mind of such people,
By accepting all the sufferings, sorrows, and joy from your hands,
May our daily life become the field of the operation of your *Pneuma* full of *agape,*
In the name of our Lord Jesus Christ, Amen.[37]

This prayer crystallizes the thought of Inoue. The essence of the activity and teaching of Jesus is seen as an acceptance of the weaknesses, imperfections, and sins of people, without making any judgment on those people. This is the essence of *agape,* the love of God. The human aspect of Jesus is empha-sized, and his communication with people, without judgment, is seen as the model for our own actions. Sorrowful aspects of human life are high-lighted, but the joy of life is not ignored. The operation of *pneuma* is con-spicuous. It works through the constellation of human relationships, a whole that is unfathomable by human intellect. Here it is interesting that Inoue does not use the usual Japanese term *seirei* for the translation of *pneuma*. He uses the word *ibuki*, which means "inspiration," "expiration," "vitality," "animation," and "energy." This word connotes some vital energy of nature. Finally, the theory of the field, which I take up in more detail below, is introduced. This prayer is a beautiful crystallization of the living faith of Inoue.

He began to write many poems from the middle of the 1990s, among them many simple prayers to *Abba*. As Inoue grew older, his thought became less abstract. He stopped using philosophical terms extensively and started writing religious poems in an easy-to-read Japanese. I introduce a representative, "The Prayer of *Namu Abba*":

Abba, Abba,
Namu Abba,
Accompanied by Jesus,
Shaking hands with all animate beings,
Embraced by the *Pneuma,*
Abba, Abba,
Namu Abba.[38]

Compared with the prayer cited earlier, this one is extremely simple.[39] Although it is short and devoid of any explanatory remarks, it represents Inoue's understanding of the Trinity. At the same time, it expresses his fellowship with nature. For an English-speaking person, the word *namu* must sound totally unfamiliar. For an ordinary Japanese person, it is not unfamiliar, but the combination *namu abba* is quite unfamiliar. Japanese usually use *namu* as part of Buddhist prayers, the most famous expressions of which are *namu amidabutsu* and *namu myōhō rengekyō*.[40] *Namu* is a transliteration of the Sanskrit word *namas*, which means "to submit oneself," "to devote oneself," and "to bend down." It also means "hail to," "praise be," et cetera. So it can be understood to mean converting and entrusting oneself to something else. Inoue uses the combination *namu abba* to express the meaning of entrusting everything to *Abba* and submitting ourselves completely to *Abba*.[41]

In a sense, this expression is redundant, for the word *abba* includes wholehearted dedication to the father. Inoue is aware of this redundancy. When he prays, he sometimes attaches *namu* to *abba*, according to his mood at the moment.[42] When he is depressed or has some serious appeal to God, he seldom utters *namu abba* but says only *abba* deeply and slowly. But when he is in a good mood and prays as he watches the shiny green leaves of the trees or the blue sky and white clouds, he is inclined to utter *namu abba*. When he prays rhythmically *Abba, Abba, namu Abba,* he feels that the cosmic rhythm of the *Pneuma* embraces him with Jesus and leads him to *Abba*. The combination of *namu* and *abba* seems to give a feeling of lightness to his prayers.[43]

Agape and the Tender Gaze of Jesus

Although Inoue is acquainted with European biblical studies, his interpretation of the Bible is sometimes not literal. It is based on his original psychological insight and imagination. Thus, his Christology is not an abstract rational construct but a concrete image of Christ based on his own religious experience.

Inoue's understanding of Jesus is expressed by his translation of the Greek word *agape* into Japanese as *hiai*. Inoue coined this word through the influence of the Buddhist concept *jihi,* which is composed of two Chinese characters: *ji* means "a love by which one gives others some benefit or comfort," and *hi* means "a sympathy by which one feels compassion toward the sufferings of others." In the *Tendai* sect of Buddhism, *ji* is compared with fatherly love, and *hi* is compared with motherly love.[44]

Inoue coined the word *hiai* by combining this *hi* with *ai,* which means "love." But in Buddhism, *ai* generally does not have a positive connotation. It means a blind impulse of human existence: passionate desire, obsession, and earthly passion. In contemporary Japanese, however, the word usually has a positive connotation, like the English word *love*. By combining these two Chinese characters, Inoue expressed the idea that *agape* is not a passionate love for something attractive but a compassionate love for something (someone) pitiful and ephemeral. In the Greek language, two kinds of love besides *agape* are known, one of which is *eros*, "a passionate love for something attractive," and the other of which is *philia*. *Philia* refers to a mutual friendly relationship based on some common values. *Philia* seems to be very good. But if someone cannot share a relationship's common value, he must be expelled from it. Both *eros* and *philia* are loves by which one pursues value, and one does not even cast a glance toward the worthless, the ugly, and the miserable. To the contrary, *agape* is a love by which one puts oneself in somebody else's place and rejoices with those who rejoice and weeps with those who weep (Romans 12:15), with an innocent mind.[45] It is a love by which one gives sympathetic and compassionate help even to the worthless, the miserable, and the suffering, just like the sun that shines on all living things without exception.[46]

Inoue points to the practice and preaching of Jesus as the typical expression of *hiai (agape)*. It was almost always Jesus who started the exchange of words between himself and weak people.[47] The gospels are the stories of conversions of the disciples and other people under Jesus' tender gaze of forgiveness. Jesus completely changed the lives of the people whom he met. Where did this power come from? Rational, objective cognition by itself does not change people.[48] Although terror and threats can subjugate people, they do not have enough power to change people in a true sense. People are changed only when they feel that their weakness, cowardliness, and ugliness are forgiven; then they experience a profound impact in the depths of their consciousness.[49] Toward the end of the Gospel of Luke (24:36-53), the resurrected Jesus appears in the midst of the disciples and says to them, "peace be to you." The disciples are startled and become frightened. Why do they become frightened? According to Luke, they think that they are seeing a ghost. But Inoue does not think that this was the main reason for their fright.

Let me reconstruct his original speculations on this point. In an intimate human relationship, Inoue notes, it is heartbreaking when one is betrayed. But what is more unbearable is the sense of guilt that one has betrayed someone because of self-love or weakness.[50] All the disciples of Jesus betrayed him when he was arrested. Earlier Peter said, "even if I have to die with You, I will not deny You!" (Mark 14:31). But then he denied Jesus three times. After the death of Jesus, the disciples were all in a state of panic and despair because of an unendurable self-hatred, a loss of hope in the future, and a sense of guilt over their betrayal.[51] So, when the resurrected Jesus appeared to them suddenly, they were afraid of resentment and punishment.[52] But Jesus did not say anything reproachful and went as far as to eat a fish in front of them. It was then that the disciples felt a sense of relief. They felt that they were forgiven and accepted. When Jesus was alive, he had taught and practised acceptance of the weaknesses, imperfections, and sins of people without becoming judgmental. The disciples realized the true meaning of it when they met the gentle gaze of the resurrected Jesus, who embraced their ugliness, filthiness, weakness, and cowardliness as manifested in their betrayal of him and forgave them.[53] Thus, the disciples were embraced and changed by the tender gaze of Jesus, the incarnation of the tender, forgiving gaze of *Abba*.[54] In this manner, the disciples realized that Jesus, a companion to those who had encountered him in Palestine while he was alive, became by his resurrection the eternal companion of all people who trudge along wearily with heavy burdens on their shoulders.[55]

If the essence of *agape (hiai)* is compassion in the sense that one shares the passion (suffering) of others, then it is natural that Jesus, who lived the utmost degree of *agape*, had to face the most miserable death, for only then could he be capable of sharing the sorrow and suffering of all people as their eternal companion. And it is important to pay attention to the fact that this interpretation of Jesus as an eternal companion is presented in a tender image, even though the passion of Jesus is included. Inoue contrasted his thought with that of the Protestant theologian Kitamori Kazoh (1916-98), whose *Theology of the Pain of God* is one of the few Japanese Christian theological works known outside Japan.[56] Kitamori presented his work as a criticism of the traditional teaching of the impassibility of God *(impassibilitas Dei)*. Although Kitamori thought that there was some affinity between his concept of pain and the concept of *hiai (agape)* put forth by Inoue, the latter emphasized differences between them. He confessed that he felt suffocated when he read Kitamori's book. He felt a sense of discomfort with Kitamori's doctrine that the essence of God is pain.[57] For Inoue, pain *(itami)* is not the property of God *(Abba)* but the property of Jesus, who forgave and embraced the disciples who had betrayed him. And both the pain of Jesus and the sorrow of the disciples were embraced by the tender light of the evening sun, *Abba*. It is true that Jesus embraced those who betrayed him even as his blood was shed on the cross.[58] But the agony of the cross itself was embraced from behind by *Abba*, whose calm silence was like the autumn sky.[59] The embrace of *Abba* gave the suffering of Jesus a kind of tenderness. The whole stage of human tragedy (including Jesus) is surrounded and embraced by the tender gaze of *Abba*. Thus, the *agape (hiai)* of Jesus embraces Man, and the *agape (hiai)* of Abba embraces Jesus. Man is thus embraced by a twofold tender gaze of love.

Inoue offers a poetic and aesthetic metaphor of Jesus. It is called "the window glass theory." He compares Jesus to a glass window and explains the special function of Jesus as mediator between God *(Abba)* and Man. Although a window is one of the features of a room, it is decisively different from other decorations or furnishings. Desks, chairs, and paintings have their own specific functions. But unlike a window, they cannot bring the light of the sun into the room. Similarly, Jesus was human, but he was different from other humans in that he was able to bring the light of the gentle gaze of *Abba* into this world.[60] In this beautiful metaphor, we can find the characteristics proper to Inoue's understanding of Jesus. Jesus was a transparent being like a window. He was so transparent and so open to *Abba* that those who saw him were able to see *Abba* himself (see John 14:9). He was the mediator between *Abba* and Man.

But the metaphor does not end there. Inoue continues it to its culmination in the passion of Christ:

> The master [Jesus], to be sure, brought the light of *Abba* unto us, unto all animate beings during his lifetime. But if the window glass is not broken, the outside wind *(pneuma)* of *Abba* cannot enter into the room and embrace the whole room warmly. It was why Master Jesus had to break himself on the cross to bring about the glory and embrace of *Abba* unto us, unto all animate beings. Only after Master Jesus, who was the incarnation of the gentle gaze of *Abba*, died a death full of suffering, disappointment, and humiliation on the cross, the *pneuma* blew through the bottom of all the animate beings, and the work of *Abba* was accomplished.[61]

Although not a rational explanation or an abstract theory of the Passion of Christ, it is amazing that Inoue was able to convey the meaning of the life and death of Jesus in such a simple metaphor. Although not a logical explanation of the mystery of the Passion, it can give us some essential intuition concerning the original experience of the salvation of the disciples. The embrace of the wind *(pneuma)* is very warm. But it is mediated by the brokenness of the window glass (Jesus). The warm wind that embraces all of us is filled with grief and sorrow. This metaphor inspires us to contemplate further the mystery of faith. And it draws our attention to another key concept put forth by Inoue: *pneuma.*

As I noted above, Inoue established a small Catholic community in Tokyo and named it the House of Pneuma. *Pneuma* is one of his most important concepts. As he points out, the Greek word *pneuma* has three meanings: "wind," "breath," and "spirit."[62] He often cites the famous passage of John 3:8: "The wind *(pneuma)* blows where it wishes and you hear the sound of it, but do not know where it comes from and where it is going; so is everyone who is born of the Spirit *(pneuma)*." And he translates Galatians 5:16 (Walk by the Spirit) as "live your life by submitting yourself completely to *pneuma*." Although it is not a literal translation of the Greek scripture, it represents the spirituality of Inoue. He cites a famous Japanese poem *(tanka)* that helps us to understand this spirituality: "Although I do not see the arrival of autumn clearly with my eyes, I have become aware of it by the sound of the wind." The poet could not find evidence of the arrival of autumn by the active operation of his own eyes, but he suddenly became aware of it when he became receptive to the sound of the wind. Similarly, Inoue maintains that we cannot find God by the active operation of our own intellect. We cannot find God as an object in front of us. But when we stop searching for

God actively and busily and stand still, we feel the breeze *(pneuma)* of God that embraces us tenderly from behind.[63]

Inoue often cites another famous Japanese poem *(haiku):* "A maple leaf falls, / casually showing / one side and the other." This poem is the swan song of Ryōkan (1758-1831), a Japanese Zen Buddhist monk. The falling maple leaf shows not only its obverse side but also its reverse side. It does not try to hide its reverse side. If it goes against *pneuma*, it might be torn to pieces. But when the falling maple leaf resigns itself completely to *pneuma*, it expresses not itself but the wind that moves it. And paradoxically enough, by submitting itself to *pneuma*, it attains its utmost beauty. It is a natural and carefree beauty. Similarly, if a man sticks to himself and goes against the breath of *pneuma*, there will be nothing but an irritating, uneasy, and discordant life. But when we get in touch with the life of a carefree man who submits himself to the large stream of *pneuma*, we can see its flow in the depth of his life.[64] And the life of Jesus was a typical expression of it.

The Mystical Body of Christ: An Alternative to Individualism and Anthropocentrism

According to Inoue, the basis of the Japanese way of thinking is not identical with that of the European way of thinking, which, since ancient Greece, has been based on substance and the individual. In Japanese culture, relationality and field are fundamental, and substance is contained within them.[65] In this sense, the Japanese way of thinking is, Inoue concludes, more comparable to the anthropology of St. Paul than to the European way of thinking.[66] In this section, I will concentrate mainly on his concepts of relationality and field by analyzing the concept of the mystical body of Christ, which ultimately is derived from St. Paul but which, like so many of his key concepts, he borrowed from the work of a European scholar, in this case Emile Mersch.[67] But as always, he developed it in his own way. We tend to think that each person lives his own life as a separate being and then meets someone accidentally as he pursues his way of life. According to St. Paul, however, it is not the case at all. Although each organ of the body performs a separate function, we are kept alive by one larger life, stamped with its hallmark, and are thus interrelated to each other. Likewise, each of our particular existences is kept alive and stamped by the single big operation of life, which he called the life of Christ. We are related to each other in the field of Christ from long before we meet in the course of life (cf. 1 Corinthians 12:14-27).[68]

Thus, all beings are relational beings. They can also be said to be responsive and dependent beings, for they are responding to, and depending on, each other, which is the case not only for human relations – all animate and inanimate beings are related in the field of Christ. Similarly, in a magnetic field, a magnet creates relationships between grains of magnetic sand. Even though each grain of sand in a magnetic field is distinct, they all exist in a mutual relationship facilitated by that field.

When Inoue studied in France, the standard interpretation of this passage from 1 Corinthians was that it referred to the different functions within the Church. But he thought that this metaphor of the body is not limited to the relationship between the individual and the Church or between the individual and society. Rather, the essence of this metaphor is grasped by referring to the relationship between the existence of each of us and Christ.[69] And what is characteristic of Inoue is that he includes not only human beings but also all animate beings in this relationship. Thus, he found an alternative to what he deemed European individualism, which emphasized the opposition between one individual and another individual and the opposition between humans and nature (anthropocentrism).

Although Inoue emphasizes the relational aspect of every being, he does not discard the reality of substance as mere illusion or fiction. He criticizes the tendency in Oriental thought to deny the reality of substance. For example, the Islamic philosopher Ibn Arabī believed that the whole world is a manifestation of some ultimate metaphysical being. Although this theory has some superficial similarities with the thinking of St. Paul, there is a fundamental difference for Inoue. In the theory of Ibn Arabī, everything (and everyone) disappears into the ultimate being and is then recaptured as manifestations of the ultimate being. Ibn Arabī has little space for the substantiality of each individual, namely, the ordinary individuals who suffer from distress, loneliness, and grief. For Inoue, human pain and loneliness should not be apprehended as mere phenomena. In the metaphor of St. Paul, an eye does not lose its substantiality by being absorbed into the life ("the field") of Christ. So, for Inoue, this is not a question of a mysticism in which all the otherness and substantiality of each being are absorbed into some ultimate reality. The metaphor of the mystery of the body of Christ includes the mind of the historical Jesus, who stressed the importance of *agape*, by which one accepts the pain and loneliness of every individual as one's own pain.

For Inoue, the key point is that the resurrection of Jesus means that the mind of Jesus was accepted by *Abba*. And the acceptance of Jesus by *Abba* is a sign of the acceptance of all people by *Abba*. According to St. Paul, "now Christ has been raised from the dead, the first fruits of those who are asleep. For since by a man came death, by a man also came the resurrection of the dead. For as in Adam all die, so also in Christ all will be made alive" (1 Corinthians 15:20-22). Also, "if the first piece of dough is holy, the lump is also; and if the root is holy, the branches are too" (Romans 11:16). These statements of St. Paul make sense only when we presuppose the theory of the body of Christ. Inoue calls this theory of St. Paul "The Theory of the First Fruits."

In the New Testament, there are several different explanations of the salvation of humans by the life of Christ. How should we understand this multiplicity? Inoue cites the statement of Karl Rahner:

> If the death of Jesus is understood this way, then perhaps it becomes clear that its soteriological significance when correctly understood is already implied in the experience of the resurrection of Jesus ... which is simply this: we are saved because this man who is one of us has been saved by God, and God has thereby made his salvific will present in the world historically, really and irrevocably. On this point too there follows for the New Testament and for later theology, as history shows, the possibility in principle of a variety of legitimate models for soteriology.[70]

According to Inoue, if we try to express this original experience in Japanese, it is difficult to accept the propitiation theory that explains the significance of the death of Jesus by superimposing onto it the practice of animal sacrifice in the Old Testament (cf. Hebrews 9:25-26), because the religion of the Old Testament is not easy for ordinary Japanese today to understand. Nor does he adopt the redemption theory that presupposes the slavery and redemption of captives that were characteristic features of the Hellenistic world (cf. Mark 10:45; Romans 3:24). The theory of vicariousness is also hard to accept, for it presupposes a concept of the curse of the law (cf. Galatians 3:13) that is not easy for us today to understand with any depth. Finding problems with all of these interpretive theories, Inoue ultimately arrives at "The Theory of the First Fruits" outlined above.

Conclusion: Theology in Japan in a Global Context

As I stated above, Inoue tried to inculturate Christianity into Japanese culture. But it does not mean that he integrated some aspects of Christianity that were incompatible with his sensitivity with a Japanese traditional culture with which he was familiar. On the contrary, as Inoue continued trying to assimilate Catholicism, he gradually became aware of his own background (i.e., he became aware of his ignorance of his own background).

Only after he went to France did Inoue become interested in Japanese culture. He encountered European culture in France and then noticed how different he was from Europeans. And at the same time, he gradually noticed how ignorant he was concerning Japanese culture even though he was Japanese and was living in the midst of the Japanese cultural tradition.[71] This was the starting point of his activity of inculturation. It was his deep desire to accept Christianity with his whole being that awoke his identity as a Japanese.

As Inoue grew older, his thought became more rooted in what he considered traditional Japanese culture. But at the same time, as we saw above, most of his basic insights into the theory and practice of inculturation were derived from Europeans: St. Thérèse of Lisieux, Henri de Lubac, Henri Bergson, Joachim Jeremias, Emile Mersch, and so on. So we should take his theory of inculturation of Christianity in Japan as an invitation to discard the European (Greek-Latin) elements of Christianity completely. His interesting theory and practice of inculturation came into existence only because he was thrown into a cultural gap and experienced internal conflict over this matter for many years.

At the outset of this chapter, I cited a statement by Karl Löwith on Japanese culture. Actually, his judgment on Japanese culture is more severe than the section cited suggests. Consider what he says in the paragraph preceding the one cited earlier:

> The way in which the Japanese, for the most part, accept European thought seems doubtful to us, insofar as we cannot regard it as genuine assimilation. The students certainly study our European books with dedication, and thanks to their intelligence, they understand them; but they fail to draw any consequences from them for their own Japanese identity. They do not make distinctions or comparisons between European terms, such as will, freedom, and spirit, and corresponding concepts in their own life, thought and speech, or where they differ from them.[72]

If we reverse this critical comment, we can get the correct image of Inoue's practice of inculturation. Namely, Inoue integrated Christian concepts, most of which were derived from Europe, with corresponding Japanese concepts and sensitivities drawn from his own life as a Japanese Catholic. Although the balance between Europe and Japan has changed gradually over the course of his life, this effort at cultural integration was the *basso continuo* of his lifelong work.

When Inoue started to construct a Japanese-flavoured theology, he characterized it as panentheism. This means that he used a European philosophical concept to express his Japanese-flavoured idea. In the later stage of his life, his thought became less abstract. And Inoue gradually discarded the philosophically abstract concepts from his thought and began to use traditional Japanese vocabulary. His continuous reappropriation of Japanese tradition moved in the direction of a de-Hellenization of his Christianity. Yet one consequence of his de-Hellenization effort is the lack of a social dimension to his thought. His theology fails to include almost any social theory. Inoue recognizes the problem of human sorrow, but the social problems that cause such sorrow are not taken up; indeed, they are treated as if they are inevitable natural phenomena. We must supplement his theology with some theory of active social commitment.[73]

It is important to emphasize that Inoue does not have an essentialist understanding of Japanese culture that cherishes the illusion that there is a pure Japanese culture out there somewhere. We must not overlook the fact that the representative expression of his Japanese-flavoured theology, *namu abba* (a combination of Sanskrit and Aramaic), is itself derived from places outside Japan. Ironically, his "Japanese mentality" led him to coin a vocabulary that does not originate from Japan. Inoue intended not to construct an abstract doctrine of a *Japanese* Christianity but sincerely to try to integrate Christianity with his own sensitivity, most (but not all) of which was derived from Japanese tradition. He says that he hopes his efforts at integration will be useful not only for himself but also for other Japanese people.[74] But I do not find any reason to limit the legitimacy of his theology to Japanese. His thinking seems to be based more on the general situation of human beings today than on a specific Japanese culture.[75]

Inoue's work on inculturation leaves us with a dilemma: if Japanese stop learning many important legacies of Western Christianity, then no inculturation or creative reinterpretation of Christianity can come about. The theory of inculturation has to be supplemented by a theory of interculturation, as it were.[76] Or perhaps we should simply say that Inoue's theory itself is the product of his intercultural experience. His theology should be described not as a "Japanese theology," which restricts its applicability to the Japanese people, but as a "theology in Japan": that is, a theology made by a Japanese person living in the cultural milieu of contemporary Japan, which means in our global intercultural context.[77]

Notes

1 Cited in Furuya, "Introduction," in *A History of Japanese Theology*, 4-5.
2 English translations of their work include Kadowaki, *Zen and the Bible*, and Okumura, *Awakening to Prayer*.
3 Inoue, *Namu no kokoro ni ikiru*, 187. The words *maternal principle* and *paternal principle* in the writings of Inoue and Endō are derived from the work of Professor Kawai Hayao (1928-2007), a leading Jungian psychoanalyst in Japan. See Kawai, *Buddhism and the Art of Psychotherapy*, and *Japanese Psyche*.
4 St. Thérèse of Lisieux, *Story of a Soul*.
5 Sister Geneviève de la Sainte Face, *A Memoir of My Sister, St. Thérèse*.
6 Inoue, *Namu no kokoro ni ikiru*, 173-74; Inoue, *Yohaku no tabi*, 53.
7 Inoue, *Yohaku no tabi*, 62-63. Inoue notes that the languages spoken in many convents in the Orient at that time were not the native languages of those countries but European languages such as English, French, and so on.
8 Ibid., 123-24.
9 Inoue, *Namu no kokoro ni ikiru*, 190.
10 Inoue, *The Face of Jesus in Japan*, 23-24. I have modified citations from this translation.
11 Inoue, *Yohaku no tabi*, 26-29.
12 He was also influenced by Japanese prominent psychologists such as Kawai Hayao, Okonogi Keigo (1930-2003), Kimura Bin (b. 1931), Shimoyama Tokuji (b. 1919), and Doi Takeo (1920-2009).
13 Inoue, *Hōnen*, 107.
14 Inoue, afterword in *Nihon to Iesu no kao*, 247. The English translation does not include the afterword.
15 Inoue, *The Face of Jesus in Japan*, 30-31.
16 Inoue, *Yohaku no tabi*, 211-12.
17 I learned much concerning this debate from Ratzinger (Pope Benedict XVI), *Truth and Tolerance*.
18 Inoue, *Hōnen*, 107-9.
19 Of course, there are other important concepts (e.g., the Kingdom of God, eternal life, etc.), but I think that they are subsumed in these three basic concepts of Inoue's theology.
20 Jeremias, *New Testament Theology*, 66-67; Inoue, *Waga shi Iesu no shōgai*, 77-78.
21 I use the New American Standard Bible when I cite the English Bible in this chapter.
22 Inoue, *Namu no kokoro ni ikiru*, 192-93.
23 Inoue, *Iesu no manazashi*, 218.
24 Inoue, *The Face of Jesus in Japan*, 83.
25 Inoue, *Namu no kokoro ni ikiru*, 126-27.
26 Inoue, *The Face of Jesus in Japan*, 110.
27 Ibid., 203-4; also Inoue, *Yohaku no tabi*, 13-14. He got this insight from the book by the Japanese psychologist Shomoyama Tokuji, who is Catholic.
28 Inoue, *The Face of Jesus in Japan*, 110.
29 Ibid., 79.
30 Ibid., 80-81.
31 Inoue, *Yohaku no tabi*, 211-12.
32 It is debatable whether we should call the religion of the Old Testament before the time of Jesus by the name of Judaism. But I will follow the usage of Inoue. Inoue, *Waga shi Iesu no shōgai*, 77.

33   The Catholic Church has rather emphasized the continuity of the Old Testament and the New Testament. In the Sunday Mass, the Old Testament is read along with the New Testament. This mode of reading led the believers to think they had equal value. I had to be careful in my remarks. I expressed my opinion gradually to avoid being regarded as heretical and being excommunicated. But when I thought about the life of Hōnen, I was made aware of my weakness, slyness, and slovenliness.

Inoue, *Namu no kokoro ni ikiru*, 194. There are some scholars who criticize Inoue's view on the Old Testament as a kind of Marcionism. Although I myself do not fully agree with his view, I will introduce it without any criticism in this chapter, for my main purpose of this chapter is to introduce the theology of Father Inoue as it is.

34   Many Islamic scholars characterize Islam as a religion of the city, but I will follow the opinion of Inoue.

35   Inoue, *The Face of Jesus in Japan*, 82.

36   Inoue, *Yohaku no tabi*, 125-33.

37   The House of Pneuma is a small community that Inoue organized in Tokyo for the inculturation of Christianity in Japan. He began this movement in 1986 with some university students after he got the approval of the archbishop of Tokyo. He wanted to shift from parish work to work where he could bring the gospel to people outside the Church. The House of Pneuma has a quarterly magazine called *Pneuma*. See Inoue, *Namu no kokoro ni ikiru*, 192-93; and Inoue, *Yohaku no tabi*, 247.

38   Inoue, *Namu Abba*, 130-31.

39   Although Inoue translated *pneuma* as *ibuki* in "The Prayer of the House of Pneuma," in "The Prayer of Namu Abba" he translated it as *omikazesama*. Both *ibuki* and *omi-kazesama* are different from the ordinary translation of this word, which is *seirei* ("the Holy Spirit"). *Seirei* is composed of two Chinese characters and sounds very abstract. Although Inoue partly uses Chinese characters to express these two concepts, they are used as *kun* readings (a native Japanese reading of a Chinese character), so they sound very tender and arouse vivid images. But there is some difference even between *ibuki* and *omikazesama*. *Ibuki* is an ordinary word of Japanese origin. But *omikazesama* is a word coined by Inoue. *Omi* is a prefix for expressing respect, *kaze* means "wind," and *sama* has two functions here, one to express respect and familiarity, the other to personify *kaze*. So *omikazesama* is, as it were, a respectful personification of wind with a nuance of familiarity.

40   *Namu amidabutsu* is a prayer that people in the True Pure Land sect of Buddhism *(Jōdo shinshū)* use often when they pray. *Amidabutsu* is a kind of Buddha that those people admire. *Namu myōhō rengekyō* is a word of prayer that the people in the *Nichiren* sect of Buddhism use when they pray. *Myōhō rengekyō* is a Buddhist scripture *(sutra)* that they deem most important.

41   Inoue, *Namu no kokoro ni ikiru*, 201. Inoue learned the exact meaning of this word from Nakamura, *Iwanami bukkyō jiten*. Nakamura was one of the most authoritative scholars on Buddhism and Eastern thought in Japan. See Nakamura, *Ways of Thinking of Eastern Peoples*.

42   Inoue, *Namu no kokoro ni ikiru*, 201.

43   Inoue, *Namu Abba*, 172-73.

44   See Nakamura et al., eds., *Iwanami bukkyō jiten*.

45   Inoue, *The Face of Jesus in Japan*, 165. Editor's note: For a sense of the importance of *agape, eros*, and *philia* in Catholic thought, see Pope Benedict XVI, "Deus Caritas Est."

46   Inoue, *The Face of Jesus in Japan*, 163.

47   For examples, see Inoue, *Waga shi Iesu no shōgai*, 189-94.

48 Inoue, *Namu no kokoro ni ikiru,* 44.
49 Inoue, *Waga shi Iesu no shōgai,* 186.
50 Inoue, *Watakushi no naka no Kirisuto,* 153.
51 Inoue, *Waga shi Iesu no shōgai,* 192.
52 Inoue, *Kirisutokyō ga yoku wakaru hon,* 68.
53 Inoue, *Watakushi no naka no Kirisuto,* 154.
54 Inoue, *Waga shi Iesu no shōgai,* 190.
55 Inoue, "Kaisetsu," in Endō, *Shikai no hotori,* 351-56; Inoue, *Yohaku no tabi,* 245.
56 Kitamori, *Theology of the Pain of God.* See Furuya, ed. and trans., *A History of Japanese Theology,* 86-89. Kitamori's theology influenced J. Moltmann, H. Küng, and others.
57 I do not intend to present a systematic interpretation of Kitamori's theology of pain here. Although one of the chapters of his book is called "Pain as the Essence of God," after Kitamori was criticized for propounding patripassianism, he stated that his concept of the pain of God is not a concept of substance but a concept of relation. That is, it is the nature of the love (relation) of God toward humans, not his essence. His position is somewhat ambiguous. See "Preface to the Fifth Edition," in Kitamori, *Theology of the Pain of God,* 15-16. What is important for the purpose of this chapter is to understand the difference between the theology of Inoue and the theology of Kitamori as understood by Inoue.
58 Toda, ed., *Nihon katorishizumu to bungaku,* 191-212.
59 Inoue and Sako, *Pauro o kataru,* 186-90.
60 Inoue, *Waga shi Iesu no shōgai,* 200-1.
61 Ibid.
62 Inoue, *Yohaku no tabi,* 223.
63 Inoue, *Kirisutokyō ga yoku wakaru hon,* 112-13.
64 Inoue, *The Face of Jesus in Japan,* 116-17.
65 See Furuya, ed. and trans., *A History of Japanese Theology,* 136. The ordinary Japanese word for human being is *ningen.* This word is interesting, for *nin* itself means "human being" and *gen* means "between." So, *ningen* means "between man and man." People usually think that each man exists as a separate being and then enters into relationships with other people. But the word *ningen* connotes that a man can be a man only because he is always already posited in the midst of other men. Watsuji created his ethics by analyzing this concept and trying to overcome European individualism. Cf. Watsuji, *Ningen no gaku to shite no rinrigaku.*
66 Inoue, *Yohaku no tabi,* 236.
67 See Mersch, *The Theology of the Mystical Body.*
68 Inoue, *Yohaku no tabi,* 234-35. This metaphor is derived from Yagi, *Kirisutokyō wa shinjiuru ka.*
69 Although Mersch's book was a historical study and not a theoretical one, Mersch emphasized that the real meaning of the mystical body of Christ is *filii in Filio* (the sons of God in the Son of God, Jesus Christ). This phrase inspired Inoue's thoughts on the subject.
70 Rahner, *Foundations of Christian Faith,* 284.
71 Inoue, *Yohaku no tabi,* 123.
72 Löwith, cited by Furuya, "Introduction," in Furuya, ed. and trans., *A History of Japanese Theology,* 4.
73 The emphasis on the non-intellectual (experiential) element of faith, also one of the consequences of de-Hellenization, entails some problems too. There are many Japanese people who do not believe in Christianity because they think it against reason. In other words, they have intellectual questions against Christianity. I am not sure if the Japanese-flavoured Christianity of Inoue, which has sensitive and

experiential characteristics, can give any answer to these people. On the other hand, there are many Japanese people who do not have any religious interest. Their indifference to Christianity is not because they think Christianity is a Western religion but because they simply are not interested in religious matters. I am not sure if the Japanese-flavoured Christianity of Inoue can give any answer to those people either.

74 Inoue, "Kaze ni yudanete: Nihon bunka no uchinaru fukuin no kaika o motomete."

75 Although *namu abba* is original to Inoue, we can find the combination of *abba* and the theme of acceptance and intimacy in the English-speaking world too. Cf. Manning, *Abba's Child;* Underhill, *Practical Mysticism;* and Wilson, *Into Abba's Arms.*

76 On interculturality as a necessary supplement to "inculturation," see Ratzinger, *Truth and Tolerance,* especially 64-79.

77 See Furuya, ed. and trans., *A History of Japanese Theology.*

9

Between Inculturation and Globalization: The Situation of Catholicism in Contemporary Japanese Society

Mark R. Mullins

For the past two decades, I have been engaged in the sociological study of religious minorities in modern Japan, particularly new religious movements and indigenous forms of Christianity. This chapter represents a preliminary attempt to extend my comparative studies and observations to the Catholic Church within the broad framework of two important processes, namely, inculturation and globalization. As someone relatively new to this field of research, I can highlight here only some prominent features of the Catholic Church in contemporary Japan and identify some significant trends that have become apparent over the past two decades.

Although my primary concern here is with the situation of the Catholic Church, it is worth noting that all religious organizations in contemporary Japan share many problems. Some are related to basic demographic realities – the low birth rate and an aging population. Religious organizations depend on natural growth, which is based on births to members and effective religious socialization. A fertility rate below 2.1 points to population decline, and Japan's birth rate declined to 1.25 in 2005. It is not surprising to find that almost all churches and religious groups are struggling to maintain participation by children and youth in this difficult situation.

In addition to these demographic realities, religious organizations are operating today in an environment in which the majority of Japanese look on them with a great deal of suspicion. These negative attitudes toward organized religion have undoubtedly been cultivated by the media coverage of deviant behaviour, financial scandals, high-profile court cases, and incidents of violence related to religious groups during the postwar period. Survey research has shown that the majority of Japanese today regard religious institutions as untrustworthy, gloomy, closed, and increasingly dangerous *(abunai)* – especially since the sarin gas attack on the Tokyo subway system by Aum Shinrikyō followers in 1995. This is the broader context in which we must understand the particular situation of the Catholic Church in Japan. Following a brief historical overview, the chapter focuses on trends and developments that characterize the situation of the Catholic Church today.

Historical Overview since the End of World War II

The development of the Catholic Church in postwar Japan has been framed by the fundamental changes in the political and legal system that resulted from Japan's defeat on 15 August 1945 and the arrival of the occupation forces. Within several months, the Supreme Commander of the Allied Powers (SCAP) issued the Directive for the Disestablishment of State Shinto (15 December 1945) and set in motion policies that effectively reduced Shinto to the status of a voluntary organization without special legal authority or financial support from the state. Articles 20 and 89 of the postwar Constitution of Japan (1947) clearly articulated the principle of religious freedom and the separation of religion and state. This new legal and political system created a free-market religious economy that allowed diverse religious groups to compete on a relatively level playing field for the first time in Japanese history.

Although the new political conditions created a favourable environment for Christian churches, the early postwar years were difficult. Many churches had been destroyed, and the Catholic Church had lost some 8,500 members from the bomb dropped on Nagasaki alone. Under MacArthur's occupation government, however, the rebuilding work of Christian churches was generally supported, and various missions received assistance with the shipment of relief supplies and religious materials. The administrators of the occupation also co-operated fully with the efforts of various churches to send personnel to assist with the postwar recovery. In fact, 326 foreign priests were admitted into Japan between 1946 and 1947. In addition to the influx of priests, some 700 foreign sisters arrived between 1946 and the end of the occupation in 1952. At this time, the ratio of foreign to native priests was approximately four to one.[1]

In the decade between 1948 and 1958, membership in the Catholic Church more than doubled from 111,209 to 227,063. This rate of growth levelled off, however, and it took another four decades for membership to double again. David Barrett notes that a relatively high annual growth rate of 10.4 percent in 1951 fell to 7.9 percent in 1953, initiating a trend that by 1971 had skidded to only 0.34 percent.[2] According to Jan Swyngedouw, the postwar Catholic growth transformed the composition and position of "two types of believers" within the Church, whom he referred to as the "Nagasaki Christians" and the "new" converts. The former refers to the descendants of the earliest converts from the premodern Kirishitan period who were rediscovered by missionaries in 1865 and grew to become the initial base and fastest-growing area of the Catholic Church in modern Japan. The latter refers to the converts who entered the Church in urban areas, particularly Tokyo and Osaka, and who by 1985 outnumbered Catholics of the Nagasaki Diocese. Swyngedouw characterizes these two types in rather broad strokes. Nagasaki Catholics are largely drawn from the lower classes, tend to be conservative and pietistic, and for the most part are willing to submit to an authoritarian Church hierarchy. The new converts in urban areas, in contrast, are largely drawn from the middle class and tend to be more open to renewal and change in the Church, such as a more significant role for the laity.[3] The rather modest growth that occurred over the last quarter of the twentieth century was concentrated in the urban areas and increased the percentage of the second type of believer. As of 2005, the Catholic Church reported a membership of 476,013. Combined with Protestant and Orthodox Christians, the total number of Japanese belonging to a Christian church of any kind is 1,138,752, which constitutes 0.892 percent of the population – a rather meagre return on the many years of missionary investments.[4]

Inculturation and the Making of a Japanese Church

As latecomers to Japan's religious scene, both Catholicism and Protestantism have experienced considerable difficulty in shedding their reputations as foreign religions. Although at times the "Westernness" of Christianity has contributed to its appeal among Japanese, for the most part it has been viewed as a problem. In fact, the relative failure of Christianity in Japan has often been blamed on its Eurocentric orientation and the clash of the Church's exclusivist teachings with traditional Japanese religiosity. The process whereby "foreign" (in this case Western) and seemingly irrelevant religions become meaningful and rooted in local culture is referred to by terms such as indigenization, inculturation, contextualization, or syncretism (the choice of nomenclature largely depending on one's academic reference group or theological commitments). Since the Second Vatican Council (1962-65), inculturation has been endorsed at many levels of Church leadership, and there is considerable evidence that the processes of de-Westernization and Japanization have made steady progress over the decades.

Although inculturation is often focused on the development of local or contextual theologies, it is important to consider this process as a multi-dimensional phenomenon that includes much more than theology. The development of new theologies is just one dimension of the larger process of cultural adaptation that occurs as the Christian faith moves from one cultural context to another. It can also involve changes and innovations in rituals, liturgies, leadership styles, and social organization (e.g., the shift from foreign to native leaders). In the case of Japanese Catholicism, theological inculturation has probably been the least significant area of development. An examination of theological education and publications reveals that theology remains Eurocentric. The curriculum in most theology departments and seminaries is still largely shaped by the study of translated works from Western theology, and postgraduate degrees are often pursued at European or North American institutions. Ernest Piryns suggested that "Catholic theologians are, perhaps, even more Western-oriented than are their Protestant colleagues." He noted that until the 1950s most priests and theologians in Japan "were trained in the Neo-Thomistic system." Writing in the late 1980s, Piryns maintained that "the first real Japanese theologians have yet to break through."[5]

Most observers of the Japanese theological scene point out that on the whole Japanese Protestants have been more creative than Catholic theologians in this area. Surveys of Japanese theology often refer to well-known Protestant examples of inculturation, such as Kitamori's 1947 *Theology of the Pain of God.*[6] Kitamori sought to develop a theology of the cross and to recover the forgotten theme of the pain and suffering of God, relating it to the Japanese experience of pain and suffering during and shortly after the war. A more recent Protestant example is Kuribayashi's "theology of a crown of thorns," a Japanese liberation theology that addresses the situation of the *burakumin,* a minority group that has experienced discrimination in Japanese society for many centuries.[7]

Few Catholic examples are forthcoming. At a loss for examples drawn from the work of Church theologians, most observers refer to the work of well-known writer and lay Catholic Endō Shūsaku. Takayanagi refers to Endō's "novelistic theology" as a "rather successful example of Japanese Catholic theology living outside of the fold of professional theology."[8] Endō struggled as much as any theologian to find appropriate ways to understand and interpret the Christian faith in the Japanese context. His novels *Silence* and *Deep River,* for example, have probably had a greater impact than any theological text on encouraging Christians and non-Christians alike to think about the meaning of Christianity for Japanese.[9] In sum, there has been a good deal of discussion about the need for inculturation in Japanese theology, but very little work has actually been done. Swyngedouw also makes the interesting point that "the diminishing number of foreign priests has not resulted in a surge toward inculturation on the level of ideas."[10] In fact, it has often been foreign priests who have encouraged the development of more local indigenous expressions of faith and dialogue with established Japanese religions. Many Japanese leaders, in contrast, often reflect a strong loyalty to "received tradition" and look toward Rome and Europe for their primary theological resources.[11]

Although inculturation in the area of theology has been slow, in other areas we see that the Catholic Church has become a more Japanese institution and addressed local cultural concerns in a number of ways. There has been a steady increase in the ratio of Japanese to foreign religious leaders (bishops, priests, and religious) over the past century. The process of Japanization was hastened by the policies of the government during World War II, which required the Church to replace all foreign ordinaries with Japanese bishops in 1940.[12] In the postwar period, the initial influx of foreign missionaries reversed the process of Japanization, but by 1985 the number of Japanese priests was roughly equal to that of foreign missionaries, and by 2005 the number of Japanese priests exceeded foreign priests by several hundred (938 to 604). The process has been even more extensive for nonclerical religious. There are currently 5,565 Japanese sisters and only 348 foreign sisters. On a much smaller scale, Japanese brothers outnumber foreign brothers 151 to 55.[13]

In addition to changes in leadership, the Catholic Church over the decades has adapted its policies in order to reduce the conflict and tension between the claims and demands of the faith in relation to traditional religious obligations (Shinto and Buddhist). Several examples are worth noting here. One has to do with the reduction of tension in relation to obligations of Shinto, which can be traced back to the well-known Yasukuni incident of 5 May 1932. On that occasion, several Catholic students at Sophia University refused to participate in the appropriate ritual of bowing before the shrine. The military officer who had taken the students to Yasukuni demanded that disciplinary action be taken against the Catholic students for their failure to pay proper respect to the spirits of the fallen Japanese soldiers enshrined there. The students had behaved, in fact, in accordance with the guidelines included in the 1896 Catholic catechism and prayer book, which stated that the faithful were not permitted to "make the bow of obeisance before Shinto Shrines."[14] The intervention of Jean Alexis Chambon, archbishop of Tokyo, helped to bring an end to this crisis. Chambon wrote to the Ministry of Education and asked for clarification regarding the meaning of the shrine visits that were expected of students.[15] On 30 September, the ministry representative responded that the ritual of *jinja sanpai* was part of the educational program and that its purpose was only to express respect for the war dead and to serve as an expression of patriotism and loyalty. This reply – that shrine visits were not "religious" but merely civil and patriotic – satisfied Chambon's theological concerns. In 1936, the Vatican Congregation for the Propagation for the Faith directed Japanese bishops to allow the faithful to participate in these "civil" rites as well as marriages and funerals at Shinto shrines.[16]

A second example has to do with the postwar policies of the Church with regard to ancestral concerns and rituals. In the Japanese context, proper care of and respect for the dead have comprised an important aspect of the religious life. It has traditionally involved taking part in a number of rituals surrounding the funeral itself, the subsequent care of the household Buddhist altar *(butsudan)* and ancestral tablets *(ihai),* as well as the performance of annual festivals and memorial rites over many years. Most transplanted Christian churches initially instructed their members to destroy these pagan altars and avoid participation in these ancestral rites. Needless to say, serious familial and communal conflict often resulted from Japanese Christians following these strict policies. In the postwar period, however, most churches have gradually relaxed these teachings and made some accommodations for these traditional Japanese practices and concerns.[17] As Berentsen notes, the Catholic tradition has a more natural affinity to the ancestral cult than Protestant forms of Christianity because of its long practice of "offering liturgical prayers and Holy Mass for the dead."[18] Undoubtedly, this has made adaptations more natural for the Catholic Church in this context.

In 1985, the Catholic Church published a remarkable document entitled *Sosen to shisha ni tsuite no katorikku shinja no tebiki* ("Guidelines for Catholics with Regard to the Ancestors and the Dead"). This short pamphlet gave official endorsement to many of the adaptations and accommodations that had occurred and been taken for granted in many Catholic households and parishes for decades. It is a practical handbook that uses a question-and-answer format to provide concrete guidance to the faithful.[19] In the earlier periods of Catholic mission work, the faithful were often instructed to dispose of household altars or at least avoid participation in family rituals connected to the Buddhist tradition. This strict teaching has been relaxed considerably, as can be seen in the following question and answer:

Question 1: What should we do with the *butsudan* (Buddhist home altar)? Answer: In case the whole family has become Catholic, it is preferable to have only a (Christian) home altar. In case it is not possible to remove the *butsudan* because of intercourse with relatives, the *butsudan* might be preserved. The home altar is the "place of prayer" for the family. When a *butsudan* is used as a home altar, Buddha images and scrolls should be removed to another place and a cross, a statue of Our Lady and other Christian symbols placed in it. If there are ancestor tablets *(ihai)*, they can be placed there together with these.[20]

The guidelines also inform Catholics that they are permitted to make offerings of fruit, liquor, or other items as signs of love and respect to the deceased. They may also ring the bell and offer rice in Buddhist ritual contexts but should pray in their hearts as Christians: "Lord, give rest to the deceased." The practical instructions for various situations are extensive, but the overall impact has clearly been to reduce the tension and potential conflict for Catholic minorities in familial and social contexts where participation in non-Christian rituals is expected.

Another example of inculturation has been the provision of functionally equivalent and alternative rituals to celebrate *Shichi-go-san,* a special blessing service traditionally held at Shinto shrines on 15 November for children at the age of seven, five, and three (girls of three and boys of five and seven). Traditionally, children would be taken to the local Shinto shrine, and prayers would be offered to the *kami* for their safety, growth, and development. Most Catholic churches (and some Protestant churches) have now incorporated their own version of the *Shichi-go-san* celebrations and rituals into the life of the church.

What stands out as one of the most prominent recent developments in the context of inculturation and Japanization has been the response of the Church to the widespread interest in marriage rites by non-Christian couples over the past two decades. As Wendy James and Douglas Johnson point out, "Christianity does not necessarily spread as an organic entity; partial elements, themes, symbols, practices, are characteristically taken up by a particular culture or civilization, ethnic class, or interest group, at a particular time."[21] In the case of Japan, most Japanese are not interested in church membership, but many members of the current generation are appropriating the marriage rites provided by the Church into the traditional division of labour in Japanese religions. Just as Shinto has traditionally dominated rituals associated with birth, and Buddhism has monopolized rituals connected to death, so too Christian churches are becoming a significant competitor in the sacralization of marriage.

Research has indicated a steady increase in the number of Japanese choosing Christian marriage rites over the past two decades.[22] In 1982, most weddings (90 percent) were still conducted by Shinto priests, and only 5.1 percent were performed with a Christian service. A 1991 survey discovered

that the percentage of Christian or church-related weddings had increased
to 35.9 percent in the Kantō region and 23.8 percent in the Kansai region.
According to the study by Fisch, by 1998 the percentage of Christian weddings had increased to 53.1 percent, whereas Shinto weddings had declined
to 32.3 percent.[23] According to Ishii Kenji's 2005 review of the most recent
surveys, the percentage of Japanese choosing Christian wedding rites has
now reached some 70 percent, and Shinto rites have declined to roughly
20 percent.[24] This trend of "Christian" weddings represents a natural
Japanese appropriation of another religious tradition into the rites of passage in contemporary society.

A change in attitudes toward Christianity among the postwar generations
provides important background for understanding significant developments
in ritual behaviour. The NHK Survey of Japanese Religious Consciousness
conducted three decades ago provides helpful information for understanding how Japanese perceptions of Christianity have changed in the postwar
environment.[25] Although exclusive commitment to an organized form of
Christianity is still rare among Japanese, the survey discovered that some
12 percent felt a certain empathy *(shitashimi)* for Christianity. Although
empathy for Buddhism and Shinto increases with age, Swyngedouw noted
in his analysis of this survey that "Christianity shows a completely reverse
trend. In the 16-19 age bracket, it reaches a favorable claim of 29.7 percent
to go gradually down to 4.5 percent and 5.4 percent for, respectively, the
60-69 and the over-70 age brackets."[26] The stigma once attached to things
Christian has largely disappeared for the generations socialized in the
postwar period. Although this has not translated into a surge in baptisms
or church membership, it has made it possible for many Japanese to incorporate elements of Christianity into their ritual lives without any consciousness of tension or incompatibility.

The Catholic Church – like many Protestant churches and enterprising
hotels with their own wedding chapels – has adapted its policies in light of
the growing interest in Christian marriage rites and celebrations. In 1975,
the Vatican granted permission for non-Christian couples to have wedding
ceremonies in Japanese churches, an accommodation to the minority status
of the Church in Japan. Apparently, Japan is the only country in the world
that has been given this special permission from the Vatican. In 1990, the
Church in Japan institutionalized this accommodation with the formal
recognition of two rites – "a Rite for the Celebration of Marriage Within
Mass and a Celebration of Marriage Outside of Mass, and the latter is nor-
mally used for the wedding of non-Catholic couples." Many Catholic leaders

have considered this development as a worthwhile opportunity for pre-evangelism and usually provide classes regarding marriage, family life, and the Catholic faith before conducting the service of Celebration of Marriage outside of Mass.[27]

This official provision of two distinct rites made it possible for local parishes and priests to respond more positively to the interest of couples outside the Church, and the number of weddings celebrated in Catholic churches increased considerably. In 2000, for example, the Church conducted a total of 7,455 marriage ceremonies nationwide. Of that number, only 793 (10.6 percent) were between individuals who shared the Catholic faith, 198 (2.7 percent) were mixed marriages between Catholics and Protestants, 2,124 (28.5 percent) were between Catholics and individuals of other religions (e.g., Buddhism and Shinto), and 4,340 (58.2 percent) were marriages in which neither party claimed the Catholic faith. Reflecting the overall demographic trends of Japanese society, the number of marriages performed each year is now in decline. By 2005, the number of weddings celebrated in Catholic churches had dropped by almost half to 3,635, and over half of these weddings were for non-Christian couples.

This brief and selective review of some postwar developments reveals that the Catholic Church has adapted in many ways to the local context, and today it clearly presents a more tolerant and generous face to Japanese society. Notwithstanding these accommodations and signs of Japanization, the Church is not experiencing significant growth in its Japanese membership. In fact, most indicators suggest a Church in transition and decline. Although membership statistics indicate a modest increase over the past few decades, other indicators suggest that the Japanese Catholic Church is on a trajectory of serious decline.[28] From 1995 to 2005, the total number of priests declined from 1,758 to 1,516. The number of seminarians training for the priesthood is also in steady decline. According to a recent report, projections are that the number of priests will decrease by one-third or one-half within the next fifteen years.[29] There are already a number of "priestless" parishes. In the Diocese of Sendai in Northern Honshū, for example, some twenty parishes conduct liturgies on Sundays without a priest.[30] Although many observers express grave concerns about this shortage, Jesuit historian Kawamura Shinzō points out that "in the 1590s there were only 45 priests to care for 225,000 people. Instead of bemoaning the shortage of priests, we should give priority to organizing the laity."[31] Some might be calling for the training of laity for ministry, but others are drawing on the resources of the much stronger Catholic Church in nearby South Korea to meet the

Table 1

Enrolment in Sunday schools and catechism classes, 1995 and 2005

Year	Primary school	Middle school	High school/above
1995	20,077	7,404	11,472
2005	15,298	5,525	5,034

Table 2

Baptisms in the Catholic Church, 1995-2005

Year	Infant	Adult	Total
1985	4,614	6,189	10,803
1995	5,090	4,419	9,509
2005	3,451	3,777	7,228

Table 3

Average Mass attendance, 1995 and 2005

Year	Sunday	Easter	Christmas
1995	142,157	232,163	320,508
2005	122,054	206,848	285,927

shortage of priests. The bishop of the Hiroshima Diocese made arrangements to receive priests from the Pusan Diocese in South Korea. The first two priests arrived in 2002, and the bishop is hopeful that in the future seminarians from Pusan will be prepared for the priesthood in Japan and serve as diocesan priests for Hiroshima.[32]

The decline in the number of priests is not the only cause for concern. Other key indicators suggest that Japanese Catholics will be a shrinking religious minority for the foreseeable future. As can be seen in Table 1, the number of children and youth enrolled in religious education and catechism classes declined dramatically in just one decade. This is obviously a reflection of the low birth rate in Japan, but it clearly means that the natural replacement of aging members will not occur, and there is very minimal new membership from evangelistic outreach to make up for the difference. Similarly, the number of baptisms (both infant and adult) continued to decline over the past ten years (see Table 2). Mass attendance (Sunday,

Easter, and Christmas) also declined significantly during this time period (see Table 3). In light of these rather pessimistic trends, Endō Shūsaku's characterization of Japan in his novel *Silence* as a "swamp" for Christianity is a compelling image.

Globalization and the Transformation of the Japanese Church

This rather gloomy picture is the context for understanding the most recent development shaping the Catholic Church in contemporary Japan, namely, globalization. This process is often thought of in terms of the impacts of the "first world" on the "third world" through the global spread of Western (American) multinational corporations and the destruction of local economies and indigenous cultures. Globalization is not, however, simply a unidirectional process of Westernization or "McDonaldization" as sometimes portrayed in the literature; rather, the development of "global society" has its share of "reverse influences" from non-Western societies. There are diverse regional and local responses to this accelerated transnational movement of information, people, and culture. The neologism "glocalization," coined by Roland Robertson and inspired in part by the Japanese term *dochakuka* ("indigenization"), draws attention to this dimension of the process and the multilateral nature of these flows and influences.[33]

As far as the Catholic Church in Japan is concerned, globalization has meant the unanticipated and rapid influx of foreign workers and new Catholic immigrants. The fact that Swyngedouw, an astute observer of the Japanese church and religious situation, did not deal with the impact of globalization in his studies just over a decade ago suggests how quickly the situation has changed. Today it is impossible to consider the character and situation of the Catholic Church apart from the impacts of globalization and immigration.

Although foreign workers were already appearing in significant numbers in the late 1980s, they were not yet seriously recognized as a challenge to and concern of the Church. The numbers rapidly increased in the 1990s as the Japanese workforce continued to shrink and foreign labourers were needed to keep the economy going and perform the jobs that Japanese were no longer able or willing to do.[34] Many of these foreign workers now remain in Japan for extended periods – both legally and illegally – and some are long-term residents by virtue of their international marriages with Japanese citizens. Between 1990 and 2000, the number of "newcomer" foreign workers increased by 50 percent (this group is to be distinguished from the Korean population, for example, that has been in Japan for several generations).[35] Many of the new immigrants come from dominantly Catholic countries in

Latin America and the Philippines, and they often seek out the Catholic Church as a "home away from home" shortly after their arrival. Although these foreign workers represent an important population that is transforming the nature of the Church, they do not appear in the annual statistics prepared by the Catholic Bishops' Conference of Japan. The figures include only Japanese Catholics or foreigners who are properly registered as members. The statistics for 2005, for example, used above to document a pattern of decline, did not include immigrants and foreign workers.[36] The Catholic Commission of Japan for Migrants, Refugees, and People on the Move, however, has been giving serious attention to this relatively new and significant category. The data prepared by the commission are presented in Table 4.[37]

According to the commission's report for 2005, "there are about 529,452 foreign Catholics in Japan. For the first time there are more foreign Catholics than the 449,925 Japanese Catholics."[38] As can be seen in Table 4, the number of foreign Catholics increased dramatically between 1996 and 2005, especially in the Dioceses of Saitama, Yokohama, Nagoya, and Tokyo. This major demographic shift in the Catholic population makes the process of inculturation extremely complicated. The Church in Japan can no longer focus primarily on Japanese cultural concerns but must address the needs of many new Catholic immigrants and their children. This is fully recognized in the commission's report, which states that in these circumstances the aim must be to create a multicultural Church. Although a multicultural and multiethnic Church might be taken for granted in a country such as the United States, it requires a serious reorientation for Japanese Catholics. How has the Japanese Church responded to this new situation, and what have been the impacts of the new Catholics on the Japanese Church? The concluding section of this chapter presents a few preliminary and tentative observations regarding the nature and response of the Catholic Church in this rapidly changing situation.

The Response of the Japanese Church

Although critics will surely point out that the Church has done too little and responded too slowly to the needs of the foreign workers and new Catholics, there is considerable evidence that the Church has responded positively in many ways. Addressing these new concerns for the Church as a whole, the Catholic Commission of Japan for Migrants, Refugees, and People on the Move has played a significant role in gathering information on the needs of as well as the resources available for churches to respond

Table 4

Japanese and foreign Catholics according to diocese, 1996-2005

Diocese	1996 members Japanese	1996 members Foreign	2001 members Japanese	2001 members Foreign	2005 members Japanese	2005 members Foreign
Sapporo	17,575	2,746	17,878	2,262	18,205	2,433
%	86	14	89	11	88	12
Sendai	12,030	6,138	11,184	6,655	10,947	9,726
%	66	34	63	37	53	47
Niigata	7,545	4,633	7,467	5,046	7,707	6,540
%	62	38	60	40	54	46
Saitama	18,710	59,772	19,162	67,821	19,814	85,104
%	24	76	22	78	19	81
Tokyo	83,872	65,948	84,962	61,813	91,586	75,134
%	56	44	58	42	55	45
Yokohama	50,234	80,007	52,717	92,614	53,512	118,934
%	39	61	36	64	31	69
Nagoya	24,233	61,109	24,703	75,143	25,380	107,386
%	28	72	25	75	19	81
Kyoto	21,197	28,490	19,634	33,111	19,194	43,047
%	43	57	37	63	31	69
Osaka	52,525	46,702	55,723	31,217	55,732	39,911
%	53	47	64	36	58	42
Hiroshima	20,637	14,714	21,461	14,520	21,702	18,106
%	58	42	60	40	55	45
Takamatsu	5,684	3,348	5,445	3,993	5,407	4,778
%	63	37	58	42	53	47
Fukuoka	31,189	7,316	31,442	6,630	31,600	8,905
%	81	19	83	17	78	22
Nagasaki	70,010	857	68,870	817	67,728	1,186
%	99	1	99	1	98	2
Oita	5,703	1,702	5,872	1,691	5,765	2,694
%	77	23	78	22	68	32
Kagoshima	9,195	1,094	9,282	1,179	9,527	2,880
%	89	11	89	11	77	23
Naha	6,204	2,609	6,104	2,460	6,119	2,688
%	70	30	71	29	69	31
Total	436,543	317,185	441,906	406,972	449,925	529,452
%	58	42	52	48	46	54

to the concerns of foreign workers.[39] At the level of the diocese, most districts have created centres to assist with the various needs of foreign workers. In the case of the Archdiocese of Tokyo, the Catholic Tokyo International Centre (CTIC) was organized at Sekiguchi Catholic Church in 1990. Since that time, additional centres have been established in Meguro, Kameido, and Chiba in an effort to address the growing needs. The diocesan staff and many volunteers provide a range of programs and services, including translation for foreign workers in dealing with government agencies, schools, and hospitals; assistance with the organization of multilingual religious services; publication of newsletters in English, Tagalog, Spanish, and Portuguese; and provision of family counselling to address the difficulties of international marriages and the specific needs of bicultural children. CTIC also prepares multilingual materials needed at the parish level for Mass and religious education, including a songbook (in English, Tagalog, and Sinugboanon) and confirmation workbooks in English for children and teens to use in preparation for the sacrament of baptism. The staff also assist foreign workers with their legal problems, which often means visiting those held in detention centres. In August 2006, CTIC even organized a new multicultural summer camp to address the needs of the growing number of children from mixed marriages.[40] In addition to programs and services addressed to the individual needs of foreign workers, all of the diocesan centres serve as resources for local churches struggling to respond to the new Catholic population.[41]

At the level of the local parish, the ability (and willingness) of churches to respond to foreign workers vary considerably. Some smaller churches are struggling to survive and are simply overwhelmed by the number of non-Japanese who have so quickly appeared. As noted earlier, the number of priests and religious (both Japanese and foreign) is already declining, and there are a number of "priestless" parishes. Furthermore, most priests have not been trained to provide pastoral care for a multilingual and multicultural congregation. Only by inviting an outside priest can some of the smaller churches provide an occasional non-Japanese Mass for the immigrants. A large church such as St. Ignatius in Tokyo, however, has the international resources of the Society of Jesus, including multilingual priests who can provide pastoral care and Mass in various languages. Currently, the pastoral staff includes five priests from Japan, one priest from the United States, five priests from Spain, and one priest from Argentina. In addition, German and Polish Jesuits have regularly assisted with foreign-language services. In addition to Japanese, Mass is provided in English, Indonesian, German, Polish, and Vietnamese.[42]

In some cases, it is not just the lack of resources but also a problem of attitude. Stories circulate about some Japanese priests who respond rather coldly and maintain that "this is Japan, and services should be conducted in Japanese." In other words, the new Catholics had better learn the language quickly if they want to be a part of the Japanese Church. Reflecting on the predicament of the Japanese Church almost a decade ago, Laguidao observed that "foreigners are still treated as guests. In many churches, there remains a strong feeling of antipathy toward foreigners from poor countries, and the veneer of tolerance that is shown is usually coupled with the hope that eventually all these foreigners will one day leave."[43] But it is no longer possible to think that the foreigners are just passing through Japan. The number of immigrant workers who are becoming long-term residents of Japan continues to increase, and they are seeking to become equal members of the Christian community.

In spite of the lack of resources and some cases of resistance, many Japanese churches have responded positively to the new challenge. Japanese-language classes are often provided for immigrants and their children, services are scheduled and co-ordinated to allow non-Japanese to gather for special activities with their ethnic communities, and, gradually, representatives of various national groups are being appointed to serve on church councils and committees in an effort to integrate more fully the foreign communities into the life of the parish. Considerable efforts have clearly been made to provide Mass in multiple languages (see Table 5, which lists the number of foreign-language Masses offered in churches once or more per month for each diocese).[44]

The Impacts of Immigrant Catholicism on the Japanese Church
Although Japanese priests and churches have responded in many ways to the needs of the new foreign workers and immigrants, it is important to recognize that these new Catholics have not been passively waiting for the Japanese Church to do something for them. Rather, many are active agents and taking the lead in organizing groups and activities, and they are bringing with them their own movements, cultural styles, and religious practices, which are reshaping the Church in Japan in significant ways. As Mark Juergensmeyer points out, "the global diasporas of peoples and cultures can transform traditions."[45] This transformation is already occurring in the Japanese Catholic Church. A Church that in the past was largely shaped by European and North American traditions and gradually Japanized through the process of inculturation is now being reshaped by new cultural influences and ways of practising Catholicism from Brazil, Peru, and the Philippines.

Table 5

Foreign-language Masses in the Japanese Catholic Church according to diocese, 2005

Diocese	Languages	Number of Masses	Diocese	Languages	Number of Masses
Sapporo	English	2	Nagoya	English	17
	Portuguese	1		Spanish	9
Sendai	English	6		Portuguese	15
	Spanish	2		Tagalog	10
	Korean	1		Korean	2
	French	1		Vietnamese	1
Niigata	English	7		French	1
	Spanish	2		Indonesian	1
	Portuguese	1	Kyoto	English	13
Saitama	English	26		Spanish	9
	Spanish	14		Portuguese	8
	Portuguese	12		Korean	1
	Tagalog	7	Osaka	English	19
	Korean	4		Spanish	9
	Vietnamese	4		Portuguese	8
	Chinese	1		Tagalog	2
Tokyo	English	29		Korean	4
	Spanish	8		Vietnamese	3
	Portuguese	3		German	1
	Tagalog	6		Chinese	1
	Korean	2		Indonesian	1
	Vietnamese	2	Hiroshima	English	17
	French	3		Spanish	6
	German	1		Portuguese	10
	Chinese	1	Takamatsu	English	7
	Indonesian	2		Spanish	2
	Miyanmarese (Burmese)	1	Fukuoka	English	8
Yokohama	English	26		Spanish	1
	Spanish	21	Nagasaki	English	1
	Portuguese	20		Spanish	1
	Tagalog	3	Oita	English	7
	Korean	3	Kagoshima	English	1
	Vietnamese	3		Spanish	1
			Naha	English	4
				Spanish	1

Several aspects of this cultural transformation are worth noting here. What was a relatively homogeneous Japanese Church is becoming a heterogeneous institution with a number of ethnic subgroups organized in parishes across Japan. Yamaoka's 1998 study of the Filipino community in St. Ignatius Church in Tokyo identified three primary social functions of these subgroups: provision of community and fellowship, maintenance of ethnic culture through language classes and social activities, and assistance in gaining access to various social services. Pluralization of the Japanese Church through the provision of Mass in Tagalog, Spanish, and English is a major change, but much more is involved. A few years earlier, Dubuc reported that the Fujisawa Catholic Church had already been transformed by the presence of the Vietnamese, Filipino, and South American communities: different styles of worship, more relaxed attitudes toward time and schedules, a new prominence of Marian devotions not usually observed in Japan, and more expressive participation in worship, music, and dancing at celebrations.[46]

In a 2006 lecture, Maria Carmelita Kasuya, an active lay Catholic from the Philippines, discussed the potential impacts of the new immigrant Catholics on the Japanese churches and expanded on some of Dubuc's observations. She offered some broad comparisons of the different cultural styles and expectations of Japanese (the receiving church) and the newer Filipino members (the church of origin). The majority of Japanese Catholics (at least those participating) tend to be older, whereas there are many more young children and families participating in the life of a church in the case of Filipino members. The Japanese services seem very formal and orderly and tend to use older hymns, whereas Filipino Catholics are more accustomed to the use of new songs and music in services. Whereas the "passing of the peace" in typical Japanese services consists of a polite bow or nod in the direction of one's neighbours, Filipino members are much more expressive and often shake hands or embrace and often perceive Japanese services as lacking in basic human warmth. And where Japanese members tend to be rather refined and educated, many Filipino members lack a solid education or instruction in the faith. At the same time, the Filipino immigrants express a high degree of popular religious devotion (what some might label as "folk Catholicism"), which includes more prayers and physical actions around and within the church in relation to sacred objects. At the moment, these very different cultural styles and expectations regarding the religious life are the sources of some conflict and misunderstanding in many churches.

Given the size of the new Catholic communities and the decline in Japanese members, it is reasonable to expect that the atmosphere and practices in Japanese churches will gradually be transformed.

Some groups are also introducing new festivals and traditions from their home countries. A number of new expressions of Catholicism are already visible in Japan. One example is the introduction of the Lord of Miracles Procession (first organized by religious brotherhoods in eighteenth-century Peru), which has been spread by recent Peruvian immigrant brotherhoods in Japan. Karsten Paerregaard has studied this central Peruvian festival and its diffusion in diasporic communities outside Peru. When Paerregaard's study was published, there were some fifty brotherhoods organized in four different continents, including eight in Japan. Some priests in Japan now co-operate with the brotherhoods and allow them to store the Lord of the Miracles icon and use their churches as bases for their activities and processions.[47] Although the usual practice is for brotherhoods to order a copy of the icon from Lima, in one case a Japanese artist was employed, and he produced a Lord of the Miracles "with *ojos jalados* (slanting eyes)."[48] This adaptation was the cause of some concern in the Peruvian community, but the icon was eventually recognized as legitimate and was accepted as the focus for worship by the devotees in one community. Peruvians have been holding Lord of the Miracles Processions in Japan since the early 1990s, and recent reports indicate gatherings of several hundred at different churches.[49] Filipino Catholics are similarly introducing processions and celebrations not observed by Japanese Catholics.[50]

The new Catholics are also introducing various lay movements into the Japanese Church. Two such movements from the Philippines include the popular charismatic El Shaddai Movement and Couples for Christ. There is already a Japan Chapter of El Shaddai that has official recognition of the Japanese Church and is permitted to hold special Masses and services on a regular basis. In the Tokyo area, El Shaddai holds weekly Masses and services between churches with supportive priests in the diocese. Although these Masses follow the standard liturgy and include a homily by the priest, they are charismatic as well. English is used for most of the service, but there is special music in Tagalog. Worship is more expressive, with hands raised high for prayer, and swaying and dancing accompanies the music. The music and celebration continue more informally after the Mass concludes, with El Shaddai worship teams leading and providing special music. A larger percentage of participants are women from the Philippines; many bring their young children with them to the services. From 200 to 300 people regularly participate in these El Shaddai Masses and services. Couples for

Christ is another movement from the Philippines that is also active in Japan. This is an organization that aims at cultivating and encouraging Christian families. Leaders and volunteers are involved in holding classes and seminars across Japan and are giving particular attention to the needs and problems faced by the growing number of international and bicultural couples and families. It remains to be seen if these Filipino movements will significantly influence the average Japanese Catholic, but they will undoubtedly shape the immigrant community and bicultural children of international marriages who are brought by their mothers to attend these services.

Finally, the impacts of the children of new immigrants and those from international marriages on Japanese churches deserve some consideration. As noted earlier, the numbers of international marriages and long-term residents have been increasing dramatically over the past decade. In 2004, for example, there were 32,209 marriages between Japanese men and foreign women. Although the largest percentage was with women from China (38 percent), the second largest category was with women from the Philippines (26 percent). Many of these women are Catholics and naturally bring their children to the church for baptism and Christian education. Older Japanese members, however, often view the large number of children accompanying mothers to Mass as noisy and disruptive. Foreigners, however, see the Church as failing to provide appropriate space, time, and programs to address the needs of the children. In a study done several years ago, Gatpatan noted that, "between 1995 and 2000, out of the total number of registered children born of Japanese and foreign nationals, 24 percent, or 31,415, are children of Filipina-Japanese couples." Gatpatan went on to project that "a decade from now there will be at least 36,000 youth in Japan born of multicultural marriages and baptized as Catholics."[51] The rate of international marriages has continued to increase since this projection was made, so the integration and nurturing of these bicultural children may well be the future of the Catholic Church in Japan.

Conclusion

The Japanese Catholic Church is clearly in a major period of transition. On the one hand, most indicators suggest that the "older" Japanese Church has already entered a phase of decline. On the other hand, the Church has unexpectedly received a whole new membership base with the arrival of many thousands of immigrants and foreign workers. The Church has responded positively in many ways to the rapidly changing situation and needs of foreign workers, but many practical difficulties remain – most related to communication problems and cultural misunderstandings. There are tensions between older Japanese members and new non-Japanese members surrounding their different expectations regarding parish life (particularly the use of sacred space, church facilities, and financial matters). Japanese churches that are in decline and struggling to survive, however, could well be revitalized by these new immigrant Catholics and their children if they are not perceived to be a "problem."[52]

The Church has only begun to reflect seriously on these new realities. Momose Fumiaki, a Catholic theologian reflecting on the tasks of theology in Asia several years ago, recognized that the number of foreign Catholics in Japan had nearly exceeded the number of Japanese Catholics, but he did not indicate the significance of this development for Japanese theology. Although he stressed that the Church should provide pastoral care, protect the human rights of these workers, and support their assimilation into Japanese society, he did not mention what these demographic trends meant for theology.[53] Takayanagi Shun'ichi, by contrast, has more recently recognized that it is clearly time for Catholic theology in Japan "to grapple with the popular religion of a new multiracial church."[54]

Preoccupation with being a "Japanese Church" is clearly inadequate in a situation where an equal number of non-Japanese are seeking to become part of the Christian community. Although Japan has had its minority groups (Ainu, Buraku, and Koreans) for many years, inculturation has been thought of largely in terms of adaptation to a "homogeneous" and relatively isolated culture and society. There are undoubtedly places where inculturation still occurs in relatively isolated cultural contexts, but Japan is certainly not one of them. Japanese churches – like churches in many other places today – are compelled to struggle with the complexities and paradoxes that inevitably emerge from exposure to multiple cultural influences – local, indigenous, national, and global. Theology in the rapidly evolving context of globalization requires a serious engagement with diverse groups and a more flexible, intercultural openness to the riches that may be drawn from many different national-ethnic-cultural contexts and traditions.[55]

Notes
1 Swyngedouw, "Katorikku kyōkai no tenkai," 327.
2 *World Christian Encylopedia*, 423.
3 Swyngedouw, "The Awakening of a Local Church," 380-81.
4 *Kirisutokyō nenkan*, 84. The Catholic presence in Japan of course extends beyond the parish churches and their members. Catholics, along with other Christian bodies, have had a major impact in the fields of education, social welfare, and medical work. As of 2005, the Catholic Church sponsored a total of 35 hospitals and medical clinics across Japan and 522 social welfare facilities (including child-care facilities and

nursing homes for the elderly); educational work continues to be a major area of contribution. Currently, there are approximately 350,000 students enrolled in one of the 870 educational institutions related to the Catholic Church, which include kindergartens (548), primary schools (54), middle schools (98), high schools (114), junior colleges (20), universities (20), and vocational and technical schools (16).

5 Piryns, "Japanese Theology and Inculturation," 540.

6 Editor's note: See Yamamoto's discussion on the Protestant Kitamori and recent Catholic theologies of inculturation and interculturation in Chapter 8 above.

7 See Kuribayashi, *Keikan no shingaku*, and his article in English, "Recovering Jesus for Outcasts in Japan: From a Theology of the Crown of Thorns."

8 Takayanagi, "Catholic Theology in Japan," 20. See also Piryns, "Japanese Theology and Inculturation," 547.

9 The significance of Endō's work for theology has been explored in some detail by Mase-Hasegawa, *Christ in Japanese Culture*. Editor's note: See also the chapter by Williams in this volume.

10 Swyngedouw, "The Awakening of a Local Church," 383.

11 It is interesting to note that the "inculturation" or Japanization of the Church does not appear to be a pressing concern of the average parishioner. One survey of Japanese Catholics in the early 1980s discovered that "only 35.5 percent look for a more Japanese type church with 14.3 percent strongly expressing their expectations in this regard. A surprising 47.8 percent are uncommitted on the subject of inculturation." O'Donoghue, *Japanese Catholics*, 34.

12 Spae, "The Catholic Church in Japan," 11.

13 "Statistics of the Catholic Church in Japan."

14 Minamiki, *The Chinese Rites Controversy*, 129.

15 Chambon's letter, addressed to Mr. Ichiro Hatoyama, is contained in the supplementary volume of historical materials related to the history of Sophia University, *Jōchi daigakushi shiryōshū*, 279.

16 Since Shinto shrines were redefined as religious (rather than civil) in the postwar period, the original rationale for allowing Catholics to participate in Shinto rites has disappeared, and there is some confusion regarding the current position of the Church. Given the current political climate – one in which Yasukuni Shrine is regularly in the news as a source of national and international conflict – the Catholic Church needs to provide clarification to the faithful on the nature of shrine rites and the appropriate response for Catholics today. For an analysis of the contemporary situation of Yasukuni Shrine visits in the context of Catholic concerns, see Doak, "A Religious Perspective on the Yasukuni Shrine Controversy"; Breen, "Popes, Bishops and War Criminals: Reflections on Catholics and Yasukuni in Postwar Japan," and Mullins, "How Yasukuni Survived the Occupation: A Critical Examination of Popular Claims."

17 See Doerner's survey of a Roman Catholic parish and the adaptations made in relation to indigenous beliefs and practices related to the dead: "Comparative Analysis of Life after Death in Folk Shinto and Christianity."

18 Berentsen, *Grave and Gospel*, 196.

19 Nihon Katorikku Sho-shūkyō Iinkai, ed., *Sosen to shisha ni tsuite no katorikku shinja no tebiki*. For a helpful explanation and translation of portions of this guide by an individual who served on the committee that prepared it, see Swyngedouw, "The Japanese Church and Ancestor Veneration Practices"; and Swyngedouw, "Japan's Roman Catholic Church and Ancestor Veneration."

20 This translation is drawn from the introduction by Swyngedouw, "The Japanese Church and Ancestor Veneration Practices," 59.

21 James and Johnson, *Vernacular Christianity*, 5.
22 What is interesting about the popularity of Christian marriage rites is that their at-
    tractiveness is connected to their being Western or different from traditional or in-
    digenous forms. This seems to be in tension with the overall concern of inculturation,
    which has been viewed primarily in terms of the Church adopting more local or
    Japanese cultural forms.
23 See Fisch, "The Rise of the Chapel Wedding in Japan."
24 Ishii, *Kekkonshiki*, 32.
25 See Nihon Hōsō Kyōkai Hōsō Yoron Chōsajo, ed., *Nihonjin no shūkyō ishiki*.
26 Swyngedouw, "The Quiet Reversal," 5-6.
27 For recent coverage of these trends, see "Church Weddings for Non-Christians
    Provide Opportunity for Couples to Reflect on Marriage."
28 Statistics for 2000-5 are provided in pdf format on the home page of the Catholic
    Bishops' Conference of Japan, http://www.cbcj.catholic.jp/.
29 This rather gloomy projection was reported in the *Katorikku Shinbun*, 6 July 2003.
    The rapid decline in the number of priests is not a problem confined to the Catholic
    Church. The two largest Protestant Churches in Japan – the United Church of Christ
    and Anglican-Episcopal Church – are also facing a serious clergy shortage in the
    coming two decades. For some comparative observations, see Hastings and Mullins,
    "The Congregational Leadership Crisis Facing the Japanese Church."
30 Reported in the *Japan Catholic News*, No. 1103, February 2005.
31 Reported in the *Japan Catholic News*, No. 1112, January 2006. Kawamura also observes
    that there are helpful historical precedents. Following the Black Death in fourteenth-
    century Europe, *confraria* were organized by the laity to cope with the shortage of
    priests and bishops.
32 The Hiroshima Diocese in Japan has only about 21,000 members and 23 priests, while
    the Pusan Diocese has some 370,000 members and 245 priests. See Donovan, "Japan
    Receives Missioner Priests."
33 Robertson, "Comments on the 'Global Triad' and 'Glocalization.'" Vasques and
    Marquardt have similarly noted that "globalization is not just about domination and
    homogenization. It also involves resistance, heterogeneity, and the active negotiation
    of space, time, and identity at the grassroots, even if these negotiations occur under
    the power constraints of neoliberal markets and all-pervading culture industries."
    Vasques and Marquardt, *Globalizing the Sacred*, 3.
34 These less desirable jobs are often referred to in terms of the three *k*s: *kitanai* ("dirty"),
    kiken ("dangerous"), and *kitsui* ("hard," "demanding").
35 The different categories of foreign and migrant workers are related to Japan's earlier
    history of colonization and the transfer of forced labourers from Korea and China
    to Japan in support of the East Asia Co-Prosperity Sphere before and during World
    War II. Approximately 500,000 "older-comers" (and their descendants) from former
    colonies currently reside in Japan as permanent residents. There are approximately
    another 1.5 million of the "newcomers" who are regarded as temporary workers
    (this number includes an estimated 200,000 who are illegal "overstayers"; see the
    helpful summary of statistical data at the following home page: http://www.jcarm.
    com/).
36 The annual statistics are available at the official home page of the Catholic Bishops'
    Conference of Japan: http://www.cbcj.catholic.jp/jpn/data/st05/statics2005.pdf.
37 The number of foreign Catholics in each diocese is a rough estimate based on several
    sources: the 2005 Ministry of Justice statistics on the number of foreigners in Japan;
    the Vatican figures on the percentage of Catholics in the immigrant workers' country

of origin; and the figures provided by the number of foreigners registered with local governments *(gaikokujin tōroku)*. By combining the data from these three sources, the Catholic Commission has produced these estimates for the approximate number of foreign Catholics currently residing in each diocese (see http://www.jcarm.com/). These figures do not include the number of illegal "overstayers" who have remained in Japan without a visa. There is probably some overlap between the figures reported here for foreign Catholics and the membership reported by each diocese since some foreigners are actually registered as members in local churches.

38 Reported by the Catholic Commission of Japan for Migrants, Refugees, and People on the Move (http://www.jcarm.com/).

39 The commission's home page, for example, provides information in Japanese as well as in English, Spanish, Portuguese, and Vietnamese. The site also lists contact information on pastoral centres in each diocese that focus on the needs of immigrants. See http://www.jcarm.com/.

40 Reported in the *CTIC Newsletter*, October 2006.

41 For example, Father Kauss Marcel of the Minoshima Pastoral Centre in Fukuoka, Kyushu, offers basic and practical advice to individual churches that are just beginning to consider how to deal with the reality of non-Japanese Catholics in their midst and how to move toward the development of a multiethnic and multilingual parish. Centre staff encourage church leaders to (1) elect or nominate an individual in the parish to take responsibility for foreigners who attend services; (2) make efforts to communicate church announcements to foreigners in a manner that they can understand; (3) provide opportunities for foreigners to participate in the Mass (e.g., give them a chance to serve in a liturgical role); (4) find creative ways to allow and encourage foreigners to participate in Bible study sessions and prayer meetings; (5) organize programs that will provide opportunities for exchange and encourage mutual understanding; (6) create a membership list of foreign participants; and (7) provide an opportunity for a representative of the foreign participants to serve on the church council. These practical suggestions are drawn from the Minoshima Pastoral Centre home page: http://www.pastorama.com/.

42 On the surface, St. Ignatius Church seems to be handling the multiethnic situation rather effectively, but most of these priests are in their seventies and eighties – having already retired from other full-time assignments – and they continue to serve because of the shortage of priests.

43 Laguidao, "Filipinos in the Land of the Rising Sun," 36.

44 The data for this table come from information reported in the *Katorikku Kyōkai Jōhō Handobukku 2006*.

45 Juergensmeyer, *Global Religions*, 7.

46 A study of the impact of Filipino immigrants on the Catholic Church in the United States provides interesting parallels to my observations here. Gonzalez points out that the Filipino presence brings more than the Mass in Tagalog. Originally Irish Catholic churches in San Francisco, he notes, had been "slightly Filipinized with statues and images of saints and the Virgin Mary. Some of them are indigenous Filipino folk figures like the Santo Nino (or Christ Child) and San Lorenzo Ruize (the first Filipino saint) ... Filipino-American parishioners, like in the Philippines, line up to touch, kiss, and wipe their handkerchief on the Virgin Mary." Gonzalez, "Transnationalization of Faith," 15. This is precisely what one can observe in connection with Filipino Catholics in Japanese churches.

47 According to Paerregaard, the "organization of brotherhoods and adoration of images outside Peru strengthen migrants' ties to their home country and reconfirm

their sense of belonging to Peru, thus transcending the national borders of the home as well as the receiving countries." Paerregaard, "In the Footsteps of the Lord of Miracles," 5.

48 Paerregaard, 25.

49 In October 2004, for example, 300 Peruvians participated in the procession from Akashi Catholic Church in Hyogo Prefecture. *Japan Catholic News,* No. 1100, November 2004. In October 2005, the procession and special Mass attracted 350 participants at the Oyama Church in the Diocese of Saitama outside Tokyo. *Japan Catholic News,* No. 1111, December 2005.

50 A Filipino festival was held at Oyama Catholic Church, Oyama City, Tochigi Prefecture, on 10 October 2004. Mass was held in Tagalog, English, and Japanese, and there was a procession held in honour of Our Lady of the Rosary and Mother of Perpetual Help, whose statue was carried around the church on a flower-decorated float. Children also offered flowers and gave offerings. After there were Filipino foods, dances, and celebrations. See the report at http://www.saitama-daichan.net/.

51 Gatpatan, "Migrants and Their Families in Japan," 205-7.

52 Grimm has forcefully made this point:

> The newcomers are still seen, by and large, as a problem that must be dealt with by the Japanese bishops, clergy, and laity. Solving the need to meet foreigners' pastoral needs is admirable, but starting from the premise that they are a problem is a big mistake. Treating these people as a problem will ultimately drive them from the Church. It is time to realize that the more than 600,000 non-Japanese Catholics in Japan are the Church in Japan. Japanese Catholics are a minority, a shrinking minority. Is the leadership of the Church in Japan – the hierarchy as well as the laity – ready to start doing its planning, training, activities, evangelization, and liturgy with the premise that the Church here is multiethnic, multicultural and only partly Japanese? Or will it continue to see the influx of "outsiders" as a problem to be dealt with from the point of view of the shrinking Japanese minority?

Grimm, "The Catholic Church in Japan Has a Future, If ... "

53 Momose, "Ajia no kyōkai to shingaku no kadai," 166.

54 Takayanagi, "Catholic Theology in Japan," 23.

55 Cruz's reflections on the theological significance of the Filipino diaspora stress this point:

> The call, therefore, especially in the context of Filipino migration, is to engage in a mission that brings about contextual borderless liberation – one that is in dialogue with other cultures and religions. Missions in the face of globalization should be a mission beyond *inculturation,* and rather a mission of *interculturation* – one that respects and embraces differences, especially in cultures and religions, and enables people to live in harmony with diversity.

Cruz, "Migration as a New Frontier for Mission," 64-65.

Bibliography

Aoki Tamotsu, and Saeki Keishi, eds. *"Ajia-teki kachi" to wa nanika.* Tokyo: TBS Britannica, 1998.

Baba Hiroaki, Tsuboi Masamichi, and Tazumi Mitsuo, eds. *Kaisō no Mizushima Kenkyūshitsu.* Tokyo: Kyōritsu Shuppan, 1990.

Ballhatchet, Helen J. "The Modern Missionary Movement in Japan: Roman Catholic, Protestant, Orthodox." In Mark R. Mullins, ed., *Handbook of Christianity in Japan,* 35-68. Leiden: Brill, 2003.

Bartholomew, James R. *The Formation of Science in Japan: Building a Research Tradition.* New Haven: Yale University Press, 1989.

Benedict XVI (see also Ratzinger, Cardinal Joseph). "Deus caritas est." 2005. http://www.vatican.va/.

Berentsen, J.M. *Grave and Gospel.* Leiden: Brill, 1985.

Bernal, John D. *The Social Function of Science.* London: Routledge and Kegan Paul, 1939.

Binzley, Ronald A. "American Catholicism's Science Crisis and the Albertus Magnus Guild, 1953-1969." *ISIS* 98, 4 (2007): 695-723.

Bosch, David. *Transforming Mission.* New York: Orbis, 1991.

Boxer, C.R. *The Christian Century in Japan, 1549-1650.* Berkeley: University of California Press; London: Cambridge University Press, 1951.

Breen, John. "The Danger is Ever Present: Catholic Critiques of Yasukuni Shrine in Postwar Japan." *Japan Mission Journal* 63, 2 (2009): 111-22.

Butow, Robert. *The John Doe Associates: Backdoor Diplomacy for Peace.* Stanford, CA: Stanford University Press, 1972.

Cary, Otis. *A History of Christianity in Japan, Volume One: Roman Catholic and Greek Orthodox Missions.* New York: Fleming H. Revell Company, 1909.

Casanova, Jose. "Religion, the New Millennium, and Globalization." *Sociology of Religion* 62, 4 (2001): 415-41.

Catechism of the Catholic Church. Washington, DC: United States Catholic Conference, 1994.

Catholic Bishops' Conference of Japan. "Statistics of the Catholic Church in Japan, 2006." 1 December 2007. http://www.cbcj.catholic.jp/jpn/data/st06/statistics2006.pdf.

"Church Weddings for Non-Christians Provide Opportunity for Couples to Reflect on Marriage." *Japan Catholic News,* July 2006. http://www.cbcj.catholic.jp/eng/jcn/jul2006.htm.

Clancey, Gregory K. *Earthquake Nation: The Cultural Politics of Japanese Seismicity, 1868-1930*. Berkeley: University of California Press, 2006.

Cobb, Jr., John B., and Christopher Ives. *The Emptying God: A Buddhist-Jewish-Christian Conversation*. Maryknoll, NY: Maryknoll Press, 1990.

Cruz, Gemma Tulud. "Migration as a New Frontier for Mission: The Filipino Experience." *Japan Mission Journal* (spring 2005): 58-65.

De Lubac, Henri. *Amida: Aspects du Bouddhisme*. Paris: Éditions du Seuil, 1955.

–. *Aspects of Buddhism*. Trans. George Lamb. London: Sheed and Ward, 1953.

Doak, Kevin M. "From the Margins: Yoshihiko Yoshimitsu's Call to Faith in a Time of Crisis." Paper presented at the 2003 Formation and Renewal Conference, University of Notre Dame. http://ethicscenter.nd.edu/archives/far.shtml.

–. *A History of Nationalism in Modern Japan: Placing the People*. Leiden: Brill, 2007.

–. "A Religious Perspective on the Yasukuni Shrine Controversy." In John Breen, ed., *Yasukuni, the War Dead, and the Struggle for Japan's Past*, 47-69. New York: Columbia University Press, 2008.

–. "Romanticism, Conservatism, and the Kyoto School of Philosophy." In Christopher Goto-Jones, ed., *Re-Politicising the Kyoto School as Philosophy*, 137-60. London: Routledge, 2007.

–. "Time, Culture, and Faith: Yoshimitsu Yoshihiko's Critique of Modernity." *University of Tokyo Center of Philosophy Bulletin* 1 (2003): 85-95.

–. "What Is a Nation and Who Belongs? National Narratives and the Ethnic Imagination in Twentieth Century Japan." *American Historical Review* 102, 2 (1997): 282-309.

Doerner, David L. "Comparative Analysis of Life after Death in Folk Shinto and Christianity." *Japanese Journal of Religious Studies* 4, 2-3 (1977): 151-82.

Donovan, Gill. "Japan Receives Missioner Priests." *National Catholic Reporter*, 15 February 2002. http://findarticles.com/.

Dower, John W. *Embracing Defeat: Japan in the Wake of World War II*. New York: W.W. Norton, 1999.

Drummond, Richard H. *A History of Christianity in Japan*. Grand Rapids, MI: William B. Eerdmans, 1971.

Dubuc, Martin. "Fujisawa Catholic Church: A Changing Parish in a Changing Society." *Japan Christian Review* 61 (1995): 35-42.

Ellis, John Tracy. "American Catholics and the Intellectual Life." *Thought* 30 (1955): 351-88.

Endō Shūsaku. *Chinmoku*. Tokyo: Shinchōsha, 1966.

–. *Deep River*. Trans. Van Gessel. London: Peter Owen, 1994.

–. *Endō Shūsaku bungaku zenshū*. Tokyo: Shinchōsha, 1975; rev. ed., 2000.

–. *Fukai kawa*. Tokyo: Kōdansha, 1993.

–. *Fukai kawa o saguru*. Tokyo: Bungei Shunjū, 1994.

–. "Fukai kawa sōsaku nikki." *Mita bungaku* 50 (1997): 10-54.

–. *Ihōjin no tachiba kara*. Tokyo: Nihon Shoseki, 1979.

–. *Kirisuto no tanjō*. Tokyo: Shinchōsha, 1978.

–. *Samurai*. Tokyo: Shinchōsha, 1980.

–. *The Samurai*. Trans. Van Gessel. London: Peter Owen, 1982; New York: Aventura, 1984.

–. *Scandal*. Trans. Van Gessel. London: Peter Owen, 1988.

–. *The Sea and the Poison*. Trans. Michael Gallagher. London: Peter Owen, 1972; reprint, New York: New Directions Paperback, 1992.

–. *Shikai no hotori*. Tokyo: Shinchōsha, 1973.

–. *Shōsetsu: Minoue sōdan*. Tokyo: Bungei Shunjū, 1978.

–. *Silence*. Trans. William Johnston. Tokyo: Sophia University and Tuttle, 1969; London: Penguin and Peter Owen, 1996.

–. *Sukyandaru*. Tokyo: Shinchōsha, 1986.

–. *Watashi no ai shita shōsetsu*. Tokyo: Shinchōsha, 1985.

Endō Shūsaku, and Kaga Otohiko. "Taidan: Saishinsaku *Fukai kawa:* Tamashii no mondai." *Kokubungaku: Kaishaku to kyōzai no kenkyū* 38, 10 (1993): 6-21.

Endō Shūsaku, Inoue Yōji, and Yasuoka Shōtarō. "'Shin' to 'katachi': *Fukai kawa* o tegakari ni." *Gunzō* 48, 9 (1993): 198-219.

Evans, David C., and Mark R. Peattie. *Kaigun: Strategy, Tactics, and Technology in the Imperial Japanese Navy, 1887-1941*. Annapolis, MD: Naval Institute Press, 1997.

Field, Norma. *In the Realm of a Dying Emperor*. New York: Pantheon Books, 1991.

Fisch, Michael. "The Rise of the Chapel Wedding in Japan." *Japanese Journal of Religious Studies* 28, 1-2 (2001): 57-76.

Flannery, Austin, ed. and trans. *Vatican Council II, Volume 1: The Concilliar and Post Concilliar Documents*. New York: Costello Publishing, 1975.

Flexner, James Thomas. *An American Saga: The Story of Helen Thomas and Simon Flexner*. Boston: Little, Brown, 1984.

Fujita, Neil S. *Japan's Encounter with Christianity: The Catholic Mission in Pre-Modern Japan*. New York: Paulist Press, 1991.

Furuno Yoshimasa. *Kin Daichū jiken no seiji ketchaku: Shuken hōkishita nihon seifu*. Tokyo: Tōhō Shuppan, 2007.

Furuya, Yasuo, ed. and trans. *A History of Japanese Theology*. Tokyo: William B. Eerdmans, 1997.

Gabriel, Philip. *Spirit Matters: The Transcendent in Modern Japanese Literature*. Honolulu: University of Hawaii Press, 2006.

Garon, Sheldon. *Molding Japanese Minds: The State in Everyday Life*. Princeton, NJ: Princeton University Press, 1979.

Gatpatan, Agnes V. "Migrants and Their Families in Japan: A New Pastoral Challenge for the Church." *Japan Mission Journal* (autumn 2003): 202-7.

Geneviève de la Sainte Face, Sister. *A Memoir of My Sister, St. Thérèse*. Authorized trans. by the Carmelite Sisters of New York of Conseils et Souvenirs. New York: P.J. Kennedy, 1959.

Germany, Charles H. *Protestant Theologies in Modern Japan: A History of Dominant Theological Currents from 1920-1960*. Tokyo: IISR Press, 1965.

Gessel, Van, et al. *Gunzō: Nihon no sakka: Endō Shūsaku 22*. Tokyo: Shogakkan, 1991.

Glynn, Paul. *The Smile of a Ragpicker*. Hunters Hill, NSW, Australia: Marist Fathers Books, 1992.

God's Fingerprints in Japan. DVD. Honolulu: Aloha ke Akua Ministries, 2005.

Goldschmidt, Richard. *In and Out of the Ivory Tower: The Autobiography of Richard Goldschmidt*. Seattle: University of Washington Press, 1960.

Gonzalez, Joaquin L. "Transnationalization of Faith: The Americanization of Christianity in the Philippines and the Filipinization of Christianity in the United States." *Asia Pacific: Perspectives* 2, 1 (2002): 9-20.

Grimm, William. "The Catholic Church in Japan Has a Future, If ... " *Japan Catholic News*, January 2006. http://www.cbcj.catholic.jp/.

Hamanaka Toshiyuki. "Nikkan yūkō no kakehashi, Kanayama Masahide-shi no kiseki to gyōseki." http://www.t-shinpo.com.

Handō Kazutoshi. *Seidan: Shōwa tennō to Suzuki Kantarō*. Tokyo: PHP Bunko, 2006.

Hane, Mikiso. *Peasants, Rebels, and Outcasts: The Underside of Modern Japan*. New York: Pantheon, 1982.

Hanlon, Kevin J. *Popular Catholicism in Japan: Their Own Voices, Their Spiritual Writers, and Their Devotional Art.* Tokyo: Enderle Book Company, 2004.

Hanron, Kebin J. (Kevin J. Hanlon). *Gaikokujin shisai ga mita nihon no katorikku shintō.* Tokyo: Enderure, 2001.

Hanzawa Takamaro. *Kindai nihon no katorishizumu: Shisōshi-teki kōsatsu.* Tokyo: Misuzu Shobō, 1993.

Harrington, Ann M. "The First Women Religious in Japan: Mother Saint Mathilde Raclot and the French Connection." *Catholic Historical* Review 87, 4 (2001): 603-23.

–. "French Mission Work in Japan: Culture and Religion in the Nineteenth Century." In Cyriac K. Pullapilly et al., eds., *Christianity and Native Cultures: Perspectives from Different Regions of the World*, 193-207. Notre Dame, IN: Cross Cultural Publications, 2004.

–. *Japan's Hidden Christians.* Chicago: Loyola University Press, 1993.

Hastings, Thomas, and Mark R. Mullins. "The Congregational Leadership Crisis Facing the Japanese Church." *International Bulletin of Missionary Research* 30, 1 (2006): 18-23.

Hayashi Kentarō, ed. *Shin-hoshushugi, gendai nihon shisō taikei 30.* Tokyo: Chikuma Shobō, 1963.

Hick, John. "Notice: The Latest Vatican Statement on Christianity and Other Religions." *New Blackfriars* (December, 1998): 1-5. http://astro.temple.edu/~arcc/hick. html.

–. *Problems of Religious Pluralism.* Basingstoke: Macmillan, 1985.

–, ed. *The Myth of Christian Uniqueness.* New York: Orbis, 1988.

Hirayama Kumiko. "Shōwa zenki Kagoshima no katoriku kōtōjogakkō appaku mondai no kenkyū." Kagoshima: *Kagoshima Junshin Girls' High School and Immaculate Heart University Research Bulletin* 23, 1 (1993): 67-83; 24, 2 (1994): 67-80; 25, 3 (1994): 15-27.

Houston, G.W., ed. *The Cross and the Lotus: Christianity and Buddhism in Dialogue.* Delhi: Motilal Banarsidass, 1985.

Howes, John F. *Japan's Modern Prophet: Uchimura Kanzō, 1861-1930.* Vancouver: UBC Press, 2005.

Hughes, Sally Smith. *The Virus: A History of the Concept.* New York: Science History Publications, 1977.

Ikeda Toshio. *Jimbutsu chūshin no nihon katorikku-shi.* Tokyo: San Pauro, 1998.

Inagaki, Bernard R. *The Constitution of Japan and the Natural Law.* Philosophical Series 164, Abstract 19. Washington, DC: Catholic University of America Press, 1955.

Inoue Yōji. *Hōnen.* Tokyo: Chikuma Shobō, 2001.

–. *Iesu no manazashi.* Tokyo: Nihon Kirisutokyōdan Shuppankyoku, 1981.

–. *Kirisutokyō ga yoku wakaru hon.* Tokyo: PHP Kenkyujo, 1989.

–. *Namu Abba.* Nagasaki: Seibo no Kishi Sha, 2000.

–. *Namu no kokoro ni ikiru.* Tokyo: Chikuma Shobō, 2003.

–. "Kaze ni yudanete: Nihon bunka no uchinaru fukuin no kaika o motomete." *Kaze* 48 (1998).

–. *Nihon to Iesu no kao.* Tokyo: Kōdansha, 1981.

–. *The Face of Jesus in Japan.* Trans. Hisako Akamatsu. Tokyo: Kindai Bungeisha, 1994.

–. *Waga shi Iesu no shōgai.* Tokyo: Nihon Kirisutokyōdan Shuppankyoku, 2005.

–. *Watakushi no naka no Kirisuto.* Tokyo: Shufu no Tomo Sha, 1978.

–. *Yohaku no tabi: Shisaku no ato.* Tokyo: Nihon Kirisutokyōdan Shuppankyoku, 1980.

Inoue Yōji, and Sako Jun'ichirō. *Pauro o kataru: Taidan.* Tokyo: Chōbunsha, 1991.

Inoue Yōji, and Yamane Michihiro. *Kaze no naka no omoi: Kirisutokyō no bunkanai kaika no kokoromi.* Tokyo: Nihon Kirisutokyōdan Shuppankyoku, 1989.

Iseki Kurō, comp. *Dai Nihon hakushi roku.* 5 vols. Tokyo: Hattensha, 1921-30.

Ishii Kenji. *Kekkonshiki: Shiawase o tsukuru gishiki.* Tokyo: NHK Books, 2005.

Ives, Christopher, ed. *Divine Emptiness and Historical Fullness: A Buddhist-Jewish-Christian Conversation with Masao Abe.* Valley Forge, PA: Trinity Press International, 1995.

Izutsu Toshihiko. *Isurāmu tetsugaku no genzō.* Tokyo: Iwanami Shoten, 1980.

James, Wendy, and Douglas H. Johnson, eds. *Vernacular Christianity: Essays in the Social Anthropology of Religion Presented to Godfrey Lienhardt.* JASO Occasional Papers 7. Oxford, UK: Institute for Social and Cultural Anthropology, 1988.

Jasper, David. *The Study of Literature and Religion.* London: Macmillan, 1989.

Jennes, Joseph. *A History of the Catholic Church in Japan: From Its Beginnings to the Early Meiji Period (1549-1873).* Missionary Bulletin Series 8. Tokyo: Committee of the Apostolate, 1959.

Jeremias, Joachim. *The Central Message of the New Testament.* London: SCM Press, 1965.

–. *New Testament Theology.* New York: Scribner, 1971.

Jōchi daigakushi shiryōshū: Hoi (1903-1969). Tokyo: Jōchi Gakuin, 1993.

John Paul II, Pope. "Redemptoris Missio: On the Permanent Validity of the Church's Missionary Mandate." Encyclical Letter, The Vatican, 1990. http://www.vatican. va/.

Juchereau-Duchesnay, Gabriel-Maria. "Rélation Annuelle de la Préfecture de Kagoshima 1932-1933 à la Sacré Congrégation de la Propagande, Rome." 31 July 1933. Archives of the Franciscans, Montreal, QC.

Juergensmeyer, Mark, ed. *Global Religions.* Oxford/New York: Oxford University Press, 2002.

Kadowaki, J.K. (Kakichi). *Zen and the Bible.* Trans. Joan Rieck. Maryknoll, NY: Orbis Books, 2002.

Kajima Heiwa Kenkyūjo, ed. *Nihon gaikōshi.* Vol. 25. Tokyo: Kajima Kenkyūjo Shuppankai, 1972.

Kamiya Mitsunobu. *Suga Atsuko to kyūnin no rerigio: Katorishizumu to shōwa no seishinshi.* Tokyo: Nichigai Asoshiētsu, 2007.

Kanao Seizō. *Nagai Nagayoshi den.* Tokyo: Nihon Yakugakkai, 1960.

Kanayama Masahide. *Dare mo kakanakatta bachikan.* Tokyo: Sankei, 1980.

–. "Kobukusha no tanoshimi." *Bungeishunjū* (July 1957): 241-45.

Karolinska Institutet. *Med. Nob. Kom. 1914 P. M. Försändelser och Betänkanden.* Stockholm: Karolinska Institutet, 1914.

Kasai, Minoru. "Endō Shūsaku's *Deep River* and the Face of Jesus." Lecture delivered at International Christian University, Tokyo, 28 May 1997.

Kasuya, Maria Carmelita. "The Filipino Migrants in the Archdiocese of Tokyo." Report presented as part of the Sophia University Research Organization Festival, Sophia University, Tokyo, 29 September 2006.

Katorikku Chūō Kyōgikai, comp. *Kyōkai jōzai chi '91.* Tokyo: Katorikku Chūō Kyōgikai, 1991.

Katorikku kyōkai kōhō handobukku 2006. Tokyo: Katorikku Chūō Kyōgikai, 2005.

Kawai, Hayao. *Buddhism and the Art of Psychotherapy.* Foreword by David Rosen. College Station: Texas A & M University Press, 1996.

–. *Japanese Psyche: Major Motifs in the Fairy Tales of Japan.* Trans. Hayao Kawai and Sachiko Reece. Dallas: Spring Publications, 1988.

Kawashima Hidekazu. "*Fukai kawa* no jikken: Ai no gensetsu o megutte." *Kirisutokyō bungaku kenkyū* 12 (1995): 13-24.

Ketelaar, James Edward. *Of Heretics and Martyrs in Meiji Japan: Buddhism and Its Persecution.* Princeton, NJ: Princeton University Press, 1990.

Kikuchi, Yoshiyuki. "Mizushima, San'ichirō." In Noretta Koertge, ed. *New Dictionary of Scientific Biography*, vol. 5, 167-71. Detroit: Charles Scribner's Sons/Thomson Gale, 2008.

Kimura Bin. *Hito to hito no aida: Seishin byōrigaku-teki nihonron.* Tokyo: Kōbundō, 1976.

–. *Kankei to shite no jiko.* Tokyo: Misuzu Shobō, 2005.

Kitahara Satoko. *Ari no machi no kodomotachi.* Nagasaki: Seibo no Kishi Sha, 2007.

Kitamori, Kazoh. *Theology of the Pain of God.* Richmond, VA: John Knox Press, 1965.

Kiyonobu Itakura, and Eri Yagi. "The Japanese Research System and the Establishment of the Institute of Physical and Chemical Research." In Nakayama Shigeru, David L. Swain, and Eri Yagi, eds., *Science and Society in Modern Japan*, 158-201. Tokyo/Cambridge, MA: University of Tokyo Press/MIT Press, 1974.

Kobori Keiichirō. *Shōwa tennō.* Tokyo: PHP Shinsho, 1999.

Koertge, Noretta, ed. *New Dictionary of Scientific Biography.* Vol. 5. Detroit: Charles Scribner's Sons/Thomson Gale, 2008.

Kosakai Sumi. *Ningen no bunsai: Shinpu Iwashita Sōichi.* Tokyo: Seibo no Kishi, 1996.

Kumagai Kenji, ed. *Omoide no Aoyama Tanemichi Sensei.* Tokyo: Aoyama Sensei Tanjō Ichihyakunensai Junbi Iinkai, 1959.

Kuribayashi Teruo. *Keikan no shingaku: Hisabetsu buraku kaihō to kirisutokyō.* Tokyo: Shinkyō Shuppansha, 1991.

–. "Recovering Jesus for Outcasts in Japan: From a Theology of the Crown of Thorns." *Japan Christian Review* 58 (1992): 19-32.

Kuroda Katsuhiro, and Hata Yoshihide, eds. *Shōwa tennō goroku.* Tokyo: Kōdansha Bunko, 2004.

Kuschel, Karl-Josef. *The Poet as Mirror.* London: SCM Press, 1997.

Laguidao, Wency. "Filipinos in the Land of the Rising Sun." *Japan Mission Journal* (spring 1997): 32-41.

Launay, A. "Society of Foreign Missions of Paris." In *The Catholic Encyclopedia.* New York: Robert Appleton, 1912. http://www.newadvent.org/cathen/14079a.htm.

Levine, Philippa, ed. *Gender and Empire.* Oxford: Oxford University Press, 2004.

Levy, Michael, executive editor. *Time Almanac 2008.* Chicago: Encyclopedia Britannica, 2008.

Magill, Frank N., ed. *The Nobel Prize Winners: Chemistry.* Vol. 1. Pasadena, CA: Salem Press, 1990.

Manning, Brennan. *Abba's Child: The Cry of the Heart for Intimate Belonging.* Colorado Springs, CO: NavPress, 2002.

Marnas, Francisque. *La Religion de Jésus Ressuscitée au Japon dans la seconde moité du XIXe siécle.* 2 vols. Paris: Delhomme et Briguet, 1896.

Marshall, Byron K. *Learning to Be Modern: Japanese Political Discourse on Education.* Boulder, CO: Westview Press, 1994.

Mary Evangeline, Sister. *Four Centuries after Xavier: Story of the Sisters of the Holy Names of Jesus and Mary in Japan 1931-1940.* Spokane, WA: Convent of the Holy Names, 1979.

Mase-Hasegawa, Emi. *Christ in Japanese Culture: Theological Themes in Shusaku Endo's Literary Works.* Leiden: Brill, 2008.

Mathy, Francis. "Shūsaku Endō: Japanese Catholic Novelist." *Thought* (winter 1967): 585-614.

Mauriac, François. *Le romancier et ses personnages*. Paris: Buchet/Chastel, 1933.
–. *Thérèse*. Trans. Gerard Hopkins. New York: Penguin Books, 1972.
McGreevy, John T. *Catholicism and American Freedom: A History*. New York: W.W. Norton, 2003.
Mélich Maixé, Antonio. "Koichi Yamamoto (1940-1983) and the Beginnings of Opus Dei in Japan." *Studia et Documenta* 1 (2007): 127-59.
Mersch, Emile. *The Theology of the Mystical Body*. Trans. Cyril Vollert. St. Louis: Herder, 1951.
Michalson, Carl. *Japanese Contributions to Christian Theology*. Philadelphia: Westminster Press, 1960.
Minamiki, George. *The Chinese Rites Controversy*. Chicago: Loyola University Press, 1985.
Miyajima Mikinosuke. *Kitasato Shibasaburō den (nempu)*. Tokyo: Iwanami Shoten, 1931.
Miyamoto, Yuki. "Rebirth in the Pure Land or God's Sacrificial Lambs? Religious Interpretations of the Atomic Bombings in Hiroshima and Nagasaki." *Japanese Journal of Religious Studies* 32, 1 (2005): 131-59.
Miyamoto Hisao. *Sonzai no kisetsu: Hayatorogia (heburai-teki sonzairon) no tanjō*. Tokyo: Chisen Shokan, 2002.
Miyazaki, Kentarō. "Roman Catholic Mission in Pre-Modern Japan." In Mark R. Mullins, ed., *Handbook of Christianity in Japan*, 1-18. Leiden: Brill, 2003.
Mizushima File, Archives of the Pontificia Accademia delle Scienze, Citta del Vaticano.
Momose Fumiaki. "Ajia no kyōkai to shingaku no kadai." *Katorikku Kenkyū* 71 (2002): 149-70.
Moriwaki Takao. "Mizushima sensei to hitori no shisai kagakusha." In Baba Hiroaki, Tsuboi Masamichi, and Tazumi Mitsuo, eds. Kaisō no Mizushima kenkyūshitsu. Tokyo: Kyōritsu Shuppan, 1990.
Mullins, Mark R. *Christianity Made in Japan: A Study of Indigenous Movements*. Honolulu: University of Hawaii Press, 1998.
–. "Contextual Theology and Theological Education in Japan." In David Kwang-sun Suh, Annette Meuthrath, and Hyondok Choe, eds., *Being Mindful of Context: Charting the Future of Theology and Theological Education in Asia*, 93-100. Delhi: Indian Society for Promoting Christian Knowledge (ISPCK), 2004.
–, ed. *Handbook of Christianity in Japan*. Leiden: Brill, 2003.
–. "How Yasukuni Shrine Survived the Occupation: A Critical Examination of Popular Claims." *Monumenta Nipponica* 65, 1 (2010): 89-136.
Nagai, Takashi. *The Bells of Nagasaki*. Trans. William Johnston. Tokyo: Kodansha International, 1984.
–. *Nagasaki no kane*. Tokyo: San Paulo, 1949; reprinted, 1995.
–. *Rozario no kusari*. Tokyo: San Paulo, 1948; reprinted, 1995.
Nakamura, Hajime. *Ways of Thinking of Eastern Peoples: India, China, Tibet, Japan*. Rev. English ed. New York: Columbia University Press, 1997.
Nakamura Hajime, et al., eds. *Iwanami bukkyō jiten*. Tokyo: Iwanami Shoten, 1989.
Nakayama, Shigeru, David L. Swain, and Eri Yagi, eds. *Science and Society in Modern Japan*. Tokyo: University of Tokyo Press; Cambridge, MA: MIT Press, 1974.
Nakayama Shigeru. *Noguchi Hideyo*. Tokyo: Asahi Shimbun Sha, 1978.
Newman, Cardinal John Henry. *Apologia Pro Vita Sua*. London: J.M. Dent and Sons, 1912.
–. *An Essay in Aid of a Grammar of Assent*. London: Burns, Oates, 1870.

Newsweek, 27 July 1953.

Nicolas, Adolfo. "Foreigners in Japan: Still Knocking at the Door (and the Heart) of the Church." *Japan Mission Journal* (summer 2002): 110-15.

Nihon Gakushiin, ed. *Nihon Gakushiin hachijūnen shi, shiryō.* Vol. 1. Tokyo: Nihon Gakushiin, 1962.

Nihon Hōsō Kyōkai Hōsō Yoron Chōsajo, ed. *Nihonjin no shūkyō ishiki.* Tokyo: NHK Books, 1984.

Nihon Katorikku Sho-shūkyō Iinkai, ed. *Sosen to shisha ni tsuite no katorikku shinja no tebiki.* Tokyo: Katorikku Chūō Kyōgikai, 1985.

O'Collins, Gerald, and Mario Farrugia. *Catholicism: The Story of Catholic Christianity.* Oxford: Oxford University Press, 2003.

O'Donoghue, Patrick F. *Japanese Catholics: A Survey of Catholic Life 1982-1983 Japan.* Tokyo: Chūō Shuppansha, 1985.

–. "Migrant Ministry in Japan." *Japan Mission Journal* (summer 2003): 112-20.

Okumura, Ichirō. *Awakening to Prayer.* Trans. Kazue Hiraki and A.M. Yamamoto. Washington, DC: ICS, 1994.

–. *Dansō: Ashimoto fukaku hore.* Tokyo: San Paulo, 1990.

–. *Inori.* Tokyo: San Paulo, 1974.

Okuno Takeo. *Joryū sakkaron: Shōsetsu wa honshitsu-teki ni josei no mono ka.* Tokyo: Daisan Bunmei Sha, 1974.

Onizuka Hideaki. *Tennō no rozario.* 2 vols. Tokyo: Seikō Shobō, 2006.

Paerregaard, Karsten. "In the Footsteps of the Lord of Miracles: The Expatriation of Religious Icons in the Peruvian Diaspora." Working Paper, Transnational Communities Programme, 2 October 2001. http://www.transcomm.ox.ac.uk/.

Parker, Gordan A. "Peter Debye." In Frank Magill, ed. *The Nobel Prize Winners: Chemistry, 1901-1937,* 391-402. Pasadena, CA/Englewood Cliffs, NJ: Salem Press, 1990.

Pinnington, Adrian. "Yoshimitsu, Benedict, Endo: Guilt, Shame, and the Post-War Idea of Japan." *Japan Forum* 13, 1 (2001): 91-105.

Piryns, Ernest D. "Japanese Theology and Inculturation." *Journal of Ecumenical Studies* 24, 4 (1987): 535-56.

Pius XI, Pope. *Rerum Ecclesiae.* http://www.vatican.va/phome_en.htm.

Plesset, Isabel R. *Noguchi and His Patrons.* Cranbury, NJ: Associated University Presses, 1980.

Pollard, John F. *The Unknown Pope: Benedict XV.* London: Geoffrey Chapman, 1999.

Quigley, Martin S. Memorandum dated 25 June 1963 on the meeting with Kanayama Masahide, Japanese Consul General Office, New York.

–. *Peace without Hiroshima: Secret Action at the Vatican in the Spring of 1945.* Lanham, MD: Madison Books, 1991.

Rahner, Karl. *Foundations of Christian Faith: An Introduction to the Idea of Christianity.* Trans. William V. Dych. New York: Crossroads, 1993.

Ratzinger, Cardinal Joseph. *Truth and Tolerance: Christian Belief and World Religions.* San Francisco: Ignatius Press, 2004.

Renan, Ernest. *Vie de Jésus.* Paris: Calmann Lévy, 1883.

Robertson, Roland. "Comments on the 'Global Triad' and 'Glocalization.'" In Inoue Nobutaka, ed., *Globalization and Indigenous Culture,* 217-25. Tokyo: Institute for Japanese Culture and Classics, Kokugakuin University, 1997.

Scannell, T.B. "Jean-Baptiste-Henri Dominique Lacordaire." In *The Catholic Encyclopedia.* http://www.newadvent.org/.

Scheiner, Irwin. *Christian Converts and Social Protest in Meiji Japan.* Berkeley: University of California Press, 1970; reprinted, Ann Arbor, MI: Center for Japanese Studies, 2002.

Shiba Ryōtarō. "Jōdo-kyō to Endō Shūsaku." *Asahi Weekly*, July 1997, 144-52.

Shillony, Ben-Ami. *Enigma of the Emperors: Sacred Subservience in Japanese History.* Kent, UK: Global Oriental, 2005.

–. "The Sons of Heaven and the Son of God: Emperors and Christianity in Modern Japan." Paper presented at the JSAA Fifteenth Biennial Conference, Australian National University, 1-4 July 2007.

Shiobara Matasaku. *Takamine Hakushi.* Tokyo: Shiobara Matasaku, 1924.

Shōwa tennō dokuhakuroku. Tokyo: Bunshun Bunko, 1995.

Sisters of Saint Maur in Japan 1872-1972: A Century of Progress. Paris: Mother House, 1972.

Smart, Ninian. *Buddhism and Christianity: Rivals and Allies.* Basingstoke, UK: Macmillan, 1993.

Smith, Anthony D. *National Identity.* Reno: University of Nevada Press, 1991.

Sono Ayako. *Aru shinwa no haikei,* reprinted as *Kadokawa Bunko 3953.* Tokyo: Kadokawa Shoten, 1977.

–. *Chi o uruosu mono.* Tokyo: Mainichi Shimbunsha, 1976.

–. *Enrai no kyakutachi, Kadokawa Bunko 2889.* Tokyo: Kadokawa Shoten, 1972.

–. *Ikenie no shima.* Tokyo: Kōdansha, 1970.

–. *Watakushi no naka no seisho.* Tokyo: Shūseisha, 1981.

Sonoda Yoshiaki. *Kakusareta kōshitsu jimmyaku: Kenpō kyūjō wa kurisuchan ga tsukutta no ka.* Tokyo: Kodansha, 2008.

Spae, Joseph J. "The Catholic Church in Japan." *Contemporary Religions in Japan* 4, 1 (1963): 1-78.

–. *Japanese Religiosity.* Tokyo: Oriens Institute for Religious Research, 1971.

Special Assembly for Asia of the Synod of Bishops. "Official Response of the Japanese Church to the Lineamenta." http://www.cbcj.catholic.jp/.

Strauss, David. *The Life of Jesus: Critically Examined.* London: Chapman Brothers, 1846.

Sundberg, Carl. "Till Medicinska Nobelkommittén Angående Simon Flexners och Hideyo Noguchis arbeten rörande akut barnförlamling, syphilis och lyssa." In Karolinska Institutet, *Med. Nob. Kom. 1914 P. M. Försändelser och Betänkanden,* 3 August 1914, 1-24.

Suzuki Norihisa, ed. *Kindai nihon kirisutokyō meicho senshū.* Tokyo: Nihon Tosho Sentā, 2003.

Swyngedouw, Jan. "The Awakening of a Local Church: Japanese Catholicism in Tension between Particularistic and Universal Values." In Thomas M. Gannon, ed., *World Catholicism in Transition,* 379-92. New York: Macmillan, 1988.

–. "The Japanese Church and Ancestor Veneration Practices: The Mahayanization of Japanese Catholicism?" *Japan Missionary Bulletin* 39, 1 (1985): 56-65.

–. "Japan's Roman Catholic Church and Ancestor Veneration: A Reappraisal." *Japanese Religions* 13, 2 (1984): 11-18.

–. "Katorikku kyōkai no tenkai: Senjika to sengo: Shūkyō shakaigaku-tekina ichi kōsatsu." In Ikado Fujio, ed., *Senryō to nihon shūkyō,* 321-42. Tokyo: Mirai Sha, 1993.

–. "The Quiet Reversal: A Few Notes on the NHK Survey of Japanese Religiosity." *Japan Missionary Bulletin* 39, 1 (1985): 4-13.

Taira, Koji. "Ragpickers and Community Development: 'Ant's Villa' in Tokyo." *Industrial and Labor Relations Review* 22, 1 (1968): 3-19.

Takagi Kazuo. *Nihon bachikan gaikōshi: Nihon to kyōkai I.* Tokyo: Seibo No Kishi, 1984.

Takahashi, Akira. "Understanding Yoshimitsu Yoshihiko's Mysticism." *Comparative Literature Studies* 39, 4 (2002): 272-81.

Takayanagi Shun'ichi. "Catholic Theology in Japan: Overview, Reflections, and Prospect." *Japan Mission Journal* (spring 2004): 14-25.

–. *"Fukai kawa:* Tensei to dōhansha." *Kirisutokyō bungaku kenkyū,* 12 (1995): 1-11.

Tanaka, Kōtarō. "Fasshizumu to katorikku no tachiba." *Yomiuri Shimbun,* May 1932; reprinted in Tanaka, *Kyōyō to bunka no kiso,* 550-60.

–. "Gendai no shisō-teki anākī to sono gen'in no kentō." *Kaizō* (1933); reprinted in Hayashi Kentarō, ed., *Shin-hoshushugi,* 235-63.

–. *Hō to shūkyō to shakai seikatsu.* Tokyo: Kaizōsha, 1927.

–. "In Search of Truth and Peace." In Ryusaku Tsunoda, William Theodore de Bary, and Donald Keene, eds., *Sources of Japanese Tradition, II,* 373-84. New York: Columbia University Press, 1958.

–. *Kyōyō to bunka no kiso.* Tokyo: Iwanami Shoten, 1937.

–. "Nihon ni okeru daigaku no jichi." In Hayashi Kentarō, ed., *Shin-hoshushugi,* 264-82.

–. *Sekai hō no riron I.* Tokyo: Iwanami Shoten, 1932; reprinted, 1950.

–. "Shin kenpō ni okeru fuhen jinrui-teki genri." *Hō tetsugaku shiki hō* 2 (1948); reprinted in Tanaka Kōtarō, *Zoku sekai hō no riron, jō,* 263-97. Tokyo: Yūhikaku, 1972.

Telle, Notto R. *Buddhism and Christianity in Japan: From Conflict to Dialogue, 1854-1899.* Honolulu: University of Hawaii Press, 1987.

Terada Takefumi. "Kaigai no ijūsha to shūkyō jissen: Nihon katorikku kyōkai ni okeru gaikokujin kyōdōtai ni tsuite." Lecture, Research Report, Sophia University, 29 September 2006.

Terasaki Hidenari. *Shōwa tennō dokuhakuroku: Terasaki Hidenari goyōgakari nikki.* Tokyo: Bungeishunjū, 1991.

Thérèse, St., of Lisieux. *Story of a Soul: The Autobiography of Saint Thérèse of Lisieux.* 3rd ed. Trans. John Clarke. Washington, DC: ICS Publications, 1996.

Toda Yoshio, ed. *Nihon katorishizumu to bungaku: Inoue Yōji, Endō Shūsaku, and Takahashi Takako.* Tokyo: Taimeidō, 1982.

Tokunaga, Michio. "A Japanese Transformation of Christianity." *Japanese Religions* 15, 3 (1989): 45-54.

Tsuji Mitsuhiko. "Iesu no mediolojī: Mediētā toshite no Endō Shūsaku." *Kokugo to Kokubungaku* (April 1998): 1-13.

Tsuruha Nobuko. *Kami no deku Sono Ayako no tamashii no sekai.* Tokyo: Shufu to Tomo Sha, 1979.

Turnbull, Stephen. *The Kakure Kirishitan of Japan: A Study of the Development, Beliefs, and Rituals to the Present Day.* Richmond, UK: RoutledgeCurzon, 1998.

Underhill, Evelyn. *Practical Mysticism: A Little Book for Normal People and Abba: Meditations Based on the Lord's Prayer.* New York: Vintage Books, 2003.

Urakawa Wasaburō. *Nihon ni okeru kōkyōkai no fukkatsu: Zenpen* (1915); reprinted as 9 in the series *Kindai nihon kirisuto-kyō meicho senshū, dai ni-ki kirisuto-kyō kyōja shihen,* ed. Suzuki Norihisa Appendix 1-62. Tokyo: Nihon Tosho Sentā, 2003.

US WAR DEPARTMENT, Office of Assistant Chief of Staff, G-2, "MAGIC" – DIPLOMATIC SUMMARY, No. 1167, 5 June 1945, SRS 1689, No. 1177, 15 June 1945, SRS 1689.

Van Hecken, Joseph L. *The Catholic Church in Japan since 1859.* Trans. and rev John van Hoydonck. Tokyo: Herder Agency Enderle Bookstore, 1963.

Varley, Paul. *Japanese Culture.* 3rd ed. Honolulu: University of Hawaii Press, 1984.

Vasques, Manuel A., and Marie Friedmann Marquardt. *Globalizing the Sacred: Religion across the Americas.* Piscataway, NJ: Rutgers University Press, 2003.

von Harnack, Adolf. *Lehrbuch der Dogmengeschichte.* Tübingen: Mohr, 1931-32.

Watsuji Tetsurō. *Climate and Culture: A Philosophical Study.* Trans. Geoffrey Bownas. New York: Greenwood Press, 1988.

–. *Ningen no gaku to shite no rinrigaku.* Tokyo: Iwanami Shoten, 1971.

Williams, Mark B. *Endō Shūsaku: A Literature of Reconciliation*. London: Routledge, 1999.

Wilson, Sandra D. *Into Abba's Arms: Finding the Acceptance You've Always Wanted.* Wheaton, IL: Tyndale House Publishers, 1998.

Woodard, William P. *The Allied Occupation of Japan 1945-1952 and Japanese Religions.* Leiden: Brill, 1972.

World Christian Encyclopedia. New York: Oxford University Press, 1982.

Yagi Seiichi. *Kirisutokyō wa shinjiuru ka.* Tokyo: Kōdansha, 1970.

Yagi, Seiichi, and Leonard Swidler. *A Bridge to Buddhist-Christian Dialogue.* New York: Paulist Press, 1990.

Yamagata Kazumi, ed. *Endō Shūsaku: Sono bungaku sekai.* Tokyo: Kokken Shuppan, 1997.

Yamaji, Aizan. *Essays on the Modern Japanese Church: Christianity in Meiji Japan.* Trans. Graham Squires, with introductory essays by Graham Squires and A. Hamish Ion. Ann Arbor, MI: Center for Japanese Studies, 1999.

Yamaoka, Masami. "A Philippine Network in Japan: A Case Study of the Philippine Network at St. Ignatius' Catholic Church in Tokyo." *Journal of Intercultural Communication* 2 (1998): 145-57.

Yanagita Tomonobu. *Christianity in Japan.* Sendai: Seisho Tosho Kankōkai (Bible Library Publishers), 1957.

Yasuoka Shōtarō, et al. "Tsuitō: Endō Shūsaku." *Gunzō* 51, 12 (1996): 102-45.

–. "Tsuitō: Endō Shūsaku." *Shinchō* 93, 12 (1996): 172-229.

Yoshimitsu Yoshihiko. *Bunka to shūkyō no rinen,* reprinted in *Yoshimitsu Yoshihiko chosakushū 1.* Tokyo: Misuzu Shobō, 1947.

–. "The Theological Grounds of Overcoming Modernity: How Can Modern Man Find God?" Trans. Richard Calichman. In Richard Calichman, ed., *Overcoming Modernity: Cultural Identity in Wartime Japan,* 77-91. New York: Columbia University Press, 2008.

Yuasa Mitsutomo, comp. *Gendai kagaku gijutsu shi nempyō.* Tokyo: San'ichi Shobō, 1961.

–. *Kagaku shi.* Tokyo: Tōyō Keizai Shimpo Sha, 1961.

Contributors

James R. Bartholomew is a professor of history at Ohio State University. Chiefly interested in the history of science, medicine, higher education, and business in Japan, he is the author of *The Formation of Science in Japan* (Pfizer Award of the History of Science Society) and was awarded a John Simon Guggenheim Memorial Fellowship to write a book on Japan and the Nobel science prizes, 1901-49.

Charles C. Campbell, a recent graduate of Georgetown University, is a teacher of French and Japanese studies at the Community School of Naples in Florida. His breadth of interest in language and culture includes religion, pop culture, and cross-cultural influence.

Kevin M. Doak is the Nippon Foundation Endowed Chair and a professor of Japanese studies at Georgetown University. His recent publications include *A History of Nationalism in Modern Japan: Placing the People* (Brill, 2007) and "A Religious Perspective on the Yasukuni Shrine Controversy," in John Breen, ed., *Yasukuni, the War Dead, and the Struggle for Japan's Past* (Columbia University Press, 2008). He co-edits the *Journal of Japanese Studies*.

Ann M. Harrington is professor emerita and past director of the Asian Studies Program at Loyola University Chicago. Her recent publications include *Creating Community: Mary Frances Clarke and Her Companions* (Mount Carmel Press, 2004) and "French Mission Work in Japan: Culture and Religion in the Nineteenth Century," in Cyriac K. Pullapilly et al., eds., *Christianity and Native Cultures: Perspectives from Different Regions of the World* (Crossroads Publications, 2004). Her current research is on the work done in Japan by Roman Catholic women religious from France in the nineteenth century and from Canada and the United States in the twentieth century.

Mariko Ikehara is a graduate of the master's program in the Edmund A. Walsh School of Foreign Service, Georgetown University, and she is now an independent writer and researcher, based in Washington, DC. She has written widely for Japanese publications on a broad range of subjects, including US politics, foreign policy, and cultural affairs. She contributed a chapter to a 2009 book analyzing the first year of the administration of President Obama. She is currently writing a book about a major performing arts institution in New York.

Mark R. Mullins is a professor in the Graduate School of Global Studies and Faculty of Liberal Arts, Sophia University, Tokyo, where his teaching and research focus on religion in modern societies. He is the author and co-editor of a number of works, including *Religion and Society in Modern Japan* (1993), *Christianity Made in Japan* (1998), and *Religion and Social Crisis in Japan* (2001). He is currently writing a book on neo-nationalism and religion in contemporary Japanese society while serving as editor of *Monumenta Nipponica*.

Toshiko Sunami is a professor of education in the Faculty of Letters of Shikoku Gakuin University, Japan. She is the author, among other works, of *Enchi Fumiko ron* (Ōfū, 1998) and *Takahashi Takako ron* (Ōfūsha, 1992). Her current research focuses on women writers in contemporary Japan.

Mark Williams is the head of the School of Modern Languages and Cultures, Leeds University, where he is also a professor of Japanese studies. The author of *Endō Shūsaku: A Literature of Reconciliation* (Routledge, 1999), he has also translated Endō's novels *Foreign Studies* and *The Girl I Left Behind* and serves as the president of the British Association of Japanese Studies. His current research looks at how Japanese writers have engaged with the concept of difference/alterity and how they have dealt with the legacy of the war.

Yoshihisa Yamamoto is an associate professor in the Department of Advanced Social and International Studies at the University of Tokyo-Komaba. He has published widely on Aquinas' ethics and metaphysics as well as on medieval Arabic philosophy. His recent publications include "Thomas Aquinas on the Ontology of *Amicitia: Unio and Communicatio*," in *Proceedings of the American Catholic Philosophical Association* (Vol. 81, 2008) and "Chūsei ni okeru ningen no songen no shisō," in Tabata Kuniharu and Tanaka Mieko, eds., *Tetsugaku: Kango to ningen ni mukau tetsugaku* (Nuveru Hirokawa, 2003).

Yoshihiko Yoshimitsu (1904-45) taught philosophy at Sophia University and was a lecturer at Tokyo Imperial University. He wrote widely on medieval philosophy and Catholic ethics and translated works by Jacques Maritain and Karl Adam. His best-known works include *Chūsei seishinshi kenkyū* ("Research on Medieval Spiritual History") and *Bunka to shūkyō* ("Culture and Religion"). His vast writings have been collected and posthumously published in the multi-volume *Yoshimitsu Yoshihiko chosakushū* (Misuzu Shobō, 1947-52).

Index